THE COMPLETE
WALLACE D. WATTLES

9 BOOKS

The Science of Getting Rich

The Science of Being Great

The Science of Being Well

How to Get What You Want

A New Christ

Jesus: The Man and his Work

Making the Man who can (How to Promote Yourself)

The New Science of Living and Healing

Hellfire Harrison (a novel)

CONTENTS

ABOUT WALLACE WATTLES

The articles of Wallace D. Wattles appeared in almost every issue of Elizabeth Towne's magazine *Nautilus –The New Thought Magazine-, from* the early 1900's until his death in 1911.

Shortly after his death, Florence Wattles, Wallace's daughter, wrote this letter that helps to provide some insights onto Wallace's life:

My dear Mrs. Towne:

Your letter of the 14th received . . . perhaps a little later I can write the romantic story of my Father's life and make it really worthwhile.

You knew, didn't you, that he lost a good position in the Methodist Church because of his "heresy"? He met George D. Herron at a convention of reformers in Chicago in 1896 and caught Herron's social vision. I shall never forget the morning he came home. It was Christmas. Mother had put her last dollar into a cuff box and we had placed it beneath an evergreen branch which served for our Christmas tree and which we had illumined with tallow candles and strung with popcorn. Finally Father came. With that beautiful smile he praised the tree, said the cuff box was just what he had been wanting—and took us all in his arms to tell us of the wonderful social message of Jesus, the message which he later embodied in "A New Christ." From that day until his death he worked unceasingly to realize the glorious vision of human brotherhood.

For years his life was cursed by poverty and the fear of poverty. He was always scheming and planning to get for his family those things which make the abundant life possible. In the first chapter of "How to be a Genius" he says: "Man's greatest happiness is found in the bestowal of benefits on those he loves." The supreme faith of the man never left him; never for a moment did he lose confidence in the power of the master Intelligence to right every wrong and to give to every man and woman his or her share of the good things of life.

When we came to Elwood (Indiana) three years ago, Father began a Sunday night lectureship in Indianapolis. This was our only source of income. Later he began to write for *Nautilus* and to work out his own philosophy. He wrote almost constantly. Then it was that he formed his mental picture. He saw himself as a successful writer, a personality of power, an advancing man, and he began to work toward the realization of this vision. ... He lived every page of "How to be a Genius." In the last three years he made lots of money, and had good health except for his extreme frailty.

I have written this hurriedly, but I think it will give you an idea of the life struggle of a great man —his failure and success. His life was truly THE POWERFUL LIFE, and surely we can say, at least in Elwood, "The name of him who loved his fellow men led all the rest."

With all good wishes, I am, Very sincerely,

FLORENCE A. WATTLES

BOOK ONE
THE SCIENCE OF
GETTING RICH

Author's Preface

THIS BOOK IS PRAGMATICAL, NOT PHILOSOPHICAL — a practical manual, not a treatise upon theories. It is intended for the men and women whose most pressing need is for money, who wish to get rich first, and philosophize afterward. It is for those who want results and who are willing to take the conclusions of science as a basis for action, without going into all the processes by which those conclusions were reached.

It is expected that the reader will take the fundamental statements upon faith, just as he would take statements concerning a law of electrical action if they were promulgated by a Marconi or an Edison, and, taking the statements upon faith, that he will prove their truth by acting upon them without fear or hesitation. Every man or woman who does this will certainly get rich, for the science herein applied is an exact science and failure is impossible.

In writing this book I have sacrificed all other considerations to plainness and simplicity of style, so that all might understand. The plan of action laid down herein was deduced from the conclusions of philosophy. It has been thoroughly tested, and bears the supreme test of practical experiment: It works.

Very Truly Yours

Wallace Wattles

1. THE RIGHT TO BE RICH

WHATEVER MAY BE SAID IN PRAISE OF POVERTY, the fact remains that it is not possible to live a really complete or successful life unless one is rich. No one can rise to his greatest possible height in talent or soul development unless he has plenty of money, for to unfold the soul and to develop talent he must have many things to use, and he cannot have these things unless he has money to buy them with.

A person develops in mind, soul, and body by making use of things, and society is so organized that man must have money in order to become the possessor of things.

Therefore, the basis of all advancement must be the science of getting rich.

The object of all life is development, and everything that lives have an inalienable right to all the development it is capable of attaining. A person's right to life means his right to have the free and unrestricted use of all the things which may be necessary to his fullest mental, spiritual, and physical unfoldment; or, in other words, his right to be rich.

In this book, I shall not speak of riches in a figurative way. To be really rich does not mean to be satisfied or contented with a little. No one ought to be satisfied with a little if he is capable of using and enjoying more.

The purpose of nature is the advancement and unfoldment of life, and everyone should have all that can contribute to the power, elegance, beauty, and richness of life. To be content with less is sinful.

The person who owns all he wants for the living of all the life he is capable of living is rich, and no person who has not plenty of money can have all he wants. Life has advanced so far and become so complex that even the most ordinary man or woman requires a great amount of wealth in order to live in a manner that even approaches completeness.

Every person naturally wants to become all that they are capable of becoming. This desire to realize innate possibilities is inherent in human nature; we cannot help wanting to be all that we can be. Success in life is becoming what you want to be. You can become what you want to be only by making use of things, and you can have the free use of things only as you become rich enough to buy them. To understand the science of getting rich is therefore the most essential of all knowledge.

There is nothing wrong in wanting to get rich. The desire for riches is really the desire for a richer, fuller, and more abundant life, and that desire is praiseworthy.

The person who does not desire to live more abundantly is abnormal, and so the person who does not desire to have money enough to buy all he wants is abnormal.

There are three motives for which we live: We live for the body, we live for the mind, we live for the soul. No one of these is better or holier than the other; all are alike desirable, and no one of the three —body, mind, or soul— can live fully if either of the others is cut short of full life and expression. It is not right or noble to live only for the soul and deny mind or body, and it is wrong to live for the intellect and deny body or soul.

We are all acquainted with the loathsome consequences of living for the body and denying both mind and soul, and we see that *real* life means the complete expression of all that a person can give forth through body, mind, and soul. Whatever that person can say, no one can be really happy or satisfied unless his body is living fully in its every function, and unless the same is true of his mind and soul. Wherever there is unexpressed possibility or function not performed, there is unsatisfied desire. Desire is possibility seeking expression or function seeking performance.

A person cannot live fully in body without good food, comfortable clothing, and warm shelter, and without freedom from excessive toil. Rest and recreation are also necessary to his physical life. One cannot live fully in mind without books and time to study them, without opportunity for travel and observation, or without intellectual companionship.

To live fully in mind a person must have intellectual recreations, and must surround itself with all the objects of art and beauty he is capable of using and appreciating. To live fully in soul, a person must have love, and love is denied fullest expression by poverty. A person's highest happiness is found in the bestowal of benefits on those he loves; love finds its most natural and spontaneous expression in giving. The individual who has nothing to give cannot fill his place as a spouse or parent, as a citizen, or as a human being.

It is in the use of material things that a person finds full life for his body, develops his mind, and unfolds his soul. It is therefore of supreme importance to each individual to be rich.

It is perfectly right that you should desire to be rich. If you are a normal person you cannot help doing so. It is perfectly right that you should give your best attention to the science of getting rich, for it is the noblest and most necessary of all studies. If you neglect this study, you are derelict in your duty to yourself, to God and humanity, for you can render to God and humanity no greater service than to make the most of yourself.

2. THERE IS A SCIENCE OF GETTING RICH

THERE IS A SCIENCE OF GETTING RICH, and it is an exact science, like algebra or arithmetic. There are certain laws which govern the process of acquiring riches, and once these laws are learned and obeyed by anyone, that person will get rich with mathematical certainty.

The ownership of money and property comes as a result of doing things in a certain way and those who do things in this certain way, whether on purpose or accidentally, get rich, while those who do not do things in this certain way, no matter how hard they work or how able they are, remain poor.

It is a natural law that like causes always produce like effects, and, therefore, any man or woman who learns to do things in this certain way will infallibly get rich.

That the above statement is true is shown by the following facts:

FIRST. Getting rich is not a matter of environment, for if it were, all the people in certain neighborhoods would become wealthy. The people of one city would all be rich, while those of other towns would all be poor, or all the inhabitants of one state would roll in wealth, while those of an adjoining state would be in poverty. But everywhere we see rich and poor living side by side, in the same environment, and often engaged in the same vocations. When two people are in the same locality and in the same business, and one gets rich while the other remains poor, it shows that getting rich is not primarily a matter of environment. Some environments may be more favorable than others, but when two people in the same business are in the same neighborhood and one gets rich while the other fails, it indicates that getting rich is the result of doing things in a certain way.

SECOND. And further, the ability to do things in this certain way is not due solely to the possession of talent, for many people who have great talent remain poor, while others who have very little talent get rich.

Studying the people who have gotten rich, we find that they are an average lot in all respects, having no greater talents and abilities than other people have. It is evident that they do not get rich because they possess talents and abilities that others do not have, but because they happen to do things in a certain way.

THIRD. Getting rich is not the result of saving, or thrift. Many very penurious people are poor, while free spenders often get rich.

FOURTH. Nor is getting rich due to doing things which others fail to do, for two people in the same business often do almost exactly the same things, and one gets rich while the other remains poor or becomes bankrupt.

From all these things, we must come to the conclusion that getting rich is the result of doing things in a certain way.

If getting rich is the result of doing things in a certain way, and if like causes always produce like effects, then any man or woman who can do things in that way can become rich, and the whole matter is brought within the domain of exact science.

The question arises here as to whether this certain way may not be so difficult that only a few may follow it. As we have seen, this cannot be true (as far as natural ability is concerned). Talented people get rich, and blockheads get rich; intellectually brilliant people get rich, and very stupid people get rich; physically strong people get rich, and weak and sickly people get rich.

Some degree of ability to think and understand is, of course, essential, but insofar as natural ability is concerned, any man or woman who has sense enough to read and understand these words can certainly get rich.

Also, we have seen that it is not a matter of environment. Yes, location counts for something. One would not go to the heart of the Sahara and expect to do successful business.

Getting rich involves the necessity of dealing with people and of being where there are people to deal with, and if these people are inclined to deal in the way you want to deal, so much the better. But that is about as far as environment goes. If anybody else in your town can get rich, so can you, and if anybody else in your state can get rich, so can you. Again, it is not a matter of choosing some particular business or profession. People get rich in every business and in every profession, while their next-door neighbors in the very same vocation remain in poverty. It is true that you will do best in a business which you like and which is congenial to you. And if you have certain talents which are well developed, you will do best in a business which calls for the exercise of those talents. Also, you will do best in a business which is suited to your locality: An ice cream parlor would do better in a warm climate than in Greenland, and a salmon fishery will succeed better in the northwest than in Florida, where there are no salmon.

But, aside from these general limitations, getting rich is not dependent upon your engaging in some particular business, but upon your learning to do things in a certain way. If you are now in business and anybody else in your locality is getting rich in the same business, while you are not getting rich, it is simply because you are not doing things in the same way that the other person is doing them.

No one is prevented from getting rich by lack of capital. True, as you get capital the increase becomes more easy and rapid, but one who has capital is already rich and does not need to consider how to become so. No matter how poor you may be, if you begin to do things in the certain way you will begin to get rich and you will begin to have capital. The getting of capital is a part of the process of getting rich and it is a part of the result which invariably follows the doing of things in the certain way.

You may be the poorest person on the continent and be deeply in debt. You may have neither friends, influence, nor resources, but if you begin to do things in this way, you must infallibly begin to get rich, for like causes must produce like effects. If you have no capital, you can get capital. If you are in the wrong business, you can get into the right business. If you are in the wrong location, you can go to the right location.

And you can do so by beginning in your present business and in your present location to do things in the certain way which always causes success. You must begin to live in harmony with the laws governing the universe.

3. IS OPPORTUNITY MONOPOLIZED?

NO ONE IS KEPT POOR BECAUSE OTHER PEOPLE HAVE MONOPOLIZED THE WEALTH and have put a fence around it. You may be shut off from engaging in business in certain lines, but there are other channels open to you.

At different periods the tide of opportunity sets in different directions, according to the needs of the whole and the particular stage of social evolution which has been reached. There is abundance of opportunity for the person who will go with the tide, instead of trying to swim against it.

So workers, either as individuals or as a class, are not deprived of opportunity. The workers are not being "kept down" by their masters; they are not being "ground" by the trusts and big business. As a class, they are where they are because they do not do things in a certain way.

The working class may become the master class whenever they will begin to do things in a certain way. The law of wealth is the same for them as it is for all others. This they must learn, and they will remain where they are as long as they continue to do as they do. The individual worker, however, is not held down by an entire class's ignorance of these laws; he can follow the tide of opportunity to riches, and this book will tell him how.

No one is kept in poverty by a shortness in the supply of riches; there is more than enough for all. A palace as large as the capitol at Washington might be built for every family on earth from the building material in the United States alone, and under intensive cultivation this country would produce wool, cotton, linen, and silk enough to clothe each person in the world finer than Solomon was arrayed in all his glory, together with food enough to feed them all luxuriously.

The visible supply is practically inexhaustible, and the invisible supply really is inexhaustible. Everything you see on earth is made from one original substance, out of which all things proceed. New forms are constantly being made, and older ones are dissolving, but all are shapes assumed by one thing.

There is no limit to the supply of formless stuff, or original substance. The universe is made out of it, but it was not all used in making the universe. The spaces in, through and between the forms of the visible universe are permeated and filled with the original substance, with the formless stuff —with the raw material of all things. Ten thousand times as much as has been made might still be made, and even then we should not have exhausted the supply of universal raw material.

No one, therefore, is poor because nature is poor or because there is not enough to go around. Nature is an inexhaustible storehouse of riches; the supply will never run short. Original substance is alive with creative energy, and is constantly producing more forms. When the supply of building material is exhausted, more will be produced. When the soil is exhausted so that food stuffs and materials for clothing will no longer grow upon it, it will be renewed or more soil will be made. When all the gold and silver has been dug from the earth, if humanity is still in such a stage of social development that it needs gold and silver, more will produced from the formless. The formless stuff responds to the needs of mankind; it will not let the world be without any good thing.

This is true of humanity *collectively*. The race as a whole is always abundantly rich, and if individuals are poor it is because they do not follow the certain way of doing things which makes the individual rich.

The formless stuff is intelligent; it is stuff which thinks. It is alive and is always impelled toward more life. It is the natural and inherent impulse of life to seek to live more; it is the nature of intelligence to enlarge itself, and of consciousness to seek to extend its boundaries and find fuller expression. The universe of forms has been made by formless living substance throwing itself into form in order to express itself more fully. The universe is a great living presence, always moving inherently toward more life and fuller functioning.

Nature is formed for the advancement of life, and its impelling motive is the increase of life. Because of this, everything which can possibly minister to life is bountifully provided. There can be no lack unless God is to contradict himself and nullify his own works.

You are not kept poor by lack in the supply of riches. It is a fact which I shall demonstrate a little farther on that even the resources of the formless supply are at the command of the man or woman who will act and think in a certain way.

4. THE FIRST PRINCIPLE IN THE SCIENCE OF GETTING RICH

THOUGHT IS THE ONLY POWER WHICH CAN PRODUCE TANGIBLE RICHES from the formless substance. The stuff from which all things are made is a substance which thinks, and a thought of form in this substance produces the form.

Original substance moves according to its thoughts; every form and process you see in nature is the visible expression of a thought in original substance. As the formless stuff thinks of a form, it takes that form; as it thinks of a motion, it makes that motion. That is the way all things were created. We live in a thought world, which is part of a thought universe. The thought of a moving universe extended throughout formless substance, and the thinking stuff — moving according to that thought— took the form of systems of planets, and maintains that form.

Thinking substance takes the form of its thought and moves according to the thought.

Holding the idea of a circling system of suns and worlds, it takes the form of these bodies, and moves them as it thinks. Thinking the form of a slow-growing oak tree, it moves accordingly, and produces the tree, though centuries may be required to do the work. In creating, the formless seems to move according to the lines of motion it has established. In other words, the thought of an oak tree does not cause the instant formation of a full-grown tree, but it does start in motion the forces which will produce the tree, along established lines of growth.

Every thought of form, held in thinking substance, causes the creation of the form, but always, or at least generally, along lines of growth and action already established.

The thought of a house of a certain construction, if it were impressed upon formless substance, might not cause the instant formation of the house, but it would cause the turning of creative energies already working in trade and commerce into such channels as to result in the speedy building of the house. And if there were no existing channels through which the creative energy could work, then the house would be formed directly from primal substance, without waiting for the slow processes of the organic and inorganic world.

No thought of form can be impressed upon original substance without causing the creation of the form.

A person is a thinking center and can originate thought. All the forms that a person fashions with his hands must first exist in his thought. He cannot shape a thing until he has thought that thing. So far, humankind has confined its efforts wholly to the work of its hands, applying manual labor to the world of forms and seeking to change or modify those already existing. Humankind has never thought of trying to cause the creation of new forms by impressing thought upon formless substance.

When a person has a thought-form, he takes material from the forms of nature and makes an image of the form which is in his mind. People have, so far, made little or no effort to cooperate with formless intelligence — to work "with the Father." The individual has not dreamed that he can "do what he seeth the Father doing." An individual reshapes and modifies existing forms by manual labor and has given no attention to the question of whether he may produce things from formless substance by communicating his thoughts to it.

We propose to prove that he may do so — to prove that *any* man or woman may do so — and to show how. As our first step, we must lay down three fundamental propositions.

First, we assert that there is one original formless stuff or substance from which all things are made. All the seemingly many elements are but different presentations of one element. All the many forms found in organic and inorganic nature are but different shapes, made from the same stuff. And this stuff is thinking stuff — *a thought held in it produces the form of the thought.* Thought, in thinking substance, produces shapes. A human being is a thinking center, capable of original thought. If a person can communicate his thought to original thinking substance, he can cause the creation, or formation, of the thing he thinks about. To summarize this:

There is a thinking stuff from which all things are made, and which, in its original state, permeates, penetrates, and fills the interspaces of the universe.

A thought in this substance produces the thing that is imaged by the thought.

A person can form things in his thought, and, by impressing his thought upon formless substance, can cause the thing he thinks about to be created.

It may be asked if I can prove these statements, and without going into details I answer that I can do so, both by logic and experience. Reasoning back from the phenomena of form and thought, I come to one original thinking substance, and reasoning forward from this thinking substance, I come to a person's power to cause the formation of the thing he thinks about.

And by experiment, I find the reasoning true. This is my strongest proof. If one person who reads this book gets rich by doing what it tells him to do, that is evidence in support of my claim, but if *every* person who *does what it tells him to do* gets rich, that is positive proof until someone goes through the process and fails. The theory is true until the process fails, and this process will not fail, for everyone *who does exactly what this book tells him to do* will get rich.

I have said that people get rich by doing things in a certain way, and to do so, people must become able to think in a certain way.

A person's way of doing things is the direct result of the way he *thinks* about things.

To do things in the way you want to do them, you will have to acquire the ability to think the way you want to think. This is the first step toward getting rich.

And to think what you *want* to think is to think TRUTH, regardless of appearances.

Every individual has the natural and inherent power to think what he wants to think, but it requires far more effort to do so than it does to think the thoughts which are suggested by appearances. To think according to appearances is easy; to think truth regardless of appearances is laborious and requires the expenditure of more power than any other work we are called upon to perform.

There is no labor from which most people shrink as they do from that of sustained and consecutive thought. It is the hardest work in the world. This is especially true when truth is contrary to appearances.

Every appearance in the visible world tends to produce a corresponding form in the mind which observes it, and this can only be prevented by holding the thought of the TRUTH.

To look upon the appearances of poverty will produce corresponding forms in your own mind, unless you hold to the truth that there is no poverty; there is only abundance.

To think health when surrounded by the appearances of disease or to think riches when in the midst of the appearances of poverty requires power, but whoever acquires this power becomes a *master mind*. That person can conquer fate and can have what he wants.

This power can only be acquired by getting hold of the basic fact which is behind all appearances, and that fact is that there is one thinking substance from which and by which all things are made. Then we must grasp the truth that *every* thought held in this substance becomes a form, and that man can so impress his thoughts upon it as to cause them to take form and become visible things.

When we realize this we lose all doubt and fear, for we know that we can create what we want to create, we can get what we want to have, and can become what we want to be. As a first step toward getting rich, you must believe the three fundamental statements given previously in this chapter, and to emphasize them, I repeat them here:

There is a thinking stuff from which all things are made, and which, in its original state, permeates, penetrates, and fills the interspaces of the universe.

A thought in this substance produces the thing that is imaged by the thought.

A person can form things in his thought, and, by impressing his thought upon formless substance, can cause the thing he thinks about to be created.

You must lay aside all other concepts of the universe, and you must dwell upon this until it is fixed in your mind and has become your habitual thought. Read these statements over and over again. Fix every word upon your memory and meditate upon them until you firmly believe what they say. If a doubt comes to you, cast it aside. Do not listen to arguments against this idea. Do not go to churches or lectures where a contrary concept of things is taught or preached. Do not read magazines or books which teach a different idea. If you get mixed up in your understanding, belief, and faith, all your efforts will be in vain.

Do not ask why these things are true nor speculate as to how they can be true. Simply take them on trust. The science of getting rich begins with the absolute acceptance of this.

5. INCREASING LIFE

YOU MUST GET RID OF THE LAST VESTIGE OF THE OLD IDEA that there is a Deity whose will it is that you should be poor or whose purposes may be served by keeping you in poverty.

The intelligent substance which is all, and in all, and which lives in all and lives in you, is a consciously living substance. Being a consciously living substance, it must have the nature and inherent desire of every living intelligence for increase of life. Every living thing must continually seek for the enlargement of its life, because life, in the mere act of living, must increase itself.

A seed, dropped into the ground, springs into activity, and in the act of living produces a hundred more seeds; life, by living, multiplies itself. It is forever becoming more. It must do so, if it continues to be at all.

Intelligence is under this same necessity for continuous increase. Every thought we think makes it necessary for us to think another thought; consciousness is continually expanding. Every fact we learn leads us to the learning of another fact; knowledge is continually increasing. Every talent we cultivate brings to the mind the desire to cultivate another talent; we are subject to the urge of life, seeking expression, which ever drives us on to know more, to do more, and to be more.

In order to know more, do more, and be more we must have more. We must have things to use, for we learn, and do, and become only by using things. We must get rich so that we can live more.

The desire for riches is simply the capacity for larger life seeking fulfillment. Every desire is the effort of an unexpressed possibility to come into action. It is power seeking to manifest which causes desire. That which makes you want more money is the same as that which makes the plant grow; it is life seeking fuller expression.

The one living substance must be subject to this inherent law of all life. It is permeated with the desire to live more, and that is why it is under the necessity of creating things. The one substance desires to live more in and through you. Therefore it wants you to have all the things you can use.

It is the desire of God that you should get rich. He wants you to get rich because he can express himself better through you if you have plenty of things to use in giving him expression. He can live more in you if you have unlimited command of the means of life.

The universe desires you to have everything you want to have. Nature is friendly to your plans.

Everything is naturally for you.

Make up your mind that this is true.

It is essential, however, that your purpose should harmonize with the purpose that is in all.

You must want real life, not mere pleasure or sensual gratification. Life is the performance of function, and the individual really lives only when he performs every function — physical, mental, and spiritual — of which he is capable, without excess in any.

You do not want to get rich in order to live swinishly, for the gratification of animal desires. That is not life. But the performance of every physical function *is* a part of life, and no one lives completely who denies the impulses of the body a normal and healthful expression.

You do not want to get rich solely to enjoy mental pleasures, to get knowledge, to gratify ambition, to outshine others, to be famous. All these are a legitimate part of life, but the person who lives for the pleasures of the intellect alone will only have a partial life, and he will never be satisfied with his lot.

You do not want to get rich solely for the good of others, to lose yourself for the salvation of mankind, to experience the joys of philanthropy and sacrifice. The joys of the soul are only a part of life, and they are no better or nobler than any other part.

You want to get rich in order that you may eat, drink, and be merry when it is time to do these things; in order that you may surround yourself with beautiful things, see distant lands, feed your mind, and develop your intellect; in order that you may love others and do kind things, and be able to play a good part in helping the world to find truth.

But remember that extreme altruism is no better and no nobler than extreme selfishness; both are mistakes. Get rid of the idea that God wants you to sacrifice yourself for others and that you can secure his favor by doing so. God requires nothing of the kind.

What God wants is that you should make the most of yourself, for yourself, and for others. And you can help others more by making the most of yourself than in any other way. You can make the most of yourself only by getting rich, so it is right and praiseworthy that you should give your first and best thought to the work of acquiring wealth.

Remember, however, that the desire of substance is for *all*, and its movements must be for more life to all. It cannot be made to work for less life to any, because it is equally in all, seeking riches and life.

Intelligent substance will make things for you, but it will not take things away from someone else and give them to you. You must get rid of the thought of competition. You are to create, not to compete for what is already created.

You do not have to take anything away from anyone. You do not have to drive sharp bargains.

You do not have to cheat or to take advantage. You do not need to let anyone work for you for less than he earns.

You do not have to covet the property of others or to look at it with wishful eyes. No one has anything of which you cannot have the like, and that without taking what he has away from him.

You are to become a creator, not a competitor. You are going to get what you want, but in such a way that when you get it every other person whom you affect will have more than he has now.

I am aware that there are those who get a vast amount of money by proceeding in direct opposition to the statements in the paragraph above, and may add a word of explanation here. Individuals of that type who become very rich do so sometimes purely by their extraordinary ability on the plane of competition, and sometimes they unconsciously relate themselves to substance in its great purposes and movements for the general up building through industrial evolution. Rockefeller, Carnegie, Morgan, have been the unconscious agents of the supreme in the necessary work of systematizing and organizing productive industry, and in the end their work will contribute immensely toward increased life for all. But their day is nearly over. They have organized production and will soon be succeeded by the agents of the multitude, who will organize the machinery of distribution.

They are like the monster reptiles of the prehistoric eras. They play a necessary part in the evolutionary process, but the same power which produced them will dispose of them. And it is well to bear in mind that they have never been really rich; a record of the private lives of most of this class will show that they have really been most abject and wretched.

Riches secured on the competitive plane are never satisfactory and permanent. They are yours today and another's tomorrow. Remember, if you are to become rich in a scientific and certain way, you must rise *entirely* out of competitive thought. You must never think for a moment that the supply is limited. Just as soon as you begin to think that all the money is being "cornered" and controlled by others, and that you must exert yourself to get laws passed to stop this process, and so on — in that moment you drop into the competitive mind and your power to cause creation is gone for the time being.

And what is worse, you will probably arrest the creative movements you have already begun. KNOW that there are countless millions of dollars' worth of gold in the mountains of the earth, not yet brought to light. And know that if there were not, more would be created from thinking substance to supply your needs.

KNOW that the money you need will come, even if it is necessary for a thousand men to be led to the discovery of new gold mines tomorrow.

Never look at the visible supply. Look always at the limitless riches in formless substance, and KNOW that they are coming to you as fast as you can receive and use them. Nobody, by cornering the visible supply, can prevent you from getting what is yours.

So never allow yourself to think for an instant that all the best building spots will be taken before you get ready to build your house, unless you hurry. Never worry about the trusts and combines, and get anxious for fear they will soon come to own the whole earth. Never get afraid that you will lose what you want because some other person "beats you to it." That cannot possibly happen. You are not seeking anything that is possessed by anybody else; you are causing what you want to be created from formless substance, and the supply is without limits. Stick to the formulated statement:

There is a thinking stuff from which all things are made, and which, in its original state, permeates, penetrates, and fills the interspaces of the universe. A thought, in this substance produces the thing that is imaged by the thought. A person can form things in his thought, and, by impressing his thought upon formless substance, can cause the thing he thinks about to be created.

6. HOW RICHES COME TO YOU

WHEN I SAY THAT YOU DO NOT HAVE TO DRIVE SHARP BARGAINS, I do not mean that you do not have to drive any bargains at all or that you are above the necessity for having any dealings with your fellow men. I mean that you will not need to deal with them unfairly. You do not have to get something for nothing, *but can give to every person more than you take from him.*

You cannot give everyone more in cash market value than you take from him, but you can give him more in use value than the cash value of the thing you take from him. The paper, ink, and other material in this book may not be worth the money you pay for it, but if the ideas suggested by it bring you thousands of dollars, you have not been wronged by those who sold it to you. They have given you a great use value for a small cash value.

Let us suppose that I own a picture by one of the great artists, which, in a developed society, is worth thousands of dollars. I take it to Baffin Bay and by "salesmanship" induce a native dweller to give a bundle of furs worth $500 for it. I have really wronged him, for he has no use for the picture. It has no use value to him; it will not add to his life. But suppose I give him a gun worth $50 for his furs. Then he has made a good bargain. He has use for the gun. It will get him many more furs and much food; it will add to his life in every way. It will make him rich.

When you rise from the competitive to the creative plane, you can scan your business transactions very strictly, and if you are selling any person anything which does not add more to his life than the thing he give you in exchange, you can afford to stop it. You do not have to beat anybody in business. And if you are in a business which does beat people, get out of it at once.

Give everyone more in use value than you take from him in cash value. Then you are adding to the life of the world by every business transaction.

If you have people working for you, you must take from them more in cash value than you pay them in wages, but you can so organize your business that it will be filled with the principle of advancement, and so that each employee who wishes to do so may advance a little every day.

You can make your business do for your employees what this book is doing for you. You can so conduct your business that it will be a sort of ladder by which every employee who will take the trouble may climb to riches himself. And given the opportunity, if he will not do so, it is not your fault.

And finally, just because you are to cause the creation of your riches from formless substance which permeates all your environment, it does not follow that they are to take shape from the atmosphere and come into being before your eyes.

If you want a sewing machine, for instance, I do not mean to tell you that you are to impress the thought of a sewing machine on thinking substance until the machine is formed without hands, in the room where you sit or elsewhere. But if you want a sewing machine, hold the mental image of it with the most positive certainty that it is being made or is on its way to you.

After once forming the thought, have the most absolute and unquestioning faith that the sewing machine is coming. Never think of it or speak of it in any other way than as being sure to arrive. Claim it as already yours.

It will be brought to you by the power of the supreme intelligence, acting upon the minds of men. If you live in Maine, it may be that a person will be brought from Texas or Japan to engage in some transaction which will result in your getting what you want. If so, the whole matter will be as much to that person's advantage as it is to yours.

Do not forget for a moment that the thinking substance is through all, in all, communicating with all, and can influence all. The desire of thinking substance for fuller life and better living has caused the creation of all the sewing machines already made, and it can cause the creation of millions more —and will, whenever people set it in motion by desire and faith and by acting in a certain way. You can certainly have a sewing machine in your house, and it is just as certain that you can have any other thing or things which you want and which you will use for the advancement of your own life and the lives of others.

You need not hesitate about asking largely. "It is your Father's pleasure to give you the kingdom," said Jesus.

Original substance wants to live all that is possible in you, and wants you to have all that you can use and will use for the living of the most abundant life.

If you fix upon your consciousness the fact that your desire for the possession of riches is one with the desire of the supreme power for more complete expression, your faith becomes invincible.

Once I saw a little boy sitting at a piano, vainly trying to bring harmony out of the keys. I saw that he was grieved and provoked by his inability to play real music. I asked him the cause of his vexation, and he answered, "I can feel the music in me, but I can't make my hands go right." The music in him was the URGE of original substance, containing all the possibilities of all life. All that there is of music was seeking expression through the child.

God, the one substance, is trying to live and do and enjoy things through humanity. He is saying "I want hands to build wonderful structures, to play divine harmonies, to paint glorious pictures. I want feet to run my errands, eyes to see my beauties, tongues to tell mighty truths and to sing marvelous songs," and so on. All that there is of possibility is seeking expression through people. God wants those who can play music to have pianos and every other instrument and to have the means to cultivate their talents to the fullest extent. He wants those who can appreciate beauty to be able to surround themselves with beautiful things. He wants those who can discern truth to have every opportunity to travel and observe. He wants those who can appreciate dress to be beautifully clothed, and those who can appreciate good food to be luxuriously fed.

He wants all these things because it is himself that enjoys and appreciates them; they are his creation. It is God who wants to play, and sing, and enjoy beauty, and proclaim truth, and wear fine clothes, and eat good foods. *"It is God that worketh in you to will and to do,"* said the apostle Paul.

The desire you feel for riches is the infinite, seeking to express himself in you as he sought to find expression in the little boy at the piano. So you need not hesitate to ask largely. Your part is to focus on and express that desire to God.

This is a difficult point with most people. They retain something of the old idea that poverty and self-sacrifice are pleasing to God. They look upon poverty as a part of the plan, a necessity of nature.

They have the idea that God has finished his work, and made all that he can make, and that the majority of people must stay poor because there is not enough to go around. They hold to so much of this erroneous thought that they feel ashamed to ask for wealth. They try not to want more than a very modest competence, just enough to make them fairly comfortable.

I recall now the case of one student who was told that he must get in mind a clear picture of the things he desired, so that the creative thought of them might be impressed on formless substance. He was a very poor man, living in a rented house and having only what he earned from day today, and he could not grasp the fact that all wealth was his. So, after thinking the matter over, he decided that he might reasonably ask for a new rug for the floor of his best room and a coal stove to heat the house during the cold weather. Following the instructions given in this book, he obtained these things in a few months.

And then it dawned upon him that he had not asked enough. He went through the house in which he lived, and planned all the improvements he would like to make in it. He mentally added a bay window here and a room there until it was complete in his mind as his ideal home, and then he planned its furnishings.

Holding the whole picture in his mind, he began living in the certain way and moving toward what he wanted — and he owns the house now and is rebuilding it after the form of his mental image. And now, with still larger faith, he is going on to get greater things. It has been unto him according to his faith, and so it is with you — and with all of us.

7. GRATITUDE

THE ILLUSTRATIONS GIVEN IN THE LAST CHAPTER will have conveyed to the reader the fact that the first step toward getting rich is to convey the idea of your wants to the formless substance. This is true, and you will see that in order to do so it becomes necessary to relate yourself to the formless intelligence in a harmonious way.

To secure this harmonious relation is a matter of such primary and vital importance that I shall give some space to its discussion here and give you instructions which, if you will follow them, will be certain to bring you into perfect unity of mind with the supreme power, or God.

The whole process of mental adjustment and attunement can be summed up in one word: Gratitude.

First, you believe that there is one intelligent substance, from which all things proceed. Second, you believe that this substance gives you everything you desire. And third, you relate yourself to it by a feeling of deep and profound gratitude.

Many people who order their lives rightly in all other ways are kept in poverty by their lack of gratitude. Having received one gift from God, they cut the wires which connect them with him by failing to make acknowledgment.

It is easy to understand that the nearer we live to the source of wealth, the more wealth we shall receive, and it is easy also to understand that the soul that is always grateful lives in closer touch with God than the one which never looks to him in thankful acknowledgment. The more gratefully we fix our minds on the supreme when good things come to us, the more good things we will receive, and the more rapidly they will come. And the reason simply is that the mental attitude of gratitude draws the mind into closer touch with the source from which the blessings come.

If it is a new thought to you that gratitude brings your whole mind into closer harmony with the creative energies of the universe, consider it well, and you will see that it is true. The good things you have already have come to you along the line of obedience to certain laws. Gratitude will lead your mind out along the ways by which things come, and it will keep you in close harmony with creative thought and prevent you from falling into competitive thought.

Gratitude alone can keep you looking toward the all, and prevent you from falling into the error of thinking of the supply as limited — and to do that would be fatal to your hopes.

There is a law of gratitude, and it is absolutely necessary that you should observe the law if you are to get the results you seek. The law of gratitude is the natural principle that action and reaction are always equal and in opposite directions.

The grateful outreaching of your mind in thankful praise to the supreme intelligence is a liberation or expenditure of force. It cannot fail to reach that to which it addressed, and the reaction is an instantaneous movement toward you.

"Draw nigh unto God, and he will draw nigh unto you." That is a statement of psychological truth. And if your gratitude is strong and constant, the reaction in formless substance will be strong and continuous; the movement of the things you want will be always toward you. Notice the grateful attitude that Jesus took, how he always seems to be saying, "I thank thee, Father, that thou hearest me." You cannot exercise much power without gratitude, for it is gratitude that keeps you connected with power.

But the value of gratitude does not consist solely in getting you more blessings in the future. Without gratitude you cannot long keep from dissatisfied thought regarding things as they are.

The moment you permit your mind to dwell with dissatisfaction upon things as they are, you begin to lose ground. You fix attention upon the common, the ordinary, the poor, the squalid, and the mean — and your mind takes the form of these things. Then you will transmit these forms or mental images to the formless. And the common, the poor, the squalid, and the mean will come to you.

To permit your mind to dwell upon the inferior is to become inferior and to surround yourself with inferior things. On the other hand, to fix your attention on the best is to surround yourself with the best, and to become the best. The creative power within us makes us into the image of that to which we give our attention. We are of thinking substance, too, and thinking substance always takes the form of that which it thinks about.

The grateful mind is constantly fixed upon the best. Therefore it tends to become the best. It takes the form or character of the best, and will receive the best.

Also, faith is born of gratitude. The grateful mind continually expects good things, and expectation becomes faith. The reaction of gratitude upon one's own mind produces faith, and every outgoing wave of grateful thanksgiving increases faith. The person who has no feeling of gratitude cannot long retain a living faith, and without a living faith you cannot get rich by the creative method, as we shall see in the following chapters.

It is necessary, then, to cultivate the habit of being grateful for every good thing that comes to you and to give thanks continuously. And because all things have contributed to your advancement, you should include all things in your gratitude.

Do not waste a lot of time thinking or talking about the shortcomings or wrong actions of those in power. Their organization of the world has created your opportunity; all you get really comes to you because of them. Do not rage against corrupt politicians. If it were not for politicians we should fall into anarchy and your opportunity would be greatly lessened.

God has worked a long time and very patiently to bring us up to where we are in industry and government, and he is going right on with his work. There is not the least doubt that he will do away with plutocrats, trust magnates, captains of industry, and politicians as soon as they can be spared, but in the meantime, they are all very necessary. Remember that they are all helping to arrange the lines of transmission along which your riches will come to you, and be grateful. This will bring you into harmonious relations with the good in everything, and the good in everything will move toward you.

8. THINKING IN THE CERTAIN WAY

TURN BACK TO CHAPTER 6 AND READ AGAIN the story of the man who formed a mental image of his house and you will get a fair idea of the initial step toward getting rich. You must form a clear and definite mental picture of what you want. You cannot transmit an idea unless you have it yourself.

You must have it before you can give it, and many people fail to impress thinking substance because they have themselves only a vague and misty concept of the things they want to do, to have, or to become.

It is not enough that you should have a general desire for wealth "to do good with." *Everybody* has that desire.

It is not enough that you should have a wish to travel, see things, live more, etc. Everybody has those desires also. If you were going to send a wireless message to a friend, you would not send the letters of the alphabet in their order and let him construct the message for himself, nor would you take words at random from the dictionary. You would send a coherent sentence, one which meant something.

When you try to impress your wants upon the thinking substance, remember that it must be done by a coherent statement. You must know what you want and be *specific* and *definite*. You can never get rich or start the creative power into action by sending out unformed longings and vague desires.

Go over your desires just as the man I have described went over his house. See just what you want and get a clear mental picture of it as you wish it to look when you get it.

That clear mental picture you must have continually in mind. As the sailor has in mind the port toward which he is sailing the ship, you must keep your face toward it all the time. You must no more lose sight of it than the helmsman loses sight of the compass.

It is not necessary to take exercises in concentration, nor to set apart special times for prayer and affirmation, nor to "go into the silence," nor to do occult stunts of any kind. Some of these things are well enough, but all you need is to know what you want and to want it badly enough so that it will stay in your thoughts.

Spend as much of your leisure time as you can in contemplating your picture. But no one needs to take exercises to concentrate his mind on a thing which he really wants. It is the things you do *not* really care about which require effort to fix your attention upon them.

And unless you *really* want to get rich, so that the desire is strong enough to hold your thoughts directed to the purpose as the magnetic pole holds the needle of the compass, it will hardly be worthwhile for you to try to carry out the instructions given in this book.

The methods set forth here are for people whose desire for riches is strong enough to overcome mental laziness and the love of ease, and to make them work.

The more clear and definite you make your picture then, and the more you dwell upon it, bringing out all its delightful details, the stronger your desire will be. And the stronger your desire, the easier it will be to hold your mind fixed upon the picture of what you want.

Something more is necessary, however, than merely to see the picture clearly. If that is all you do, you are only a dreamer, and will have little or no power for accomplishment.

Behind your clear vision must be the purpose to realize it, to bring it out in tangible expression. And behind this purpose must be an invincible and unwavering FAITH that the thing is already yours, that it is "at hand" and you have only to take possession of it.

Live in the new house, mentally, until it takes form around you physically. In the mental realm, enter at once into full enjoyment of the things you want.

"Whatsoever things ye ask for when ye pray, believe that ye receive them, and ye shall have them" said Jesus.

See the things you want as if they were actually around you all the time. See yourself as owning and using them. Make use of them in imagination just as you will use them when they are your tangible possessions. Dwell upon your mental picture until it is clear and distinct, and then take the mental attitude of ownership toward everything in that picture. Take possession of it, in mind, in the full faith that it is actually yours. Hold to this mental ownership. Do not waiver for an instant in the faith that it is real.

And remember what was said in a proceeding chapter about gratitude: Be as thankful for it all the time as you expect to be when it has taken form. The person who can sincerely thank God for the things which as yet he owns only in imagination has real faith. He will get rich. He will cause the creation of whatever he wants.

You do not need to pray repeatedly for things you want. It is not necessary to tell God about it every day.

Your part is to intelligently formulate your desire for the things which make for a larger life and to get these desire arranged into a coherent whole, and then to impress this whole desire upon the formless substance, which has the power and the will to bring you what you want.

You do not make this impression by repeating strings of words; you make it by holding the vision with unshakable PURPOSE to attain it and with steadfast FAITH that you do attain it.

The answer to prayer is not according to your faith while you are *talking*, but according to your faith while you are *working*.

You cannot impress the mind of God by having a special Sabbath day set apart to tell him what you want, and then forgetting him during the rest of the week. You cannot impress him by having special hours to go into your closet and pray, if you then dismiss the matter from your mind until the hour of prayer comes again. Oral prayer is well enough, and has its effect, especially upon yourself, in clarifying your vision and strengthening your faith, but it is not your oral petitions which get you what you want.

In order to get rich you do not need a "sweet hour of prayer;" you need to "pray without ceasing." And by prayer I mean holding steadily to your vision, with the purpose to cause its creation into solid form, and the faith that you are doing so. "Believe that ye receive them."

Once you have clearly formed your vision, the whole matter turns on *receiving*. When you have formed it, it is well to make an oral statement, addressing the supreme in gratitude. Then, from that moment on you must, in mind, receive what you ask for.

Live in the new house, wear the fine clothes, ride in the automobile, go on the journey, and confidently plan for greater journeys. Think and speak of all the things you have asked for in terms of actual present ownership. Imagine an environment and a financial condition exactly as you want them, and live all the time in that mental environment and financial condition until they take physical shape.

Mind, however, that you do not do this as a mere dreamer and castle builder. Hold to the FAITH that the imaginary is being realized and to your PURPOSE to realize it. Remember that it is faith and purpose in the use of the imagination which make the difference between the scientist and the dreamer.

And having learned this fact, it is here that you must learn the proper use of the will.

9. HOW TO USE THE WILL

TO SET ABOUT GETTING RICH IN A SCIENTIFIC WAY, you do not try to apply your will power to anything outside of yourself.

You have no right to do so, anyway. It is wrong to apply your will to other men and women in order to get them to do what you wish done.

It is as flagrantly wrong to coerce people by mental power as it is to coerce them by physical power. If compelling people by physical force to do things for you reduces them to slavery, compelling them by mental means accomplishes exactly the same thing; the only difference is in methods. If taking things from people by physical force is robbery, them taking things by mental force is robbery also. There is no difference in principle.

You have no right to use your will power upon another person, even "for his own good," for you do not know what is for his good. The science of getting rich does not require you to apply power or force to any other person, in any way whatsoever. There is not the slightest necessity for doing so. Indeed, any attempt to use your will upon others will only tend to defeat your purpose.

You do not need to apply your will to things in order to compel them to come to you. That would simply be trying to coerce God and would be foolish and useless. You do not have to try to compel God to give you good things, any more than you have to use your will power to make the sun rise. You do not have to use your will power to conquer an unfriendly Deity, or to make stubborn and rebellious forces do your bidding. Substance is friendly to you, and is more anxious to give you what you want than you are to get it.

To get rich, you need only to use your will power upon *yourself.*

When you know what to think and do, then you must use your will to compel yourself to think and do the right things. That is the legitimate use of the will in getting what you want —to use it in holding yourself to the right course.

Use your will to keep yourself thinking and acting in the certain way. Do not try to project your will, or your thoughts, or your mind out into space to "act" on things or people. Keep your mind at home. It can accomplish more there than elsewhere.

Use your mind to form a mental image of what you want and to hold that vision with faith and purpose. And use your will to keep your mind working in the *right* way.

The more steady and continuous your faith and purpose, the more rapidly you will get rich because you will make only POSITIVE impressions upon substance, and you will not neutralize or offset them by negative impressions.

The picture of your desires, held with faith and purpose, is taken up by the formless, and permeates it to great distances — throughout the universe, for all we know.

As this impression spreads, all things are set moving toward its realization. Every living thing, every inanimate thing, and the things yet uncreated are stirred toward bringing into being that which you want. All force begins to be exerted in that direction. All things begin to move toward you. The minds of people everywhere are influenced toward doing the things necessary to the fulfilling of your desires, and they work for you, unconsciously.

But you can check all this by starting a negative impression in the formless substance. Doubt or unbelief is as certain to start a movement *away* from you as faith and purpose are to start one *toward* you. It is by not understanding this that most people make their failure. Every hour and moment you spend in giving heed to doubts and fears, every hour you spend in worry, every hour in which your soul is possessed by unbelief, sets a current *away from you* in the whole domain of intelligent substance. All the promises are unto them that believe and unto them only.

Since belief is all important, it behooves you to guard your thoughts, and as your beliefs will be shaped to a very great extent by the things you observe and think about, it is important that you should carefully govern to what you give your attention.

And here the will comes into use, for it is by your will that you determine upon what things your attention shall be fixed. If you want to become rich, you must not make a study of poverty. Things are not brought into being by thinking about their opposites.

Health is never to be attained by studying disease and thinking about disease; righteousness is not promoted by studying sin and thinking about sin; and no one ever got rich by studying poverty and thinking about poverty. Medicine as a science of disease has increased disease; religion as a science of sin has promoted sin, and economics as a study of poverty will fill the world with wretchedness and want.

Do not talk about poverty, do not investigate it, or concern yourself with it. Never mind what its causes are; you have nothing to do with them. What concerns you is the cure.

Do not spend your time in so called charitable work or charity movements; most charity only tends to perpetuate the wretchedness it aims to eradicate. I do not say that you should be hard-hearted or unkind and refuse to hear the cry of need, but you must not try to eradicate poverty in any of the *conventional* ways. Put poverty behind you, and put all that pertains to it behind you, and "make good."

Get rich. That is the best way you can help the poor. And you cannot hold the mental image which is to make you rich if you fill your mind with pictures of poverty and all its attendant ills. Do not read books or papers which give circumstantial accounts of the wretchedness of the tenement dwellers, of the horrors of child labor, and so on. Do not read anything which fills your mind with gloomy images of want and suffering.

You cannot help the poor in the least by knowing about these things, and the widespread knowledge of them does not tend at all to do away with poverty. What tends to do away with poverty is not the getting of pictures of poverty into your mind, but getting pictures of wealth, abundance, and possibility into the minds of the poor. You are not deserting the poor in their misery when you refuse to allow your mind to be filled with pictures of that misery.

Poverty can be done away with, not by increasing the number of well-to-do people who think about poverty, but by increasing the number of poor people who purpose with faith to get rich.

The poor do not need charity; they need inspiration. Charity only sends them a loaf of bread to keep them alive in their wretchedness, or gives them an entertainment to make them forget for an hour or two. But inspiration can cause them to rise out of their misery. If you want to help the poor, demonstrate to them that they can become rich. Prove it by getting rich yourself.

The only way in which poverty will ever be banished from this world is by getting a large and constantly increasing number of people to practice the teachings of this book.

People must be taught to become rich by creation, not by competition. Every person who becomes rich by competition knocks down the ladder by which he rises, and keeps others down, but every person who gets rich by creation opens a way for thousands to follow — and inspires them to do so.

You are not showing hardness of heart or an unfeeling disposition when you refuse to pity poverty, see poverty, read about poverty, or think or talk about it, or to listen to those who do talk about it. Use your will power to keep your mind OFF the subject of poverty and to keep it fixed with faith and purpose ON the vision of what you want and are creating.

10. FURTHER USE OF THE WILL

YOU CANNOT RETAIN A TRUE AND CLEAR vision of wealth if you are constantly turning your attention to opposing pictures, whether they be external or imaginary.

Do not tell of your past troubles of a financial nature, if you have had them. Do not think of them at all. Do not tell of the poverty of your parents or the hardships of your early life. To do any of these things is to mentally class yourself with the poor for the time being, and it will certainly check the movement of things in your direction. Put poverty and all things that pertain to poverty completely behind you. You have accepted a certain theory of the universe as being correct, and are resting all your hopes of happiness on its being correct. What can you gain by giving heed to conflicting theories?

Do not read books which tell you that the world is soon coming to an end, and do not read the writing of muckrakers and pessimistic philosophers who tell you that it is going to the devil. The world is not going to the devil; it is going to God. It is a wonderful becoming.

True, there may be a good many things in existing conditions which are disagreeable, but what is the use of studying them when they are certainly passing away and when the study of them only tends to slow their passing and keep them with us? Why give time and attention to things which are being removed by evolutionary growth, when you can hasten their removal only by promoting the evolutionary growth as far as your part of it goes?

No matter how horrible in seeming may be the conditions in certain countries, sections, or places, you waste your time and destroy your own chances by dwelling on them.

You should interest yourself in the world's becoming rich.

Think of the riches the world is coming into instead of the poverty it is growing out of, and bear in mind that the only way in which you can assist the world in growing rich is by growing rich yourself through the creative method, not the competitive one.

Give your attention wholly to riches. Do not focus on poverty. Whenever you think or speak of those who are poor, think and speak of them as those who are becoming rich, as those who are to be congratulated rather than pitied. Then they and others will catch the inspiration, and begin to search for the way out.

Because I say that you are to give your whole time and mind and thought to riches, it does not follow that you are to be sordid or mean. To become really rich is the noblest aim you can have in life, for it includes everything else.

On the competitive plane, the struggle to get rich is a Godless scramble for power over others, but when we come into the creative mind, all this is changed. All that is possible in the way of greatness, of service and lofty endeavor, comes by way of getting rich, because all is made possible by the use of things. You can aim at nothing so great or noble, I repeat, as to become rich, and you must fix your attention upon your mental picture of wealth to the exclusion of all that may tend to dim or obscure the vision.

Some people remain in poverty because they are ignorant of the fact that there is wealth for them, and these can best be taught by showing them the way to affluence in your own person and practice.

Others are poor because, while they feel that there is a way out, they are too intellectually indolent to put forth the mental effort necessary to find that way and travel it. For these, the very best thing you can do is to arouse their desire by showing them the happiness that comes from being rightly rich.

Others still are poor because, while they have some notion of science, they have become so swamped and lost in the maze of theories that they do not know which road to take. They try a mixture of many systems and fail in all. For these, again, the very best thing to do is to show the right way in your own person and practice. An ounce of doing things is worth a pound of theorizing.

The very best thing you can do for the whole world is to make the most of yourself. You can serve God and humanity in no more effective way than by getting rich; that is, if you get rich by the creative method and not by the competitive one.

Another thing. We assert that this book gives in detail the principles of the science of getting rich, and if that is true, you do not need to read any other book upon the subject. This may sound narrow and egotistical, but consider: There is no more scientific method of computation in mathematics than by addition, subtraction, multiplication, and division; no other method is possible. There can be but one shortest distance between two points. There is only one way to think scientifically, and that is to think in the way that leads by the most direct and simple route to the goal. No one has yet formulated a briefer or less complex "system" than the one set forth here. It has been stripped of all non-essentials. When you commence on this, lay all others aside. Put them out of your mind altogether.

Read this book every day. Keep it with you. Commit it to memory, and do not think about other "systems" and theories. If you do, you will begin to have doubts and to be uncertain and wavering in your thought, and then you will begin to make failures. After you have made good and become rich, you may study other systems as much as you please.

And read only the most optimistic comments on the world's news — those in harmony with your picture. Also, do not dabble in theosophy, spiritualism, or kindred studies. Perhaps the dead still live and are near, but if they are, let them alone; mind your own business.

Wherever the spirits of the dead may be, they have their own work to do, and we have no right to interfere with them. We cannot help them, and it is very doubtful whether they can help us, or whether we have any right to trespass upon their time if they can. Let the dead and the hereafter alone, and solve your own problem: Get rich. If you begin to mix with the occult, you will start mental cross-currents which will surely bring your hopes to shipwreck.

Now, this and the preceding chapters have brought us to the following statement of basic facts:

There is a thinking stuff from which all things are made, and which, in its original state, permeates, penetrates, and fills the interspaces of the universe. A thought in this substance produces the thing that is imaged by the thought.

A person can form things in his thought, and, by impressing his thought upon formless substance, can cause the thing he thinks about to be created.

In order to do this, a person must pass from the competitive to the creative mind; he must form a clear mental picture of the things he wants, and hold this picture in his thoughts with the fixed PURPOSE to get what he wants, and the unwavering FAITH that he does get what he wants, closing his mind against all that may tend to shake his purpose, dim his vision, or quench his faith.

And in addition to all this, we shall now see that he must live and *act* in a certain way.

11. ACTING IN THE CERTAIN WAY

THOUGHT IS THE CREATIVE POWER or the impelling force which causes the creative power to act. Thinking in a certain way will bring riches to you, but you must not rely upon thought alone, paying no attention to personal action. That is the rock upon which many otherwise scientific thinkers meet shipwreck — the failure to connect thought with personal action.

We have not yet reached the stage of development, even supposing such a stage to be possible, in which a person can create directly from formless substance without nature's processes or the work of human hands. A person must not only think, but his personal action must supplement his thought.

By thought you can cause the gold in the hearts of the mountains to be impelled toward you, but it will not mine itself, refine itself, coin itself into double eagles, and come rolling along the roads, seeking its way into your pocket.

Under the impelling power of the supreme spirit, people's affairs will be so ordered that someone will be led to mine the gold for you. Other people's business transactions will be so directed that the gold will be brought toward you. And you must so arrange your own business affairs that you may be able to receive it when it comes to you. Your thought makes all things, animate and inanimate, work to bring you what you want, but your personal activity must be such that you can rightly receive what you want when it reaches you. You are not to take it as charity, nor to steal it. You must give every man more in use value than he gives you in cash value.

The scientific use of thought consists in forming a clear and distinct mental image of what you want, in holding fast to your purpose to get what you want, and in realizing with grateful faith that you do get what you want.

Do not try to "project" your thought in any mysterious or occult way, with the idea of having it go out and do things for you. That is wasted effort and will weaken your power to think with sanity.

The action of thought in getting rich is fully explained in the preceding chapters: Your faith and purpose positively impress your vision upon formless substance, which has *the same desire for more life that you have,* and this vision, received from you, sets all the creative forces at work *in and through their regular channels of action,* but directed toward you.

It is not your part to guide or supervise the creative process. All you have to do with that is to retain your vision, stick to your purpose, and maintain your faith and gratitude.

But you must *act in a certain way,* so that you can appropriate what is yours when it comes to you and so that you can meet the things you have in your picture and put them in their proper places as they arrive.

You can really see the truth of this. When things reach you, they will be in the hands of others, who will ask an equivalent for them. And you can only get what is yours by giving the other person what is rightfully his.

Your pocketbook is not going to be transformed into a Fortunata's purse, which shall be always full of money without effort on your part.

This is the crucial point in the science of getting rich — right here, where thought and personal action must be combined. There are very many people who, consciously or unconsciously, set the creative forces in action by the strength and persistence of their desires, but who remain poor because they do not provide for the reception of the thing they want when it comes.

By thought the thing you want is brought to you. By action, you receive it.

Whatever your action is to be, it is evident that you must act NOW. You cannot act in the past, and it is essential to the clearness of your mental vision that you dismiss the past from your mind. You cannot act in the future, for the future is not here yet. And you cannot tell how you will want to act in any future contingency until that contingency has arrived.

Because you are not in the right business or the right environment now, do not think that you must postpone action until you get into the right business or environment. And do not spend time in the present taking thought as to the best course in possible future emergencies; have faith in your ability to meet any emergency when it arrives.

If you act in the present with your mind on the future, your present action will be with a divided mind, and will not be effective.

Put your whole mind into present action.

Do not give your creative impulse to original substance, and then sit down and wait for results. If you do, you will never get them. Act now. There is never any time but now, and there never will be any time but now. If you are ever to begin to make ready for the reception of what you want, you must begin NOW.

And your action, whatever it is, must most likely be in your present business or employment, and must be upon the persons and things in your present environment.

You cannot act where you are not, you cannot act where you have been, and you cannot act where you are going to be. You can act only where you are.

Do not bother as to whether yesterday's work was well done or ill done; do today's work well. Do not try to do tomorrow's work now; there will be plenty of time to do that when you get to it. Do not try, by occult or mystical means, to act on people or things that are out of your reach.

Do not wait for a change of environment, before you act; get a change of environment by action. You can so act upon the environment in which you are now, as to cause yourself to be transferred to a better environment.

Hold with faith and purpose the vision of yourself in the better environment, but act upon your present environment with all your heart, and with all your strength and with all your mind. Do not spend any time in day dreaming or castle building, hold to the one vision of what you want and act now.

Do not cast about, seeking some new thing to do or some strange, unusual, or remarkable action to perform as a first step toward getting rich. It is probable that your actions, at least for some time to come, will be the same ones you have been performing for some time past, but you are to begin now to perform these actions in the certain way, which will surely make you rich.

If you are engaged in some business, and feel that it is not the right one for you, do not wait until you get into the right business before you begin to act.

Do not feel discouraged or sit down and lament because you are misplaced. No one is so misplaced that he cannot find the right place, and no one is so involved in the wrong business that he cannot get into the right business.

Hold the vision of yourself in the right business, with the purpose to get into it and the faith that you *will* get into it and *are* getting into it, but ACT in your present business. Use your present business as the means of getting a better one, and use your present environment as the means of getting into a better one. Your vision of the right business, if held with faith and purpose, will cause the supreme power to move the right business toward you. And your action, if performed in the certain way, will cause you to move toward the business.

If you are an employee or wage earner and feel that you must change places in order to get what you want, do not "project" your thought into space and rely upon it to get you another job. It will probably fail to do so.

Hold the vision of yourself in the job you want while you ACT with faith and purpose on the job you have, and you will certainly get the job you want.

Your vision and faith will set the creative force in motion to bring it toward you, and your action will cause the forces in your own environment to move you toward the place you want. In closing this chapter, we will add another statement to our syllabus:

There is a thinking stuff from which all things are made, and which, in its original state, permeates, penetrates, and fills the interspaces of the universe. A thought in this substance produces the thing that is imaged by the thought.

A person can form things in his thought, and, by impressing his thought upon formless substance, can cause the thing he thinks about to be created.

In order to do this, a person must pass from the competitive to the creative mind; he must form a clear mental picture of the things he wants, and hold this picture in his thoughts with the fixed PURPOSE to get what he wants, and the unwavering FAITH that he does get what he wants, closing his mind to all that may tend to shake his purpose, dim his vision, or quench his faith. So that he may receive what he wants when it comes, a person must act NOW upon the people and things in his present environment.

12. EFFICIENT ACTION

YOU MUST USE YOUR THOUGHT AS DIRECTED in previous chapters and begin to do what you can do where you are, and you must do ALL that you can do where you are.

You can advance only by being larger than your present place, and no one is larger than his present place who leaves undone any of the work pertaining to that place. The world is advanced only by those who more than fill their present places.

If no one quite filled his present place, you can see that there must be a going backward in everything. Those who do not quite fill their present places are dead weight upon society, government, commerce, and industry. They must be carried along by others at a great expense. The progress of the world is slowed only by those who do not fill the places they are holding. They belong to a former age and their tendency is toward degeneration. No society could advance if everyone was smaller than his place; social evolution is guided by the law of physical and mental evolution.

In the animal world, evolution is caused by excess of life. When an organism has more life than can be expressed in the

41

functions of its own plane, it develops the organs of a higher plane, and a new species is originated.

There never would have been new species had there not been organisms which more than filled their places. The law is exactly the same for you: Your getting rich depends upon your applying this principle to your own affairs.

Every day is either a successful day or a day of failure, and it is the successful days which get you what you want. If every day is a failure you can never get rich, while if every day is a success, you cannot fail to get rich.

If there is something that may be done today and you do not do it, you have failed insofar as that thing is concerned — and the consequences may be more disastrous than you imagine.

You cannot foresee the results of even the most trivial act. You do not know the workings of all the forces that have been set moving in your behalf. Much may be depending on your doing some simple act, and it may be the very thing which is to open the door of opportunity to very great possibilities. You can never know all the combinations which supreme intelligence is making for you in the world of things and of human affairs. Your neglect or failure to do some small thing may cause a long delay in getting what you want. **Do, every day, ALL that can be done that day.**

There is, however, a limitation or qualification of the above that you must take into account.

You are not to overwork, nor to rush blindly into your business in the effort to do the greatest possible number of things in the shortest possible time. You are not to try to do tomorrow's work today, nor to do a week's work in a day. It is really not the number of things you do, but the EFFICIENCY of each separate action that counts.

Every act is, in itself, either a success or a failure. Every act is, in itself, either effective and efficient or ineffective and inefficient.

Every inefficient act is a failure, and if you spend your life in doing inefficient acts, your whole life will be a failure. The more things you do, the worse for you, if all your acts are inefficient ones.

On the other hand, every efficient act is a success in itself, and if every act of your life is an efficient one, your whole life *must* be a success.

The cause of failure is doing too many things in an inefficient manner and not doing enough things in an efficient manner.

You will see that it is a self-evident proposition that if you do not do any inefficient acts and if you do a sufficient number of efficient acts, you will become rich. If, now, it is possible for you to make each act an efficient one, you see again that the getting of riches is reduced to an exact science, like mathematics.

The matter turns, then, on the question of whether you can make each separate act a success in itself. And this you can certainly do. You can make each act a success, because ALL power is working with you, and ALL power cannot fail.

Power is at your service, and to make each act efficient you have only to put power into it.

Every action is either strong or weak, and when every action is strong, you are acting in the certain way which will make you rich.

Every act can be made strong and efficient by holding your vision while you are doing it and putting the whole power of your FAITH and PURPOSE into it.

It is at this point that the people who separate mental power from personal action fail. They use the power of mind in one place and at one time, and they act in another way in another place and at another time. So their acts are not successful in themselves; too many of them are inefficient. But if ALL power goes into every act, no matter how commonplace, every act will be a success in itself. And since it is the nature of things that every success opens the way to other successes, your progress toward what you want and the progress of what you want toward you, will become increasingly rapid.

Remember that successful action is cumulative in its results. Since the desire for more life is inherent in all things, when a person begins to move toward larger life, more things attach themselves to him, and the influence of his desire is multiplied.

Do, every day, all that you can do that day, and do each act in an efficient manner.

In saying that you must hold your vision while you are doing each act, however trivial or commonplace, I do not mean to say that it is necessary at all times to see the vision distinctly to its smallest details. It should be the work of your leisure hours to use your imagination on the details of your vision and to contemplate them until they are firmly fixed upon memory. If you wish speedy results, spend practically all your spare time in this practice.

By continuous contemplation you will get the picture of what you want — even to the smallest details — so firmly fixed upon your mind and so completely transferred to the mind of formless sub- stance, that in your working hours you need only to mentally refer to the picture to stimulate your faith and purpose and cause your best effort to be put forth. Contemplate your picture in your leisure hours until your consciousness is so full of it that you can grasp it instantly. You will become so enthused with its bright promises that the mere thought of it will call forth the strongest energies of your whole being.

Let us again repeat our syllabus, and by slightly changing the closing statements bring it to the point we have now reached.

There is a thinking stuff from which all things are made, and which, in its original state, permeates, penetrates, and fills the interspaces of the universe.

A thought in this substance produces the thing that is imaged by the thought.

A person can form things in his thought, and, by impressing his thought upon formless substance, can cause the thing he thinks about to be created.

In order to do this, a person must pass from the competitive to the creative mind. He must form a clear mental picture of the things he wants, and must do — with faith and purpose — all that can be done each day, doing each separate thing in an efficient manner.

13. GETTING INTO THE RIGHT BUSINESS

SUCCESS, IN ANY PARTICULAR BUSINESS, depends for one thing upon your possessing, in a well-developed state, the faculties required in that business.

Without good musical faculty no one can succeed as a teacher of music. Without well-developed mechanical faculties no one can achieve great success in any of the mechanical trades. Without tact and the commercial faculties no one can succeed in mercantile pursuits. But to possess in a well-developed state the faculties required in your particular vocation does not insure getting rich. There are musicians who have remarkable talent, and who yet remain poor. There are blacksmiths, carpenters, and so on who have excellent mechanical ability, but who do not get rich. And there are merchants with good faculties for dealing with people who nevertheless fail.

The different faculties are tools. It is essential to have good tools, but it is also essential that the tools should be used in the right way. One man can take a sharp saw, a square, a good plane, and so on, and build a handsome article of furniture. Another man can take the same tools and set to work to duplicate the article, but his production will be a botch. He does not know how to use good tools in a successful way.

The various faculties of your mind are the tools with which you must do the work which is to make you rich. So it will be easier for you to succeed if you get into a business for which you are well equipped with mental tools.

Generally speaking, you will do best in that business which will use your strongest faculties — the one for which you are naturally "best fitted." But there are limitations to this statement also. No one should regard his vocation as being irrevocably fixed by the tendencies with which he was born.

You can get rich in ANY business, for if you have not the right talent, you can develop that talent. It merely means that you will have to make your tools as you go along, instead of confining yourself to the use of those with which you were born. It will be EASIER for you to succeed in a vocation for which you already have the talents in a well-developed state; but you CAN succeed in any vocation, for you can develop any rudimentary talent, and there is no talent of which you have not at least the rudiment.

You will get rich most easily in terms of effort, if you do that for which you are best fitted, but you will get rich most satisfactorily if you do that which you WANT to do. Doing what you want to do is life, and there is no real satisfaction in living if we are compelled to be forever doing something which we do not like to do and can never do what we want to do. And it is certain that you can do what you want to do. The desire to do it is proof that you have within you the power which *can* do it.

Desire is a manifestation of power. The desire to play music is the power which can play music seeking expression and development. The desire to invent mechanical devices is the mechanical talent seeking expression and development.

Where there is no power, either developed or undeveloped, to do a thing, there is never any desire to do that thing, and where there is strong desire to do a thing, it is certain proof that the power to do it is strong and only requires to be developed and applied in the right way.

All other things being equal, it is best to select the business for which you have the best developed talent, but if you have a strong desire to engage in any particular line of work, you should select that work as the ultimate end at which you aim. You can do what you want to do, and it is your right and privilege to follow the business or avocation which will be most congenial and pleasant. You are not obliged to do what you do not like to do, and should not do it except as a means to bring you to the doing of the things you want to do.

If there are past mistakes whose consequences have placed you in an undesirable business or environment, you may be obliged for some time to do what you do not like to do, but you can make the doing of it pleasant by knowing that it is making it possible for you to come to the doing of what you want to do.

If you feel that you are not in the right vocation, do not act too hastily in trying to get into another one. The best way, generally, to change business or environment is by growth.

Do not be afraid to make a sudden and radical change if the opportunity is presented and you feel after careful consideration that it is the right opportunity, but never take sudden or radical action when you are in doubt as to the wisdom of doing so.

There is never any hurry on the creative plane, and there is no lack of opportunity.

When you get out of the competitive mind you will understand that you never need to act hastily. No one else is going to beat you to the thing you want to do; there is enough for all. If one space is taken, another and a better one will be opened for you a little farther on; there is plenty of time. When you are in doubt, wait. Fall back on the contemplation of your vision, and increase your faith and purpose. And by all means, in times of doubt and indecision, cultivate gratitude.

A day or two spent in contemplating the vision of what you want and in earnest thanksgiving that you are getting it will bring your mind into such close relationship with the supreme that you will make no mistake when you do act.

There is a mind which knows all there is to know, and you can come into close unity with this mind by faith and the purpose to advance in life, if you have deep gratitude.

Mistakes come from acting hastily or from acting in fear or doubt or in forgetfulness of the right motive, which is more life to all, and less to none.

As you go on in the certain way, opportunities will come to you in increasing number, and you will need to be very steady in your faith and purpose, and to keep in close touch with the supreme mind by reverent gratitude.

Do all that you can do in a perfect manner every day, but do it without haste, worry, or fear. Go as fast as you can, but never hurry.

Remember that in the moment you begin to hurry you cease to be a creator and become a competitor. You drop back upon the old plane again.

Whenever you find yourself hurrying, call a halt. Fix your attention on the mental image of the thing you want and begin to give thanks that you are getting it. The exercise of GRATITUDE will never fail to strengthen your faith and renew your purpose.

14. THE IMPRESSION OF INCREASE

WHETHER YOU CHANGE YOUR VOCATION OR NOT, your actions for the present must be those pertaining to the business in which you are now engaged.

You can get into the business you want by making constructive use of the business you are already established in — by doing your daily work in the certain way. And insofar as your business consists in dealing with other people, whether personally or by letter, the key thought of all your efforts must be to convey to their minds the *impression of increase.*

Increase is what all men and all women are seeking; it is the urge of the formless intelligence within them seeking fuller expression.

The desire for increase is inherent in all nature; it is the fundamental impulse of the universe. All human activities are based on this desire. People are seeking more food, more clothes, better shelter, more luxury, more beauty, more knowledge, more pleasure —increase in something, more life. Every living thing is under this necessity for continuous advancement; where increase of life ceases, dissolution and death set in at once.

Man instinctively knows this, and therefore he is forever seeking more. This law of perpetual increase is set forth by Jesus in the parable of the talents: Only those who gain more retain any; from him who has not shall be taken away even that which he has.

The normal desire for increased wealth is not an evil or a reprehensible thing. It is simply the desire for more abundant life. It is aspiration.

And because it is the deepest instinct of their natures, all men and women are attracted to those who can give them more of the means of life.

In following the certain way as described in the foregoing pages, you are getting continuous increase for yourself, and you are giving it to all with whom you deal. You are a creative center from which increase is given off to all.

Be sure of this, and convey assurance of the fact to every man, woman, and child with whom you come in contact. No matter how small the transaction, even if it be only the selling of a stick of candy to a little child, put into it the thought of increase, and make sure that the customer is impressed with the thought.

Convey the impression of advancement with everything you do, so that all people shall receive the impression that you are an "advancing personality," and that you advance all who deal with you. Even to the people whom you meet in a social way — without any thought of business and to whom you do not try to sell anything — give the thought of increase.

You can convey this impression by holding the unshakable faith that you, yourself, are in the way of increase and by letting this faith inspire, fill, and permeate every action.

Do everything that you do in the firm conviction that you are an advancing personality and that you are giving advancement to everybody. Feel that you are getting rich, and that in so doing you are making others rich and conferring benefits on all. Do not boast or brag of your success or talk about it unnecessarily; true faith is never boastful. Wherever you find a boastful person, you find one who is secretly doubtful and afraid. Simply feel the faith, and let it work out in every transaction.

Let every act and tone and look express the quiet assurance that you are getting rich — that you are already rich. Words will not be necessary to communicate this feeling to others. They will feel the sense of increase when in your presence, and will be attracted to you again.

You must so impress others that they will feel that in associating with you they will get increase for themselves. See that you give them a use value greater than the cash value you are taking from them.

Take an honest pride in doing this and let everybody know it, and you will have no lack of customers. People will go where they are given increase, and the supreme, which desires increase in all and which knows all, will move toward you men and women who have never heard of you. Your business will increase rapidly, and you will be surprised at the unexpected benefits which will come to you. You will be able from day to day to make larger combinations, secure greater advantages, and to go on into a more congenial vocation if you desire to do so. But doing thing all this, you must never lose sight of your vision of what you want or your faith and purpose to get what you want.

Let me here give you another word of caution in regard to motives: Beware of the insidious temptation to seek for power over other people.

Nothing is so pleasant to the unformed or partially developed mind as the exercise of power or dominion over others. The desire to rule for selfish gratification has been the curse of the world. For countless ages kings and lords have drenched the earth with blood in their battles to extend their dominions — not to seek more life for all, but to get more power for themselves.

Today, the main motive in the business and industrial world is the same: Men marshal their armies of dollars and lay waste the lives and hearts of millions in the same mad scramble for power over others. Commercial kings, like political kings, are inspired by the lust for power.

Look out for the temptation to seek for authority, to become a "master," to be considered as one who is above the common herd, to impress others by lavish display, and so on. The mind that seeks for mastery over others is the competitive mind, and the competitive mind is not the creative one. In order to master your environment and your destiny, it is not at all necessary that you should rule over your fellow men, and, indeed, when you fall into the world's struggle for the high places, you begin to be conquered by fate and environment and your getting rich becomes a matter of chance and speculation.

Beware of the competitive mind! No better statement of the principle of creative action can be formulated than the favorite declaration of the late "Golden Rule" Jones of Toledo: "What I want for myself, I want for everybody."

15. THE ADVANCING PERSONALITY

WHAT I HAVE SAID IN THE LAST CHAPTER APPLIES as well to the professional person and the wage- earner as to the person who is engaged in selling or any other form of business.

No matter whether you are a physician, a teacher, or a clergyman, if you can give increase of life to others and make them sensible of that fact, they will be attracted to you, and you will get rich. The physician who holds the vision of himself as a great and successful healer, and who works toward the complete realization of that vision with faith and purpose, as described in former chapters, will come into such close touch with the source of life that he will be phenomenally successful; patients will come to him in throngs.

No one has a greater opportunity to carry into effect the teaching of this book than the practitioner of medicine. It does not matter to which of the various schools he may belong, for the principle of healing is common to all of them and may be reached by all alike. The "advancing man" in medicine, who holds to a clear mental image of himself as successful, and who obeys the laws of faith, purpose, and gratitude, will cure every curable case he undertakes.

In the field of religion, the world cries out for the clergyman who can teach his hearers the true science of abundant life. He who masters the details of the science of getting rich, together with the allied sciences of being well, of being great, and of winning love, and who teaches these details from the pulpit, will never lack for a congregation. This is a gospel that the world needs; it will give increase of life, and people will hear it gladly and give liberal support to the person who brings it to them.

What is now needed is a demonstration of the science of life from the pulpit. We want preachers who can not only tell us how, but who in their own persons will show us how. We need the preacher who will himself be rich, healthy, great, and beloved, to teach us how to attain to these things, and when he comes he will find a numerous and loyal following.

The same is true of the teacher who can inspire the children with the faith and purpose of the advancing life. He will never be "out of a job." And any teacher who has this faith and purpose can give it to his pupils. He cannot help giving it to them if it is part of his own life and practice. What is true of the teacher, preacher, and physician is true of the lawyer, dentist, real estate agent, insurance agent — of everybody.

The combined mental and personal action I have described is infallible; it cannot fail. Every man and woman who follows these instructions steadily, perseveringly, and to the letter, will get rich. The law of the increase of life is as mathematically certain in its operation as the law of gravity. Getting rich is an exact science.

The wage-earner will find this as true of his case as of any of the others mentioned. Do not feel that you have no chance to get rich because you are working where there is no visible opportunity for advancement, where wages are small and the cost of living high. Form your clear mental vision of what you want, and begin to act with faith and purpose.

Do all the work you can do, every day, and do each piece of work in a perfectly successful manner. Put the power of success and the purpose to get rich into everything that you do.

But do not do this merely with the idea of currying favor with your employer, in the hope that he, or those above you, will see your good work and advance you. It is not likely that they will do so.

The person who is merely a "good" worker, filling his place to the very best of his ability and satisfied with that, is valuable to his employer, and it is not to the employer's interest to promote him. He is worth more where he is.

To secure advancement, something more is necessary than to be too large for your place.

The person who is certain to advance is the one who is too big for his place, who has a clear concept of what he wants to be, who knows that he can become what he wants to be, and who is determined to BE what he wants to be.

Do not try to more than fill your present place with a view to pleasing your employer. Do it with the idea of advancing yourself. Hold the faith and purpose of increase during work hours, after work hours, and before work hours. Hold it in such a way that every person who comes in contact with you, whether foreman, fellow worker, or social acquaintance, will feel the power of purpose radiating from you — so that everyone will get the sense of advancement and increase from you. People will be attracted to you, and if there is no possibility for advancement in your present job, you will very soon see an opportunity to take another job.

There is a power which never fails to present opportunity to the advancing personality who is moving in obedience to law. God cannot help helping you if you act in a certain way. He must do so in order to help himself.

There is nothing in your circumstances or in the industrial situation that can keep you down. If you cannot get rich working for the steel trust, you can get rich on a ten-acre farm. And if you begin to move in the *certain way*, you will certainly escape from the "clutches" of the steel trust and get on to the farm or wherever else you wish to be.

If a few thousands of its employees would enter upon the certain way, the steel trust would soon be in a bad plight. It would have to give its workers more opportunity or go out of business. Nobody has to work for a trust. The trusts can keep people in so called hopeless conditions only so long as there are people who are ignorant of the science of getting rich or too intellectually slothful to practice it.

Begin this way of thinking and acting, and your faith and purpose will make you quick to see any opportunity to better your condition. Such opportunities will speedily come, for the supreme power, working in all and working for you, will bring them before you. Do not wait for an opportunity to be *all* that you want to be. When an opportunity to be more than you are now is presented and you feel impelled toward it, take it. It will be the first step toward a greater opportunity.

There is no such thing possible in this universe as a lack of opportunities for the person who is living the advancing life. It is inherent in the constitution of the cosmos that all things shall be for him and work together for his good, and he must certainly get rich if he acts and thinks in the certain way.

So let wage-earning men and women study this book with great care and enter with confidence upon the course of action it prescribes. It will not fail.

16. SOME CAUTIONS AND CONCLUDING OBSERVATIONS

MANY PEOPLE WILL SCOFF at the idea that there is an exact science of getting rich. Holding the impression that the supply of wealth is limited, they will insist that social and governmental institutions must be changed before even any considerable number of people can acquire a competence. But this is not true. It is true that existing governments keep the masses in poverty, but this is because the masses do not think and act in the certain way.

If the masses begin to move forward as suggested in this book, neither governments nor industrial systems can check them; all systems must be modified to accommodate the forward movement.

If the people have the advancing mind, have the faith that they can become rich, and move forward with the fixed purpose to become rich, nothing can possibly keep them in poverty. Individuals may enter upon the certain way at any time and under any government and make themselves rich. And when any considerable number of individuals do so under any government, they will cause the system to be so modified as to open the way for others.

The more people who get rich on the competitive plane, the worse for others. The more who get rich on the creative plane, the better for others. The economic salvation of the masses can only be accomplished by getting a large number of people to practice the scientific method set down in this book and become rich. These will show others the way and inspire them with a desire for real life, with the faith that it can be attained, and with the purpose to attain it.

For the present, however, it is enough to know that neither the government under which you live nor the capitalistic or competitive system of industry can keep you from getting rich. When you enter upon the creative plane of thought you will rise above all these things and become a citizen of another kingdom.

But remember that your thought must be held upon the creative plane. You are never for an instant to be betrayed into regarding the supply as limited or into acting on the moral level of competition.

Whenever you do fall into old ways of thought, correct yourself instantly. For when you are in the competitive mind, you have lost the cooperation of the supreme mind.

Do not spend any time in planning as to how you will meet possible emergencies in the future, except as the necessary policies may affect your actions today. You are concerned with doing today's work in a perfectly successful manner and not with emergencies which may arise tomorrow. You can attend to them as they come.

Do not concern yourself with questions as to how you shall surmount obstacles which may loom upon your business horizon unless you can see plainly that your course must be altered today in order to avoid them.

No matter how tremendous an obstruction may appear at a distance, you will find that if you go on in the certain way it will disappear as you approach it, or that a way over, under, through or around it will appear.

No possible combination of circumstances can defeat a person who is proceeding to get rich along strictly scientific lines. No person who obeys the law can fail to get rich, any more than one can multiply two by two and fail to get four.

Give no anxious thought to possible disasters, obstacles, panics, or unfavorable combinations of circumstances. There is time enough to meet such things when they present themselves before you in the immediate present, and you will find that every difficulty carries with it the wherewithal for its overcoming.

Guard your speech. Never speak of yourself, your affairs, or of anything else in a discouraged or discouraging way. Never admit the possibility of failure or speak in a way that infers failure as a possibility. Never speak of the times as being hard or of business conditions as being doubtful. Times may be hard and business doubtful for those who are on the competitive plane, but they can never be so for you. You can create what you want, and you are above fear.

When others are having hard times and poor business, you will find your greatest opportunities. Train yourself to think of and to look upon the world as a something which is becoming, which is growing, and to regard seeming evil as being only that which is undeveloped. Always speak in terms of advancement. To do otherwise is to deny your faith, and to deny your faith is to lose it.

Never allow yourself to feel disappointed. You may expect to have a certain thing at a certain time and not get it at that time, and this will appear to you like failure. But if you hold to your faith you will find that the failure is only apparent.

Go on in the certain way, and if you do not receive that thing, you will receive something so much better that you will see that the seeming failure was really a great success.

A student of this science had set his mind on making a certain business combination which seemed to him at the time to be very desirable, and he worked for some weeks to bring it about. When the crucial time came, the thing failed in a perfectly inexplicable way. It was as if some unseen influence had been working secretly against him. But he was not disappointed. On the contrary, he thanked God that his desire had been overruled, and went steadily on with a grateful mind. In a few weeks an opportunity so much better came his way that he would not have made the first deal on any account, and he saw that a mind which knew more than he knew had prevented him from losing the greater good by entangling himself with the lesser.

That is the way every seeming failure will work out for you, if you keep your faith, hold to your purpose, have gratitude, and do — every day — all that can be done that day, doing each separate act in a successful manner.

When you make a failure, it is because you have not asked for enough. Keep on, and a larger thing then you were seeking will certainly come to you. Remember this. You will not fail because you lack the necessary talent to do what you wish to do. If you go on as I have directed, you will develop all the talent that is necessary to the doing of your work.

It is not within the scope of this book to deal with the science of cultivating talent, but it is as certain and simple as the process of getting rich. However, do not hesitate or waver for fear that when you come to any certain place you will fail for lack of ability. Keep right on, and when you come to that place, the ability will be furnished to you. The same source of ability which enabled the untaught Lincoln to do the greatest work in government ever accomplished by a single man is open to you. You may draw upon all the mind there is for wisdom to use in meeting the responsibilities which are laid upon you. Go on in full faith.

Study this book. Make it your constant companion until you have mastered all the ideas contained in it. While you are getting firmly established in this faith, you will do well to give up most recreations and pleasure and to stay away from places where ideas conflicting with these are advanced in lectures or sermons. Do not read pessimistic or conflicting literature or get into arguments upon the matter.

Spend most of your leisure time in contemplating your vision, in cultivating gratitude, and in reading this book. It contains all you need to know of the science of getting rich, and you will find all the essentials summed up in the following chapter.

17. A SUMMARY OF THE SCIENCE OF GETTING RICH

THERE IS A THINKING STUFF FROM WHICH ALL THINGS ARE MADE, and which, in its original state, permeates, penetrates, and fills the interspaces of the universe.

A thought in this substance produces the thing that is imaged by the thought.

A person can form things in his thought, and by impressing his thought upon formless substance can cause the thing he thinks about to be created.

In order to do this, a person must pass from the competitive to the creative mind. Otherwise he cannot be in harmony with formless intelligence, which is always creative and never competitive in spirit.

A person may come into full harmony with the formless substance by entertaining a lively and sincere gratitude for the blessings it bestows upon him. Gratitude unifies the mind of man with the intelligence of substance, so that man's thoughts are received by the formless. A person can remain upon the creative plane only by uniting himself with the formless intelligence through a deep and continuous feeling of gratitude.

A person must form a clear and definite mental image of the things he wishes to have, to do, or to become, and he must hold this mental image in his thoughts, while being deeply grateful to the supreme that all his desires are granted to him. The person who wishes to get rich must spend his leisure hours in contemplating his vision, and in earnest thanksgiving that the reality is being given to him. Too much stress cannot be laid on the importance of frequent contemplation of the mental image, coupled with unwavering faith and devout gratitude. This is the process by which the impression is given to the formless and the creative forces set in motion.

The creative energy works through the established channels of natural growth, and of the industrial and social order. All that is included in his mental image will surely be brought to the person who follows the instructions given above, and whose faith does not waver. What he wants will come to him through the ways of established trade and commerce.

In order to receive his own when it is ready to come to him, a person must be in action in a way that causes him to more than fill his present place. He must keep in mind the purpose to get rich through realization of his mental image. And he must do, every day, all that can be done that day, taking care to do each act in a successful manner. He must give to every person a use value in excess of the cash value he receives, so that each transaction makes for more life, and he must hold the advancing thought so that the impression of increase will be communicated to all with whom he comes into contact.

The men and women who practice the foregoing instructions will certainly get rich, and the riches they receive will be in exact proportion to the definiteness of their vision, the fixity of their purpose, the steadiness of their faith, and the depth of their gratitude.

BOOK TWO
THE SCIENCE OF BEING WELL

Author's Preface

This volume is the second of a series, the first of which is The Science of Getting Rich. As that book is intended solely for those who want money, so this is for those who want health, and who want a practical guide and handbook, not a philosophical treatise.

It is an instructor in the use of the universal Principle of Life, and my effort has been to explain the way in so plain and simple a fashion that the reader, though he may have given no previous study to New Thought or metaphysics, may readily follow it to perfect health. While retaining all essentials, I have carefully eliminated all non-essentials. I have used no technical, abstruse, or difficult language, and have kept the one point in view at all times.

As its title asserts, the book deals with science, not speculation. The monistic theory of the universe — the theory that matter, mind, consciousness, and life are all manifestations of One Substance — is now accepted by most thinkers, and if you accept this theory, you cannot deny the logical conclusions you will find here.

Best of all, the methods of thought and action prescribed have been tested by the author in his own case and in the case of hundreds of others during twelve years of practice, with continuous and unfailing success.

I can say of the Science of Being Well that it works, and that wherever its laws are complied with, it can no more fail to work than the science of geometry can fail to work. If the tissues of your body have not been so destroyed that continued life is impossible, you can get well, and if you will think and act in a Certain Way, you will get well.

Those who wish more detailed information as to the performance of the voluntary function of eating, I would recommend the writings of Horace Fletcher and of Edward Hooker Dewey. Read these, if you like, as a sort of buttress to your faith, but let me warn you against making the mistake of studying many conflicting theories, and practicing, at the same time, parts of several different "systems." For if you get well, it must be by giving your WHOLE MIND to the right way of thinking and living.

Remember that the Science of Being Well claims to be a complete and sufficient guide in every particular. Concentrate upon the way of thinking and acting it prescribes, and follow it in every detail, and you will get well, or if you are already well, you will remain so.

Trusting that you will go on until the priceless blessing of perfect health is yours, I remain,

Truly Yours,

Wallace D. Wattles

1. THE PRINCIPLE OF HEALTH

In the personal application of the Science of Being Well, as in that of the *Science of Getting Rich*, certain fundamental truths must be known in the beginning, and accepted without question. Some of these truths we state here:

The perfectly natural performance of function constitutes health, and the perfectly natural performance of function results from the natural action of the Principle of Life.

There is a Principle of Life in the universe, and it is the One Living Substance from which all things are made. This Living Substance permeates, penetrates, and fills the interspaces of the universe. It is in and through all things, like a very refined and diffusible ether. All life comes from it — its life is all the life there is.

A human being is a form of this Living Substance, and has within him a Principle of Health. (The word Principle is used as meaning source.) The Principle of Health in a person, when in full constructive activity, causes all the voluntary functions of his life to be perfectly performed. It is the Principle of Health in a person which really works all healing, no matter what "system" or "remedy" is employed, and this Principle of Health is brought into Constructive Activity by thinking in a Certain Way.

I proceed now to prove this last statement. We all know that cures are wrought by all the different, and often opposite, methods employed in the various branches of the healing art. The allopath, who gives a strong dose of a counter- poison, cures his patient. And the homeopath, who gives a diminutive dose of the poison most similar to that of the disease, also cures it. If allopathy ever cured any given disease, it is certain that homeopathy never cured that disease. And if homeopathy ever cured an ailment, allopathy could not possibly cure that ailment.

The two systems are radically opposite in theory and practice, and yet both "cure" most diseases. And even the remedies used by physicians in any one school are not the same.

Go with a case of indigestion to half a dozen doctors, and compare their prescriptions. It is more than likely that none of the ingredients of any one of them will also be in the others. Must we not conclude that their patients are healed by a Principle of Health within themselves, and not by something in the varying "remedies"?

Not only this, but we find the same ailments cured by the osteopath with manipulations of the spine, by the faith healer with prayer, by the food scientist with bills of fare, by the Christian Scientist with a formulated creed statement, by the mental scientist with affirmation, and by the hygienists with differing plans of living.

What conclusion can we come to in the face of all these facts but that there is a Principle of Health which is the same in all people, and which really accomplishes all the cures; and that there is something in all the "systems" which, under favorable conditions, arouses the Principle of Health to action? That is, medicines, manipulations, prayers, bills of fare, affirmations, and hygienic practices cure whenever they cause the Principle of Health to become active, and fail whenever they do not cause it to become active.

Does not all this indicate that the results depend upon the way the patient thinks about the remedy, rather than upon the ingredients in the prescription?

There is an old story which furnishes so good an illustration on this point that I will give it here. It is said that in the middle ages, the bones of a saint, kept in one of the monasteries, were working miracles of healing. On certain days a great crowd of the afflicted gathered to touch the relics, and all who did so were healed.

On the eve of one of these occasions, some sacrilegious rascal gained access to the case in which the wonder-working relics were kept and stole the bones, and in the morning, with the usual crowd of sufferers waiting at the gates, the fathers found themselves shorn of the source of the miracle-working power.

They resolved to keep the matter quiet, hoping that by doing so they might find the thief and recover their treasures, and hastening to the cellar of the convent they dug up the bones of a murderer, who had been buried there many years before. These they placed in the case, intending to make some plausible excuse for the failure of the saint to perform his usual miracles on that day; and then they let in the waiting assemblage of the sick and infirm.

To the intense astonishment of those in on the secret, the bones of the malefactor proved as effective as those of the saint, and the healing went on as before. One of the fathers is said to have left a history of the occurrence, in which he confessed that, in his judgment, the healing power had been in the people themselves all the time, and never in the bones at all.

Whether the story is true or not, the conclusion applies to all the cures wrought by all the systems. The Power that Heals is in the patient himself, and whether it shall become active or not does not depend upon the physical or mental means used, but upon the way the patient thinks about these means. There is a Universal Principle of Life, as Jesus taught — a great spiritual Healing Power — and there is a Principle of Health in every human being which is related to this Healing Power. This is dormant or active, according to the way a person thinks. He can always quicken it into activity by thinking in a Certain Way.

Your getting well does not depend upon the adoption of some system, or the finding of some remedy; people with your identical ailments have been healed by all systems and all remedies. It does not depend upon climate; some people are well and others are sick in all climates. It does not depend upon avocation, unless in case of those who work under poisonous conditions; people are well in all trades and professions.

Your getting well depends upon your beginning to think — and act — in a Certain Way. The way a person thinks about things is determined by what he believes about them. His thoughts are determined by his faith, and the results depend upon his making a personal application of his faith.

If a person has faith in the efficacy of a medicine, and is able to apply that faith to himself, that medicine will certainly cause him to be cured. But though his faith be great, he will not be cured unless he applies it to himself. Many sick people have faith for others but none for themselves. So, if he has faith in a system of diet, and can personally apply that faith, it will cure him. And if he has faith in prayers and affirmations and personally applies his faith, prayers and affirmations will cure him.

Faith, personally applied, cures. And no matter how great the faith or how persistent the thought, it will not cure without personal application. The Science of Being Well, then, includes the two fields of thought and action.

To be well it is not enough that a person should merely think in a Certain Way. He must apply his thought to himself, and he must express and externalize it in his outward life by acting in the same way that he thinks.

2. THE FOUNDATIONS OF FAITH

Before a person can think in the Certain Way which will cause his diseases to be healed, he must believe in certain truths which are here stated:

All things are made from one Living Substance, which, in its original state, permeates, penetrates, and fills the interspaces of the universe. While all visible things are made from It, yet this Substance — in its first formless condition — is in and through all the visible forms that It has made. Its life is in All, and its intelligence is in All.

This Substance creates by thought, and its method is by taking the form of that which it thinks about. The thought of a form held by this substance causes it to assume that form; the thought of a motion causes it to institute that motion. Forms are created by this substance in moving itself into certain orientations or positions.

When original Substance wishes to create a given form, it thinks of the motions which will produce that form. When it wishes to create a world, it thinks of the motions, perhaps extending through ages, which will result in its coming into the attitude and form of the world — and these motions are made. When it wishes to create an oak tree, it thinks of the sequences of movement, perhaps extending through ages, which will result in the form of an oak tree — and these motions are made. The particular sequences of motion by which differing forms should be produced were established in the beginning; they are changeless. Certain motions instituted in the Formless Substance will forever produce certain forms.

The human body is formed from the Original Substance, and is the result of certain motions, which first existed as thoughts of Original Substance. The motions which produce, renew, and repair the body are called functions, and these functions are of two classes: voluntary and involuntary.

The involuntary functions are under the control of the Principle of Health in a person, and are performed in a perfectly healthy manner so long as a person thinks in a certain way. The voluntary functions of life are eating, drinking, breathing, and sleeping. These, entirely or in part, are under the direction of a person's conscious mind, and he can perform them in a perfectly healthy way if he will. If he does not perform them in a healthy way, he cannot long be well.

So we see that if a person thinks in a certain way, and eats, drinks, breathes, and sleeps in a corresponding way, he will be well.

The involuntary functions of a person's life are under the direct control of the

Principle of Health, and so long as a person thinks in a perfectly healthy way, these functions are perfectly performed, for the action of the Principle of Health is largely directed by a person's conscious thought, affecting his subconscious mind.

A person is a thinking center, capable of originating thought, and as he does not know everything, he makes mistakes and

66

thinks error. Not knowing everything, he believes things to be true which are not true. A person holds in his thought the idea of diseased and abnormal functioning and conditions, and so perverts the action of the Principle of Health, causing diseased and abnormal functioning and conditions within his own body.

In the Original Substance there are held only the thoughts of perfect motion, perfect and healthy function, complete life. God never thinks disease or imperfection. But for countless ages people have held thoughts of disease, abnormality, old age, and death. And the perverted functioning resulting from these thoughts has become a part of the inheritance of the human race. Our ancestors have, for many generations, held imperfect ideas concerning human form and functioning, and we begin life with racial sub-conscious impressions of imperfection and disease.

This is not natural, not a part of the plan of nature.

The purpose of nature can be nothing else than the perfection of life. This we see from the very nature of life itself. It is the nature of life to continually advance toward more perfect living; advancement is the inevitable result of the very act of living. Increase is always the result of active living; whatever lives must live more and more.

The seed, lying in the granary, has life, but it is not living. Put it into the soil and it becomes active, and at once begins to gather to itself from the surrounding substance, and to build a plant form. It will so cause increase that a seed head will be produced containing 30, 60, or a hundred seeds, each having as much life as the first. Life, by living, increases.

Life cannot live without increasing, and the fundamental impulse of life is to live. It is in response to this fundamental impulse that Original Substance works, and creates. God must live, and God cannot live except as God creates and increases. In multiplying forms, God is moving on to live more.

The universe is a Great Advancing Life, and the purpose of nature is the advancement of life toward perfection, toward perfect functioning. The purpose of nature is perfect health.

The purpose of Nature, so far as a human being is concerned, is that he should be continuously advancing into more life, and progressing toward perfect life; and that he should live the most complete life possible in his present sphere of action. This must be so, because That which lives in a person is seeking more life.

Give a little child a pencil and paper, and he begins to draw crude figures. That which lives in him is trying to express Itself in art. Give him a set of blocks, and he will try to build something. That which lives in him is seeking expression in architecture. Seat him at a piano, and he will try to draw harmony from the keys. That which lives in him is trying to express Itself in music.

That which lives in a person is always seeking to live more, and since a person lives most when he is well, the Principle of Nature in him can seek only health. The natural state of a human being is a state of perfect health, and everything in him and in nature tends toward health. Sickness can have no place in the thought of Original Substance, for it is by its own nature continually impelled toward the fullest and most perfect life — therefore, toward health. A human being, as he exists in the thought of the Formless Substance, has perfect health. Disease, which is abnormal or perverted function — motion imperfectly made, or made in the direction of imperfect life — has no place in the thought of the Thinking Stuff.

The Supreme Mind never thinks of disease. Disease was not created or ordained by God, or sent forth from God. It is wholly a product of separate consciousness, of the individual thought of a person. God, the Formless Substance, does not see disease, think disease, know disease, or recognize disease. Disease is recognized only by the thought of humanity; God thinks nothing but health.

From all the foregoing, we see that health is a fact or TRUTH in the Original Substance from which we are all formed, and that disease is imperfect functioning, resulting from the imperfect thoughts of people, past and present. If a person's thoughts of himself had always been those of perfect health, a person could not possibly now be otherwise than perfectly healthy.

A human being in perfect health is the thought of Original Substance, and a human being in imperfect health is the result of his own failure to think perfect health, and to perform the voluntary functions of life in a healthy way. We will here arrange in a syllabus the basic truths of the Science of Being Well:

There is a Thinking Substance from which all things are made, and which, in its original state, permeates, penetrates, and fills the interspaces of the universe. It is the life of All.

The thought of a form in this Substance causes the form; the thought of a motion produces the motion. In relation to humanity, the thoughts of this Substance are always of perfect functioning and perfect health.

A person is a thinking center, capable of original thought; and his thought has power over his own functioning. By thinking imperfect thoughts he has caused imperfect and perverted functioning; and by performing the voluntary functions of life in a perverted manner, he has assisted in causing disease.

If a person will think only thoughts of perfect health, he can cause within himself the functioning of perfect health; all the Power of Life will be exerted to assist him. But this healthy functioning will not continue unless a person performs the external, or voluntary, functions of living in a healthy manner.

A person's first step must be to learn how to think perfect health; and his second step to learn how to eat, drink, breathe, and sleep in a perfectly healthy way. If a person takes these two steps, he will certainly become well, and remain so.

3. LIFE AND ITS ORGANISMS

The human body is the abiding place of an energy which renews it when worn, which eliminates waste or poisonous matter, and which repairs the body when broken or injured. This energy we call life. Life is not generated or produced within the body; *it produces the body.*

The seed which has been kept in the storehouse for years will grow when planted in the soil; it will produce a plant. But the life in the plant is not generated by its growing; it is the life which makes the plant grow.

The performance of function does not cause life; it is life which causes function to be performed. Life is first; function afterward.

It is life which distinguishes organic from inorganic matter, but it is not produced after the organization of matter.

Life is the principle or force which causes organization; it builds organisms. It is a principle or force inherent in Original Substance; all life is One.

This Life Principle of the All is the Principle of Health in a person, and becomes constructively active whenever a person thinks in a Certain Way. Whoever, therefore, thinks in this Certain Way will surely have perfect health if his external functioning is in conformity with his thought. But the external functioning must conform to the thought; a person cannot hope to be well by thinking health, if he eats, drinks, breathes, and sleeps like a sick person.

The universal Life Principle, then, is the Principle of Health in a human being. It is one with original substance. There is one Original Substance from which all things are made; this substance is alive, and its life is the Principle of Life of the universe. This Substance has created from itself all the forms of organic life by thinking them, or by thinking the motions and functions which produce them.

Original Substance thinks only health, because It knows all truth. There is no truth which is not known in the Formless, which is All, and in all. It not only knows all truth, but it has all power. Its vital power is the source of all the energy there is. A conscious life which knows all truth and which has all power cannot go wrong or perform function imperfectly. Knowing all, it knows too much to go wrong, and so the Formless cannot be diseased or think disease.

A human being is a form of this Original Substance, and has a separate consciousness of his own, but his consciousness is limited, and therefore imperfect. By reason of his limited knowledge a person can and does think wrongly, and so he causes perverted and imperfect functioning in his own body. A human being has not yet known enough not to go wrong. The diseased or imperfect functioning may not instantly result from an imperfect thought, but it is bound to come if the thought becomes habitual.

Any thought continuously held by a person tends to the establishment of the corresponding condition in his body.

Also, the human being has failed to learn how to perform the voluntary functions of his life in a healthy way. He does not know when, what, and how to eat. He knows little about breathing and less about sleep. He does all these things in a wrong way, and under wrong conditions, and this because he has neglected to follow the only sure guide to the knowledge of life. He has tried to live by logic rather than by instinct. He has made living a matter of art, and not of nature. And he has gone wrong.

His only remedy is to begin to go right, and this he can surely do. It is the work of this book to teach the whole truth, so that the person who reads it shall know too much to go wrong.

The thoughts of disease produce the forms of disease. A person must learn to think health; and being Original Substance which takes the form of its thoughts, he will become the form of health and manifest perfect health in all his functioning. The people who were healed by touching the bones of the saint were really healed by thinking in a Certain Way, and not by any power emanating from the relics. There is no healing power in the bones of dead men, whether they be those of saint or sinner.

The people who were healed by the doses of either the allopath or the homeopath were also really healed by thinking in a Certain Way; there is no drug which has within itself the power to heal disease. The people who have been healed by prayers and affirmations were also healed by thinking in a certain way; there is no curative power in strings of words. All the sick who have been healed, by whatsoever "system," have thought in a Certain Way; and a little examination will show us what this way is.

The two essentials of the Way are Faith and a Personal Application of the Faith.

The people who touched the saint's bones had faith, and so great was their faith that in the instant they touched the relics they SEVERED ALL MENTAL RELATIONS WITH DISEASE, AND MENTALLY UNIFIED THEMSELVES WITH HEALTH.

This change of mind was accompanied by an intense devotional FEELING which penetrated to the deepest recesses of their souls, and so aroused the Principle of Health to powerful action. By faith they claimed that they were healed, or appropriated health to themselves, and in full faith they ceased to think of themselves in connection with disease and thought of themselves only in connection with health.

These are the two essentials to thinking in the Certain Way which will make you well: first, claim or appropriate health by faith, and, second, sever all mental relations with disease and enter into mental relations with health.

That which we make ourselves, mentally, we become physically, and that with which we unite ourselves mentally we become unified with physically. If your thought always relates you to disease, then your thought becomes a fixed power to cause disease within you. And if your thought always relates you to health, then your thought becomes a fixed power exerted to keep you well.

In the case of the people who are healed by medicines, the result is obtained in the same way. They have, consciously or unconsciously, sufficient faith in the means used that they sever mental relations with disease and enter into mental relations with health.

Faith may be unconscious. It is possible for us to have a sub-conscious or inbred faith in things like medicine, in which we do not believe to any extent objectively, and this sub-conscious faith may be quite sufficient to quicken the Principle of Health into constructive activity.

Many who have little conscious faith are healed in this way, while many others who have great faith in the means are not healed because they do not make the personal application to themselves. Their faith is general, but not specific for their own cases.

In the Science of Being Well we have two main points to consider: first, how to think with faith, and, second, how to so apply the thought to ourselves as to quicken the Principle of Health into constructive activity.

We begin by learning What to Think.

4. WHAT TO THINK

In order to sever all mental relations with disease, you must enter into mental relations with health, making the process positive, not negative — one of assumption, not of rejection. You are to receive or appropriate health rather than to reject and deny disease. Denying disease accomplishes next to nothing; it does little good to cast out the devil and leave the house vacant, for he will presently return with others worse than himself. When you enter into full and constant mental relations with health, you must of necessity cease all relationship with disease.

The first step in the Science of Being Well, then, is to enter into complete thought connection with health.

The best way to do this is to form a mental image or picture of yourself as being well, imagining a perfectly strong and healthy body, and to spend sufficient time in contemplating this image to make it your habitual thought of yourself.

This is not so easy as it sounds. It necessitates the taking of considerable time for meditation, and not all persons have the imaging faculty well enough developed to form a distinct mental picture of themselves in a perfect or idealized body. It is much easier, as in *The Science of Getting Rich*, to form a mental image of the things one wants to have, for we have seen these things or their counterparts and know how they look. We can picture them very easily from memory. But if we have never seen ourselves in a perfect body, a clear mental image is hard to form.

It is not necessary or essential, however, to have a clear mental image of yourself as you wish to be; it is only essential to form a CONCEPTION of perfect health, and to relate yourself to it. This Conception of Health is not a mental picture of a particular thing. It is an understanding of health, and carries with it the idea of perfect functioning in every part and organ.

You may TRY to picture yourself as perfect in physique — that helps — and you MUST *think of yourself as doing everything in the manner of a perfectly strong and healthy person.*

You can picture yourself as walking down the street with an erect body and a vigorous stride. You can picture yourself as doing your day's work easily and with surplus vigor, never tired or weak. You can picture in your mind how all things would be done by a person full of health and power, and you can make yourself the central figure in the picture, doing things in just that way.

Never think of the ways in which weak or sickly people do things; always think of the way strong people do things. Spend your leisure time in thinking about the Strong Way, until you have a good conception of it, and always think of yourself in connection with the Strong Way of Doing Things. That is what I mean by having a Conception of Health.

In order to establish perfect functioning in every part, a person does not have to study anatomy or physiology so that he can form a mental image of each separate organ and address himself to it. He does not have to "treat" his liver, his kidneys, his stomach, or his heart. There is one Principle of Health in a human being, which has control over all the involuntary functions of his life, and the thought of perfect health, impressed upon this Principle, will reach each part and organ. A person's liver is not controlled by a liver-principle, his stomach by a digestive principle, and so on. The Principle of Health is One.

The less you go into the detailed study of physiology, the better for you. Our knowledge of this science is very imperfect, and leads to imperfect thought.

Imperfect thought causes imperfect functioning, which is disease.

Let me illustrate: Until quite recently, physiology fixed ten days as the extreme limit of a human being's endurance without food. It was considered that only in exceptional cases could a person survive a longer fast. So the impression became universally disseminated that one who was deprived of food must die in from five to ten days. And numbers of people, when cut off from food by shipwreck, accident, or famine, did die within this period.

But the performances of Dr. Tanner, the 40-day faster, and the writings of Dr. Dewey and others on the fasting cure, together with the experiments of numberless people who have fasted from 40 to 60 days, have shown that a human's ability to live without food is vastly greater than had been supposed. Any person, properly educated, can fast from 20 to 40 days with little loss in weight, and often with no apparent loss of strength at all.

The people who starved to death in ten days or less did so because they believed that death was inevitable. An erroneous physiology had given them a wrong thought about themselves. When a person is deprived of food he will die in from 10 to 50 days, according to the way he has been taught, or, in other words, according to the way he thinks about it. So you see that an erroneous physiology can work very mischievous results.

No Science of Being Well can be founded on current physiology; it is not sufficiently exact in its knowledge. With all its pretensions, comparatively little is really known as to the interior workings and processes of the body. It is not known just how food is digested. It is not known just what part food plays, if any, in the generation of force. It is not known exactly what the liver, spleen, and pancreas are for, or what part their secretions play in the chemistry of assimilation. On all these and most other points we theorize, but we do not really know.

When a person begins to study physiology, he enters the domain of theory and disputation. He comes among conflicting opinions, and he is bound to form mistaken ideas concerning himself. These mistaken ideas lead to the thinking of wrong thoughts, and this leads to perverted functioning and disease.

All that the most perfect knowledge of physiology could do for a person would be to enable him to think only thoughts of perfect health, and to eat, drink, breathe, and sleep in a perfectly healthy way. And this, as we shall show, he can do without studying physiology at all.

This, for the most part, is true of all hygiene. There are certain fundamental propositions which we should know, and these will be explained in later chapters, but aside from these propositions, ignore physiology and hygiene. They tend to fill your mind with thoughts of imperfect conditions, and these thoughts will produce the imperfect conditions in your own body. You cannot study any "science" which recognizes disease, if you are to think nothing but health.

Drop all investigation as to your present condition, its causes, or possible results, and set yourself to the work of forming a conception of health.

Think about health and the possibilities of health, of the work that may be done and the pleasures that may be enjoyed in a condition of perfect health. Then make this conception your guide in thinking of yourself. Refuse to entertain for an instant any thought of yourself which is not in harmony with it. When any idea of disease or imperfect functioning enters your mind, cast it out instantly by calling up a thought which is in harmony with the Conception of Health.

Think of yourself at all times as realizing this conception, as being a strong and perfectly healthy personage, and do not harbor a contrary thought.

KNOW that as you think of yourself in unity with this conception, the Original Substance which permeates and fills the tissues of your body is taking form according to the thought, and know that this Intelligent Substance or mind stuff will cause function to be performed in such a way that your body will be rebuilt with perfectly healthy cells.

The Intelligent Substance, from which all things are made, permeates and penetrates all things; and so it is in and through your body. It moves according to its thoughts, and so if you hold only the thoughts of perfectly healthy function, it will cause the movements of perfectly healthy function within you.

Hold with persistence to the thought of perfect health in relation to yourself. Do not permit yourself to think in any other way. Hold this thought with perfect faith that it is the fact, the truth. It is the truth so far as your mental body is concerned.

You have a mind-body and a physical body. The mind-body takes form just as you think of yourself, and any thought which you hold continuously is made visible by the transformation of the physical body into its image. Implanting the thought of perfect functioning in the mind-body will, in due time, cause perfect functioning in the physical body.

The transformation of the physical body into the image of the ideal held by the mind-body is not accomplished instantaneously — we cannot transfigure our physical bodies at will as Jesus did. In the creation and recreation of forms, Substance moves along the fixed lines of growth it has established, and the impression upon it of the health thought causes the healthy body to be built cell by cell. Holding only thoughts of perfect health will ultimately cause perfect functioning, and perfect functioning will in due time produce a perfectly healthy body.

It may be as well to condense this chapter into a syllabus:

Your physical body is permeated and filled with an Intelligent Substance, which forms a body of mind-stuff. This mind-stuff controls the functioning of your physical body. A thought of disease or of imperfect function, impressed upon the mind-stuff, causes disease or imperfect functioning in the physical body.

If you are diseased, it is because wrong thoughts have made impressions on this mind-stuff. These may have been either your own thoughts or those of your parents — we begin life with many sub-conscious impressions, both right and wrong. But the natural tendency of all mind is toward health, and if no thoughts are held in the conscious mind save those of health, all internal functioning will come to be performed in a perfectly healthy manner.

The Power of Nature within you is sufficient to overcome all hereditary impressions, and if you will learn to control your thoughts, so that you shall think only those of health, and if you will perform the voluntary functions of life in a perfectly healthy way, you can certainly be well.

5. FAITH

The Principle of Health is moved by Faith. Nothing else can call it into action, and only faith can enable you to relate yourself to health, and sever your relation with disease, in your thoughts.

You will continue to think of disease unless you have faith in health. If you do not have faith, you will doubt. If you doubt, you will fear. And if you fear, you will relate yourself in mind to that which you fear.

If you fear disease, you will think of yourself in connection with disease, and that will produce within yourself the form and motions of disease. Just as Original Substance creates from itself the forms of its thoughts, so your mind-body, which is original substance, takes the form and motion of whatever you think about. If you fear disease, dread disease, have doubts about your safety from disease, or if you even contemplate disease, you will connect yourself with it and create its forms and motions within you.

Let me enlarge somewhat upon this point. The potency, or creative power, of a thought is given to it *by the faith that is in it.*

Thoughts which contain no faith create no forms.

The Formless Substance, which knows all truth and therefore thinks only truth, has perfect faith in every thought, because it thinks only truth, and so all its thoughts create.

But if you will imagine a thought in Formless Substance in which there was no faith, you will see that such a thought could not cause the Substance to move or take form.

Keep in mind the fact that only those thoughts which are conceived in faith have creative energy. Only those thoughts which have faith with them are able to change function, or to quicken the Principle of Health into activity.

If you do not have faith in health, you will certainly have faith in disease. If you do not have faith in health, it will do you no good to think about health, for your thoughts will have no potency, and will cause no change for the better in your conditions.

If you do not have faith in health, I repeat, you will have faith in disease. And if, under such conditions, you think about health for ten hours a day and think about disease for only a few minutes, the disease thought will control your condition because it will have the potency of faith, while the health thought will not. Your mind-body will take on the form and motions of disease and retain them, because your health thought will not have sufficient dynamic force to change form or motion.

In order to practice the Science of Being Well, you must have complete faith in health.

Faith begins in belief; and we now come to the question: *What must you believe in order to have faith in health?*

You must believe that there is more health-power than disease-power in both yourself and your environment; and you cannot help believing this if you consider the facts. These are the facts:

There is a Thinking Substance from which all things are made, and which, in its original state, permeates, penetrates, and fills the interspaces of the universe.

The thought of a form, in this Substance, produces the form; the thought of a motion institutes the motion. In relation to the human being, the thoughts of Original Substance are always of perfect health and perfect functioning. This Substance, within and without a human being, always exerts its power toward health.

A person is a thinking center, capable of original thought. He has a mind-body of Original Substance permeating a physical body, and the functioning of his physical body is determined by the FAITH of his mind-body. If a person thinks with faith of the functioning of health, he will cause his internal functions to be performed in a healthy manner, provided that he performs the external functions in a corresponding manner. But if a person thinks, with faith, of disease, or of the power of disease, he will cause his internal functioning to be the functioning of disease.

The Original Intelligent Substance is in a human being, moving toward health — and it is pressing upon him from every side. The human being lives, moves, and has his being in a limitless ocean of health-power, and he uses this power according to his faith. If he appropriates it and applies it to himself it is all his, and if he unifies himself with it by unquestioning faith, he cannot fail to attain health, for the power of this Substance is all the power there is.

A belief in the above statements is a foundation for faith in health. If you believe them, you believe that health is the natural state of humanity, and that a human being lives in the midst of Universal Health — that all the power of nature makes for health, and that health is possible to all, and can surely be attained by all.

You will believe that the power of health in the universe is 10,000 times greater than that of disease — in fact, that disease has no power whatever, being only the result of perverted thought and faith. And if you believe that health is possible to you, and that it may surely be attained by you, and that you know exactly what to do in order to attain it, you will have faith in health. You will have this faith and knowledge if you read this book through with care and determine to believe in and practice its teachings.

It is not merely the possession of faith, but the personal application of faith which works healing. You must claim health in the beginning, and form a conception of health, and, as far as may be, of yourself as a perfectly healthy person. And then, by faith, you must claim that you ARE REALIZING this conception.

Do not assert with faith that you are going to get well; assert with faith that you ARE well. Having faith in health, and applying it to yourself, means having faith that you are healthy. And the first step in this is to claim that it is the truth.

Mentally take the attitude of being well, and do not say anything or do anything which contradicts this attitude. Never speak a word or assume a physical attitude which does not harmonize with the claim: "I am perfectly well."

When you walk, go with a brisk step, and with your chest thrown out and your head held up. Watch that at all times your physical actions and attitudes are those of a healthy person. When you find that you have relapsed into the attitude of weakness or disease, change instantly: straighten up, and think of health and power. Refuse to consider yourself as other than a perfectly healthy person.

One great aid —perhaps the greatest aid— in applying your faith you will find in the exercise of gratitude. Whenever you think of yourself, or of your advancing condition, give thanks to the Great Intelligent Substance for the perfect health you are enjoying.

Remember that there is a continual inflow of life from the Supreme, which is received by all created things according to their forms, and by every person according to his faith. Health from God is continually being urged upon you, and when you think of this, lift up your mind reverently, and give thanks that you have been led to the Truth and into perfect health of mind and body. Be, all the time, in a grateful frame of mind, and let gratitude be evident in your speech. Gratitude will help you to own and control your own field of thought.

Whenever the thought of disease is presented to you, instantly claim health, and thank God for the perfect health you have. Do this so that there shall be no room in your mind for a thought of ill. Every thought connected in any way with ill health is unwelcome, and you can close the door of your mind in its face by asserting that you are well, and by reverently thanking God that it is so. Soon the old thoughts will return no more.

Gratitude has a twofold effect: it strengthens your own faith, and it brings you into close and harmonious relations with the Supreme. You believe that there is one Intelligent Substance from which all life and all power come, you believe that you receive your own life from this substance, and you relate yourself closely to It by feeling continuous gratitude.

It is easy to see that the more closely you relate yourself to the Source of Life the more readily you may receive life from it. And it is easy also to see that your relation to It is a matter of mental attitude.

We cannot come into physical relationship with God, for God is mind-stuff and we also are mind-stuff. Our relation with God must therefore be a mind relation. It is plain, then, that the person who feels deep and hearty gratitude will live in closer touch with God than the person who never looks up to God in thankfulness.

The ungrateful or unthankful mind really denies that it receives at all, and so cuts its connection with the Supreme. The grateful mind is always looking toward the Supreme, is always open to receive from it, and it will receive continually.

The Principle of Health in a human being receives its vital power from the Principle of Life in the universe, and a person relates himself to the Principle of Life by faith in health, and by gratitude for the health he receives.

A person may cultivate both faith and gratitude by the proper use of his will.

6. USE OF THE WILL

In the practice of the Science of Being Well, the will is not used to compel yourself to go when you are not really able to go or to do things when you are not physically strong enough to do them. You do not direct your will upon your physical body or try to compel the proper performance of internal function by will power.

You direct the will upon the mind, and use it in determining what you shall believe, what you shall think, and to what you shall give your attention.

The will should never be used upon any person or thing external to you, and it should never be used upon your own body. The sole legitimate use of the will is in determining to what you shall give your attention and what you shall think about the things to which your attention is given.

All belief begins in the will to believe.

You cannot always and instantly believe what you will to believe; but you can always will to believe what you want to believe. You want to believe truth about health, and you can will to do so. The statements you have been reading in this book are the truth about health, and you can will to believe them. This must be your first step toward getting well.

These are the statements you must will to believe:

That there is a Thinking Substance from which all things are made, and that a human being receives the Principle of Health, which is his life, from this Substance.

That a human being himself is Thinking Substance — a mind-body permeating a physical body, and that as a person's thoughts are, so will the functioning of his physical body be.

That if a person will think only thoughts of perfect health, he must and will cause the internal and involuntary functioning of his body to be the functioning of health, provided that his external and voluntary functioning and attitude are in accordance with his thoughts.

When you will to believe these statements, you must also begin to act upon them. You cannot long retain a belief unless you act upon it, you cannot increase a belief until it becomes faith unless you act upon it, and you certainly cannot expect to reap benefits in any way from a belief so long as you act as if the opposite were true.

You cannot long have faith in health if you continue to act like a sick person. If you continue to act like a sick person, you cannot help continuing to think of yourself as a sick person. And if you continue to think of yourself as a sick person, you will continue to be a sick person.

The first step toward acting externally like a well person is to begin to act internally like a well person. Form your conception of perfect health, and get into the way of thinking about perfect health until it begins to have a definite meaning to you. Picture yourself as doing the things a strong and healthy person would do, and have faith that you can and will do those things in that way. Continue this until you have a vivid CONCEPTION of health, and what it means to you.

When I speak in this book of a conception of health, I mean a conception that carries with it the idea of the way a healthy person looks and does things. Think of yourself in connection with health until you form a conception of how you would live, appear, act, and do things as a perfectly healthy person. Think about yourself in connection with health until you conceive of yourself, in imagination, as always doing everything in the manner of a well person — until the thought of health conveys the idea of what health means to you. As I have said in a former chapter, you may not be able to form a clear mental image of yourself in perfect health, but you can form a conception of yourself as acting like a healthy person.

Form this conception, and then think only thoughts of perfect health in relation to yourself, and, so far as may be possible, in relation to others. When a thought of sickness or disease is presented to you, reject it. Do not let it get into your mind. Do not entertain or consider it at all. Meet it by thinking health, by thinking that you are well, and by being sincerely grateful for the health you are receiving.

Whenever suggestions of disease are coming thick and fast upon you, and you are in a "tight place," fall back upon the exercise of gratitude. Connect yourself with the Supreme, give thanks to God for the perfect health God gives you, and you will soon find yourself able to control your thoughts, and to think what you want to think. In times of doubt, trial, and temptation, the exercise of gratitude is always a sheet anchor which will prevent you from being swept away.

Remember that the great essential thing is to SEVER ALL MENTAL RELATIONS WITH DISEASE, AND TO ENTER INTO FULL MENTAL RELATIONSHIP WITH HEALTH. This is the KEY to all mental healing; it is the whole thing.

Here we see the secret of the great success of Christian Science. More than any other formulated system of practice, it insists that its converts shall sever relations with disease, and relate themselves fully with health. The healing power of Christian Science is not in its theological formulae nor in its denial of matter, but in the fact that it induces the sick to ignore disease as an unreal thing and accept health by faith as a reality. Its failures are made because its practitioners, while thinking in the Certain Way, do not eat, drink, breathe, and sleep in the same way.

While there is no healing power in the repetition of strings of words, yet it is a very convenient thing to have the central thoughts so formulated that you can repeat them readily, and so that you can use them as affirmations whenever you are surrounded by an environment which gives you adverse suggestions. When those around you begin to talk of sickness and death, close your ears and mentally assert something like the following:

There is One Substance, and I am that Substance. That Substance is eternal, and it is Life; I am that Substance, and I am Eternal Life. *That Substance knows no disease; I am that Substance, and I am Health.*

Exercise your will power in choosing only those thoughts which are thoughts of health, and arrange your environment so that it shall suggest thoughts of health. Do not have about you books, pictures, or other things which suggest death, disease, deformity, weakness, or age. Have only those which convey the ideas of health, power, joy, vitality, and youth. When you are confronted with a book, or anything else which suggests disease, do not give it your attention.

Think of your conception of health, and your gratitude, and affirm as above. Use your will power to fix your attention upon thoughts of health. In a future chapter I shall touch upon this point again. What I wish to make plain here is that you must think only health, recognize only health, and give your attention only to health, and that you must control thought, recognition, and attention by the use of your will.

Do not try to use your will to compel the healthy performance of function within you. The Principle of Health will attend to that if you give your attention only to thoughts of health.

Do not try to exert your will upon the Formless to compel It to give you more vitality or power. It is already placing all the power there is at your service.

You do not have to use your will to conquer adverse conditions, or to subdue unfriendly forces. There are no unfriendly forces; there is only One Force, and that force is friendly to you. It is a force which makes for health.

Everything in the universe wants you to be well. You have absolutely nothing to overcome but your own habit of thinking in a certain way about disease, and you can do this only by forming a habit of thinking in another Certain Way about health.

A person can cause all the internal functions of his body to be performed in a perfectly healthy manner by continuously thinking in a Certain Way and by performing the external functions in a certain way. He can think in this Certain Way by controlling his attention, and he can control his attention by the use of his will.

He can decide what things he will think about.

7. HEALTH FROM GOD

I will give a chapter here to explain how a human being may receive health from the Supreme. By the Supreme I mean the Thinking Substance from which all things are made, and which is in all and through all, seeking more complete expression and fuller life. This Intelligent Substance, in a perfectly fluid state, permeates and penetrates all things, and is in touch with all minds. It is the source of all energy and power, and constitutes the "inflow" of life, vitalizing all things. It is working to one definite end and for the fulfillment of one purpose, and that purpose is the advancement of life toward the complete expression of Mind. When a person harmonizes himself with this Intelligence, it can and will give him health and wisdom. When a person holds steadily to the purpose to live more abundantly, he comes into harmony with this Supreme Intelligence.

The purpose of the Supreme Intelligence is the most Abundant Life for all. The purpose of this Supreme Intelligence for you is that you should live more abundantly. If, then, your own purpose is to live more abundantly, you are unified with the Supreme — you are working with It, and it must work with you.

But as the Supreme Intelligence is in all, *if you harmonize with it you must harmonize with all, and you must desire more abundant life for all as well as for yourself.* Two great benefits come to you from being in harmony with the Supreme Intelligence.

First, you will receive wisdom. By wisdom I do not mean knowledge of facts so much as ability to perceive and understand facts, and to judge soundly and act rightly in all matters relating to life. Wisdom is the power to perceive truth, and the ability to make the best use of the knowledge of truth. It is the power to perceive at once the best end to aim at, and the means best adapted to attain that end.

With wisdom comes poise, and the power to think rightly, to control and guide your thoughts, and to avoid the difficulties which come from wrong thinking. With wisdom you will be able to select the right courses for your particular needs, and to so govern yourself in all ways as to secure the best results. You will know how to do what you want to do. You can readily see that wisdom must be an essential attribute of the Supreme Intelligence, since That which knows all truth must be wise, and you can also see that just in proportion as you harmonize and unify your mind with that Intelligence you will have wisdom.

But I repeat that since this Intelligence is All, and in all, you can enter into Its wisdom only by harmonizing with all. If there is anything in your desires or your purpose which will bring oppression to any, or work injustice to, or cause lack of life for any, you cannot receive wisdom from the Supreme. Furthermore, your purpose for your own self must be the best.

A person can live in three general ways: for the gratification of his body, for that of his intellect, or for that of his soul.

The first is accomplished by satisfying the desires for food, drink, and those other things which give enjoyable physical sensations. The second is accomplished by doing those things which cause pleasant mental sensations, such as gratifying the desire for knowledge or those for fine clothing, fame, power, and so on. The third is accomplished by giving way to the instincts of unselfish love and altruism.

A person lives most wisely and completely when he functions most perfectly along all of these lines, without excess in any of them. The person who lives swinishly, for the body alone, is unwise and out of harmony with God. That person who lives solely for the cold enjoyments of the intellect, though he be absolutely moral, is unwise and out of harmony with God. And the person who lives wholly for the practice of altruism, and who throws himself away for others, is as unwise and as far from harmony with God as those who go to excess in other ways.

To come into full harmony with the Supreme, you must purpose to LIVE — to live to the utmost of your capabilities in body, mind, and soul. This must mean the full exercise of function in all the different ways, but without excess, for excess in one causes deficiency in the others. Behind your desire for health is your own desire for more abundant life, and behind that is the desire of the Formless Intelligence to live more fully in you.

So, as you advance toward perfect health, hold steadily to the purpose to attain complete life, physical, mental, and spiritual; to advance in all ways, and in every way to live more. If you hold this purpose you will be given wisdom. "He that willeth to do the will of the Father shall KNOW," said Jesus. Wisdom is the most desirable gift that can come to a person, for it makes him rightly self-governing.

But wisdom is not all you may receive from the Supreme Intelligence. You may receive physical energy, vitality, life force. The energy of the Formless Substance is unlimited, and permeates everything. You are already receiving or appropriating to yourself this energy in an automatic and instinctive way, but you can do so to a far greater degree if you set about it intelligently. The measure of a person's strength is not what God is willing to give him, but what he, himself, has the will and the intelligence to appropriate to himself. God gives you all there is. Your only question is how much to take of the unlimited supply.

Professor James has pointed out that there is apparently no limit to the powers of the human being, and this is simply because the human being's power comes from the inexhaustible reservoir of the Supreme.

The runner who has reached the stage of exhaustion, when his physical power seems entirely gone, by running on in a Certain Way may receive his "second wind." His strength is renewed in a seemingly miraculous fashion, and he can go on indefinitely. And by continuing in the Certain Way, he may receive a third, fourth, and fifth "wind." We do not know where the limit is, or how far it may be possible to extend it.

The conditions are that the runner must have absolute faith that the strength will come, that he must think steadily of strength and have perfect confidence that he has it, and that he must continue to run on. If he admits a doubt into his mind, he falls exhausted, and if he stops running to wait for the accession of strength, it will never come.

His faith in strength, his faith that he can keep on running, his unwavering purpose to keep on running, and his action in keeping on seem to connect him to the source of energy in such a way as to bring him a new supply.

In a very similar manner, the sick person who has unquestioning faith in health, whose purpose brings him into harmony with the source, and who performs the voluntary functions of life in a certain way, will receive vital energy sufficient for all his needs, and for the healing of all his diseases. God, who seeks to live and express himself fully in humanity, delights to give human beings all that is needed for the most abundant life.

Action and reaction are equal, and when you desire to live more, if you are in mental harmony with the Supreme, the forces which make for life begin to concentrate about you and upon you. The One Life begins to move toward you, and your environment becomes surcharged with it. Then, if you appropriate it by faith, it is yours. "Ye shall ask what ye will, and it shall be done unto you." Your Father doesn't give his spirit by measure; he delights to give good gifts to you.

8. SUMMARY OF THE MENTAL ACTIONS

Let me now summarize the mental actions and attitudes necessary to the practice of the Science of Being Well: first, you believe that there is a Thinking Substance, from which all things are made, and which, in its original state, permeates, penetrates, and fills the interspaces of the universe. This Substance is the Life of All, and is seeking to express more life in all. It is the Principle of Life of the universe, and the Principle of Health in a human being. A human being is a form of this Substance, and draws his vitality from it. He is a mind-body of original substance, permeating a physical body, and the thoughts of his mind- body control the functioning of his physical body. If a person thinks no thoughts save those of perfect health, the functions of his physical body will be performed in a manner of perfect health.

In order to consciously relate yourself to the All-Health, your purpose must be to live fully on every plane of your being. You must want all that there is in life for body, mind, and soul, and this will bring you into harmony with all the life there is.

The person who is in conscious and intelligent harmony with All will receive a continuous inflow of vital power from the Supreme Life, and this inflow is prevented by angry, selfish or antagonistic mental attitudes. If you are against any part, you have severed relations with all — you will receive life, but only instinctively and automatically, not intelligently and purposefully.

You can see that if you are mentally antagonistic to any part, you cannot be in complete harmony with the Whole. Therefore, as Jesus directed, be reconciled to everybody and everything before you offer worship. *Want for everybody all that you want for yourself.*

The reader is recommended to read what we have said in a former work (The Science of Getting Rich) concerning the Competitive mind and the Creative mind. It is very doubtful whether one who has lost health can completely regain it so long as he remains in the competitive mind. Being on the Creative or Good-Will plane in mind, the next step is to form a conception of yourself as in perfect health, and to hold no thoughts which are not in full harmony with this conception. Have FAITH that if you think only thoughts of health you will establish in your physical body the functioning of health; and use your will to determine that you will think only thoughts of health.

Never think of yourself as sick, or as likely to be sick; never think of sickness in connection with yourself at all. And, as far as may be, shut out of your mind all thoughts of sickness in connection with others. Surround yourself as much as possible with the things which suggest the ideas of strength and health.

Have faith in health, and accept health as an actual present fact in your life. Claim health as a blessing bestowed upon you by the Supreme Life, and be deeply grateful at all times. Claim the blessing by faith, know that it is yours, and never admit a contrary thought to your mind.

Use your will-power to withhold your attention from every appearance of disease in yourself and others. Do not study disease, think about it, nor speak of it. At all times, when the thought of disease is thrust upon you, move forward into the mental position of prayerful gratitude for your perfect health.

The mental actions necessary to being well may now be summed up in a single sentence: Form a conception of yourself in perfect health, and think only those thoughts which are in harmony with that conception. That — with faith and gratitude and the purpose to really live — covers all the requirements.

It is not necessary to take mental exercises of any kind, except as described in Chapter 6, or to do wearying "stunts" in the way of affirmations, and so on. It is not necessary to concentrate the mind on the affected parts. It is far better not to think of any part as affected. It is not necessary to "treat" yourself by auto-suggestion, or to have others treat you in any way whatever. The power that heals is the Principle of Health within you, and to call this Principle into Constructive Action it is only necessary, having harmonized yourself with the All- Mind, to claim by FAITH the All-Health and to hold that claim until it is physically manifested in all the functions of your body.

In order to hold this mental attitude of faith, gratitude, and health, however, your external acts must be only those of health. You cannot long hold the internal attitude of a well person if you continue to perform the external acts of a sick person. It is essential not only that your every thought should be a thought of health, but that your every act should be an act of health, performed in a healthy manner. If you will make every thought a thought of health, and every conscious act an act of health, it must infallibly follow that every internal and unconscious function shall come to be healthy, for all the power of life is being continually exerted toward health. We shall next consider how you may make every act an act of health.

9. WHEN TO EAT

You cannot build and maintain a perfectly healthy body by mental action alone, or by the performance of the unconscious or involuntary functions alone. There are certain actions, more or less voluntary, which have a direct and immediate relation with the continuance of life itself. These are eating, drinking, breathing, and sleeping.

No matter what a person's thought or mental attitude may be, he cannot live unless he eats, drinks, breathes, and sleeps, and, moreover, he cannot be well if he eats, drinks, breathes, and sleeps in an unnatural or wrong manner. It is therefore vitally important that you should learn the right way to perform these voluntary functions, and I shall proceed to show you this way, beginning with the matter of eating, which is most important.

There has been a vast amount of controversy as to when to eat, what to eat, how to eat, and how much to eat, and all this controversy is unnecessary, for the Right Way is very easy to find. You have only to consider the Law which governs all attainment, whether of health, wealth, power, or happiness; and that law *is that you must do what you can do now, where you are now; do every separate act in the most perfect manner possible, and put the power of faith into every action.*

The processes of digestion and assimilation are under the supervision and control of an inner division of a person's mentality, which is generally called the sub-conscious mind, and I shall use that term here in order to be understood. The sub-conscious mind is in charge of all the functions and processes of life, and when more food is needed by the body, it makes the fact known by causing a sensation called hunger.

Whenever food is needed and can be used, there is hunger, and whenever there is hunger it is time to eat. When there is no hunger it is unnatural and wrong to eat, no matter how great may APPEAR to be the need for food.

Even if you are in a condition of apparent starvation, with great emaciation, if there is no hunger you may know that FOOD CANNOT BE USED, and it will be unnatural and wrong for you to eat. Though you have not eaten for days or weeks, if you have no hunger you may be perfectly sure that food cannot be used, and will probably not be used if taken. Whenever food is needed, if there is power to digest and assimilate it, so that it can be normally used, the sub- conscious mind will announce the fact by a decided hunger.

Food, taken when there is no hunger, will sometimes be digested and as simulated, because Nature makes a special effort to perform the task which is thrust upon her against her will, but if food is habitually taken when there is no hunger, the digestive power is at last destroyed, and numberless evils caused.

If the foregoing be true — and it is indisputably so — it is a self-evident proposition that the natural time (and the healthy time) to eat is when one is hungry, and that it is never a natural or a healthy action to eat when one is not hungry. You see, then, that it is an easy matter to scientifically settle the question when to eat. ALWAYS eat when you are hungry, and NEVER eat when you are not hungry. This is obedience to nature, which is obedience to God.

We must not fail, however, to make clear the distinction between hunger and appetite.

Hunger is the call of the sub-conscious mind for more material to be used in repairing and renewing the body, and in keeping up the internal heat. Hunger is never felt unless there is need for more material, and unless there is power to digest it when taken into the stomach.

Appetite is a desire for the gratification of sensation. The drunkard has an appetite for liquor, but he cannot have a hunger for it. A normally fed person cannot have a hunger for candy or sweets. The desire for these things is an appetite. You cannot hunger for tea, coffee, spiced foods, or for the various taste-tempting devices of the skilled cook. If you desire these things, it is with appetite, not with hunger.

Hunger is nature's call for material to be used in building new cells, and nature never calls for anything which may not be legitimately used for this purpose.

Appetite is often largely a matter of habit. If one eats or drinks at a certain hour, and especially if one takes sweetened or spiced and stimulating foods, the desire comes regularly at the same hour, but this habitual desire for food should never be mistaken for hunger.

Hunger does not appear at specified times. It only comes when work or exercise has used sufficient energy to make the taking in of new raw material a necessity.

For instance, if a person has been sufficiently fed on the preceding day, it is impossible that he should feel a genuine hunger on arising from refreshing sleep. In sleep the body is recharged with vital power, and the assimilation of the food which has been taken during the day is completed — the system has no need for food immediately after sleep, unless the person went to his rest in a state of starvation. With a system of feeding which is even a reasonable approach to a natural one, no one can have a real hunger for an early morning breakfast. There is no such thing possible as a normal or genuine hunger immediately after arising from sound sleep.

The early morning breakfast is always taken to gratify appetite, never to satisfy hunger. No matter who you are, or what your condition is; no matter how hard you work, or how much you are exposed, unless you go to your bed starved, you cannot arise from your bed hungry.

Hunger is not caused by sleep, but by work. And it does not matter who you are, or what your condition, or how hard or easy your work, the so-called no-breakfast plan is the right plan for you. It is the right plan for everybody, because it is based on the universal law that hunger never comes until it is EARNED. I am aware that a protest against this will come from the large number of people who "enjoy" their breakfasts, whose breakfast is their "best meal," who believe that their work is so hard that they cannot "get through the forenoon on an empty stomach, " and so on. But all their arguments fall down before the facts.

They enjoy their breakfast as the toper enjoys his morning dram, because it gratifies a habitual appetite and not because it supplies a natural want. It is their best meal for the same reason that his morning dram is the toper's best drink. And they CAN get along without it, because millions of people, of every trade and profession, DO get along without it, and are vastly better for doing so.

If you are to live according to the Science of Being Well, you must NEVER EAT UNTIL YOU HAVE AN EARNED HUNGER.

But if I do not eat on arising in the morning, when shall I take my first meal?

In 99 cases out of a hundred twelve o'clock noon is early enough, and it is generally the most convenient time. If you are doing heavy work, you will get by noon a hunger sufficient to justify a good-sized meal. And if your work is light, you will probably still have hunger enough for a moderate meal. The best general rule or law that can be laid down is that you should eat your first meal of the day at noon if you are hungry, and if you are not hungry, wait until you become so.

And when shall I eat my second meal?

Not at all, unless you are hungry for it — and that with a genuine earned hunger. If you do get hungry for a second meal, eat at the most convenient time, but do not eat until you have a really earned hunger.

The reader who wishes to fully inform himself as to the reasons for this way of arranging the mealtimes will find the best books thereon cited in the preface to this work. From the foregoing, however, you can easily see that the Science of Being Well readily answers the question, When, and how often shall I eat? The answer: Eat when you have an earned hunger, and never eat at any other time.

10. WHAT TO EAT

The current sciences of medicine and hygiene have made no progress toward answering the question, What shall I eat? The contests between the vegetarians and the meat eaters, the cooked food advocates, raw food advocates, and various other "schools" of theorists, seem to be interminable. And from the mountains of evidence and argument piled up for and against each special theory, it is plain that if we depend on these scientists we shall never know what is the natural food of humans. Turning away from the whole controversy, then, we will ask the question of Nature herself, and we shall find that she has not left us without an answer.

On the question of what to eat, the answer is simple: Eat what Nature provides. The One Living Substance from which all things are made has made an abundance of perfect foods for every person in every place humans can live, and has given every person the physical and mental faculties to know what foods he should eat and how and when he should eat them.

Whenever people have attempted to "improve" on Nature, they go wrong. For humanity does not yet know enough not to go wrong. Nature is the physical form of the One Living Substance, operating according to the rules of the One Living Substance, with the energy of the One Living Substance. Nature provides every person exactly what is needed for perfect health.

The Great Intelligence, which is in and through all, has in reality practically settled the question as to what we shall eat. In ordering the affairs of nature, It has decided that a human being's food shall be according to the zone in which he lives. These are the foods best for the requirements of the climate. These are the foods which will be the freshest when a person eats them, and therefore most filled with the life force of the One Living Substance. In acquiring these foods a person can be in closest association with the Principle of Life that created them. Therefore, a person need only ask himself what food grows and lives where he lives.

How shall a person know which of these foods to eat, according to his age, gender, ancestry, condition of health, exposure to cold, physical and mental activity?

Again, we see that the Great Intelligence operating in Nature answers the question. It provides a variety of foods in every zone, and it provides a human being with hunger and taste.

A person needs food as a raw material for the Principle of Health in his own body to direct in providing energy, heat, defense, and tissue repair and growth. He needs protein, carbohydrates, fats, vitamins, and minerals. These are found in the flesh, milk, blood, eggs, bones, and organs of water and land creatures, and in the roots, stems, leaves, flowers, seeds, grains, nuts, and fruits of land and water plants. The Great Intelligence guides the masses of people to discover ways of procuring and preparing these foods in harmony with Nature. A person's own Principle of Health guides his hunger and taste to the particular foods that will fill its needs.

With all the various ways food is prepared, how shall a person know the proper way?

He should procure and prepare his food in ways that cooperate with Nature. It is only when people work against Nature that they go wrong. To illustrate this point let us compare the health of people working in cooperation with Nature with the health of these same people working against Nature.

In every climate there are tribes who have learned over thousands of years the wisdom of nature and the best ways to gather, prepare, and eat the foods of the region in perfect harmony with the seasons and cycles of Nature.

The perfect health of these people provides a shining example of what is possible in physical strength and endurance, perfect eyesight and teeth, longevity, skill and agility, mental development, morality, and overall well-being. Moreover, they have learned the secrets of healthy reproduction and child- rearing such that there are not only happy, healthy children, but the absence of unsociable behavior.

What secrets of eating are followed by these perfectly healthy people?

• They eat only foods that occur in nature or that can be simply made from these.

• They eat only the best foods, and parts of foods, with the greatest nutrient content.

• They eat both animal and plant foods.

• Many foods from both plant and animal sources are eaten raw.

• From wild animals, bones, and organs are as important as (and often preferred over) muscle meat.

• From domesticated animals, fresh milk (and in some cases, even blood) is drawn. When milk products are used, they are made from milk taken from vitally healthy animals after they have been well fed on newly growing spring grasses.

• Cheese, butter, and other milk products that can be stored for later use are made from this milk. During other seasons, the animals are fed the highest quality hay.

• For some groups, insects in both adult and immature forms are important food sources, even where other animal foods are available.

• In zones near the sea, sea creatures are the source of animal food. Fish eggs are a rich source of nutrients. Where they are not available year- round, both the flesh and eggs of fish are dried for winter use in a way that preserves or increases nutrient content.

• Plant foods are eaten liberally during the season in which they grow and are ripe. Where they are not growing year-round, some are preserved for winter use in ways that preserves their nutrients.

• Sweet foods of all kinds are eaten only sparingly on special occasions.

Refined sugar is avoided altogether, as are all foods made by adding refined sugar.

• Land used for plant cultivation is fertilized liberally with natural substances, and allowed periods of rest.

• Grains are eaten whole, or ground immediately before use. The entire grain is used.

• Women are supplied with extra high nutrient diets for several months before marriage and pregnancy, and during pregnancy and lactation. Childbirth is carefully spaced three years apart so that the mother can nurse her child, then replenish her body in preparation for the next pregnancy.

• Young men are also fed extra-high nutrient diets in preparation for fathering children.

Children are nursed, then given high nutrient foods to help them grow.

There are times of natural decrease in food supply, and ceremonial times, when the people eat less, or not at all.

- The people actively participate in the physical pursuit of growing, gathering, hunting, and preparing their food. They have community ceremonies of gratitude and celebration.

These are the practices of the healthiest people on earth.

What happens when these same people abandon their way of living and eating and replace their foods with unnatural foods? They develop disease, deformity, misery, and unsociable behavior.

What are the unnatural foods that cause these effects? They are refined and preserved foods from which natural life has been removed or lost, or sugar and flavors added to hide the absence of nutrients. They are foods so old that no life force remains in them. They are foods from unhealthy plants and animals, containing life force that bears the impression of weakness or disease.

What is needed for perfect health is vital food, brimming with life force, eaten according to the practices of healthy people.

How shall the modern city dweller acquire this vital food and incorporate these practices into his life? First is to remember that he is to eat the food Nature provides in the zone in which he lives.

He must align himself with the Principle of Life with gratitude that there is abundant food for all and with faith that he will be perfectly guided to the best sources available in his area. Perfect health requires a relationship with the Source of all food with faith, gratitude, and joy. Food must be gathered with the attitude of more life to all and less to none.

A person must either learn to grow and gather, raise animals, hunt and fish, or find those who do. If he does not procure his own food directly from Nature, he must form a friendly relationship with those who do. He can then knowingly choose to deal with those who operate in harmony with Nature, exercising gratitude and wisdom.

The person who does not know how to identify a farmer or hunter following the natural laws of producing and finding food can be guided by these simple concepts:

Choosing your food providers

• The food provider is healthy, happy, and of a generous spirit.

• He uses no poisons of any kind in the production of foods.

• If he raises animals, they are healthy and treated with kindness, respect, and gratitude.

They are fed only the best foods for their health, not for abnormal growth or food production. They are not confined in unhealthy conditions, but given freedom to move about normally, and only sheltered for their protection.

• If he fishes or hunts, he catches or kills lake, river, land or sea creatures in their natural environment. He uses means that ensure the healthy survival of all the species caught, whether or not they are the ones to be eaten.

• If he farms, he uses only healthy, living soil uncontaminated by previous poisons. He replenishes the life of the soil so that his crops are rich in natural nutrients. His crops and soil are so healthy that they do not attract pests, and he farms in such a way that birds and other creatures eating the insects on his farm are unharmed. Any water running off his land contains no chemicals that will harm any other part of life.

These are the characteristics of a person who knows the laws of Nature in the production and procurement of food.

You must also know how to determine the correct people with whom to associate in any other steps of obtaining your food.

Do not associate with anyone in the process of procuring food who speaks of disease, fear, or lack in any way. Associate only with those who gratefully and joyfully appreciate the life-giving qualities of food, are happy to grow it, harvest it, prepare it, serve it, eat it, and know that there is an abundance of the best food for all. This is important whether you are dealing with someone who is selling you land on which to farm, or a farmer, or butcher, or truck driver, or store clerk, or cook, or waiter in a restaurant.

You must not eat foods produced or transported carelessly, or treated in any other way than as precious, life-giving substances. This is easily accomplished when you are the one procuring the food from its natural source or if you are in direct and harmonious relationship with all those who are.

The city dweller who thinks it is too difficult or too expensive to obtain food in this way need only review The Science of Getting Rich. All his doubts will there be answered. He will be guided in the correct manner of acquiring all the money he wants, and in attracting to himself all other resources he desires.

Once a person is supplied with a variety of vital foods from which to choose, how shall he know what to eat at a given meal? **Here is the only needed guideline: Eat what your body wants.** Your body wants what the Principle of Health requires to create perfect health.

What your body wants is determined very simply. The thought of the food, when you are truly hungry, is appealing.

The taste of the food while chewing it is pleasant. After eating, your body feels energized and satisfied. There is no sleepiness, irritability, congestion, pain, discomfort of any kind, from the moment you begin to eat until the next day. Over a period of days, weeks and months, you continue to feel well.

This is how you will know you are eating the correct foods. Then you will not need to give the least thought to what you should or should not eat. You will want the right foods. The Principle of Health in your own body will guide you to know what to eat just as surely as it will guide you to know when to eat.

If you do not eat until you have an EARNED hunger, you will not find your taste demanding unnatural or unhealthy foods. If you make an association with your source of food that brings joy and gratitude, you will further increase your desire to eat what is natural and healthy.

It is when a person becomes lazy and allows himself to be tempted by taste and convenience rather than following the Great Intelligence with which he is bestowed, that he pays the price of decreased health.

When you learn to cooperate with Nature you will want what is good for you, and you will eat what you want. This you can do with perfect results if you eat in the right way, and how to do this will be explained in the next chapter.

11. HOW TO EAT

It is a settled fact that a person naturally chews his food. The few faddists who maintain that we should bolt our nourishment, after the manner of the dog and others of the lower animals, can no longer get a hearing. We know that we should chew our food. And if it is natural that we should chew our food, the more thoroughly we chew it the more completely natural the process must be. If you will chew every mouthful to a liquid, you need not be in the least concerned as to whether you are getting enough nutrients, for you have already chosen the best foods according to Natural Law. Whether or not this chewing shall be an irksome and laborious task or a most enjoyable process, depends upon the mental attitude in which you come to the table.

If your mind and attitude are on other things, or if you are anxious or worried about business or domestic affairs, you will find it almost impossible to eat without bolting more or less of your food. You must learn to live so scientifically that you will have no business or domestic cares to worry about. This you can do.

You must also arrange your life so that you are not in the presence of others who distract from the enjoyment of your meal. This way, you can learn to give your undivided attention to the act of eating while at the table.

The matter of eating only when in a peaceful state of mind must be emphasized. You must focus on gratitude before eating the food on your table and on the full enjoyment of each bite while eating. After eating, you must again focus on gratitude for the vital force from the food supplied to you through the One Living Substance. These mental actions will assist in the physical extraction of vital force from your food, and in bringing the Principle of Health within you into full Constructive Activity.

You must therefore eat with an eye single to the purpose of getting all the enjoyment you can from that meal. Dismiss everything else from your mind, and do not let anything take your attention from the food and its taste until your meal is finished. Be cheerfully confident, for if you follow these instructions you may KNOW that the food you eat is exactly the right food, and that it will "agree" with you to perfection.

Sit down to the table with confident cheerfulness, and take a moderate portion of the food. Take whatever thing looks most desirable to you. Do not select some food because you think it will be good for you — select that which will taste good to you. If you are to get well and stay well, you must drop the idea of doing things because they are good for your health, and do things because you want to do them. Select the food you want most, gratefully give thanks to God that you have learned how to eat it in such a way that digestion shall be perfect, and take a moderate mouthful of it.

Do not fix your attention on the act of chewing; fix it on the TASTE of the food. And taste and enjoy it until it is reduced to a liquid state and passes down your throat by involuntary swallowing. No matter how long it takes, do not think of the time. Think of the taste. Do not allow your eyes to wander over the table, speculating as to what you shall eat next. Do not worry for fear there is not enough, and that you will not get your share of everything. Do not anticipate the taste of the next thing. Keep your mind centered on the taste of what you have in your mouth.

And that is all of it. Scientific and healthful eating is a delightful process after you have learned how to do it, and after you have overcome the bad old habit of gobbling down your food unchewed. It is best not to have too much conversation going on while eating. Be cheerful, but not talkative.

Do the talking afterward.

In most cases, some use of the will is required to form the habit of correct eating. The bolting habit is an unnatural one, and is without doubt mostly the result of fear. Fear that we will be robbed of our food, fear that we will not get our share of the good things, fear that we will lose precious time — these are the causes of haste. Then there is anticipation of the dainties that are to come for dessert and the consequent desire to get at them as quickly as possible. And there is mental abstraction, or thinking of other matters while eating. All these must be overcome.

When you find that your mind is wandering, call a halt. Think for a moment of the food and of how good it tastes, of the perfect digestion and assimilation that are going to follow the meal, and begin again. Begin again and again, though you must do so 20 times in the course of a single meal. And again and again, though you must do so every meal for weeks and months. It is perfectly certain that you CAN form the "Fletcher habit" if you persevere, and when you have formed it, you will experience a healthful pleasure you have never known.

This is a vital point, and I must not leave it until I have thoroughly impressed it upon your mind. Given the right materials, perfectly prepared, the Principle of Health will positively build you a perfectly healthy body, and you cannot prepare the materials perfectly in any other way than the one I am describing.

If you are to have perfect health, you MUST eat in just this way. You can, and the doing of it is only a matter of a little perseverance. What use for you to talk of mental control unless you will govern yourself in so simple a matter as ceasing to bolt your food? What use to talk of concentration unless you can keep your mind on the act of eating for so short a space as 15 or 20 minutes, especially with all the pleasures of taste to help you?

Go on, and conquer. In a few weeks, or months, as the case may be, you will find the habit of scientific eating becoming fixed, and soon you will be in so splendid a condition, mentally and physically, that nothing would induce you to return to the bad old way.

We have seen that if a person will think only thoughts of perfect health, his internal functions will be performed in a healthy manner, and we have seen that in order to think thoughts of health, a person must perform the voluntary functions in a healthy manner. The most important of the voluntary functions is that of eating, and we see, so far, no special difficulty in eating in a perfectly healthy way.

I will here summarize the instructions as to when to eat, what to eat, and how to eat, with the reasons why:

NEVER eat until you have an EARNED hunger, no matter how long you go without food. This is based on the fact that whenever food is needed in the system, if there is power to digest it, the sub-conscious mind announces the need by the sensation of hunger.

Learn to distinguish between genuine hunger and the gnawing and craving sensations caused by unnatural appetite. Hunger is never a disagreeable feeling, accompanied by weakness, faintness, or gnawing feelings at the stomach. It is a pleasant, anticipatory desire for food. It does not come at certain hours or at stated intervals. It only comes when the body is ready to receive, digest, and assimilate food.

Eat whatever foods you want, making your selection from the full variety of the best foods found in the zone in which you live. The Supreme Intelligence has guided humanity to the selection of these foods, and they are the right ones. I am referring, of course, to the foods which are taken to satisfy hunger, not to those which have been contrived merely to gratify appetite or perverted taste. The instinct which has guided people to make use of the great staples of food to satisfy their hunger is a divine one. God has made no mistake; if you eat these foods you will not go wrong.

Eat your food with cheerful confidence in a pleasant atmosphere, and get all the pleasure that is to be had from the taste of every mouthful. Chew each morsel to a liquid, keeping your attention fixed on the enjoyment of the process. This is the only way to eat in a perfectly complete and successful manner; and when anything is done in a completely successful manner, the general result cannot be a failure.

In the attainment of health, the law is the same as in the attainment of riches: if you make each act a success in itself, the sum of all your acts must be a success. When you eat in the mental attitude I have described, and in the manner I have described, nothing can be added to the process — it is done in a perfect manner, and it is successfully done. And if eating is successfully done, digestion, assimilation, and the building of a healthy body are successfully begun.

We next take up the question of the quantity of food required.

12. HUNGER AND APPETITES

It is very easy to find the correct answer to the question, How much shall I eat? You are never to eat until you have an earned hunger, and you are to stop eating the instant you BEGIN to feel that your hunger is abating. Never gorge yourself. Never eat to repletion. When you begin to feel that your hunger is satisfied, know that you have enough. For until you have enough, you will continue to feel the sensation of hunger.

If you eat as directed in the last chapter, it is probable that you will begin to feel satisfied before you have taken half your usual amount, but stop there, all the same. No matter how delightfully attractive the dessert, or how tempting the pie or pudding, do not eat a mouthful of it if you find that your hunger has been in the least degree assuaged by the other foods you have taken.

Whatever you eat after your hunger begins to abate is taken to gratify taste and appetite, not hunger and is not called for by nature at all. It is therefore excess — mere debauchery — and it cannot fail to work mischief.

This is a point you will need to watch with nice discrimination, for the habit of eating purely for sensual gratification is very deeply rooted with most of us. The usual "dessert" of sweet and tempting foods is prepared solely with a view to inducing people to eat after hunger has been satisfied, and all the effects are evil. For the effect of eating these unwholesome foods is often an increase in appetite.

The same is true of alcohol taken before eating. Both will trick you to eat far more than you would otherwise want, and make it difficult to focus your attention on the satisfaction of your true hunger. You will find that if you eat as directed in the preceding chapters, the plainest food will soon come to taste like kingly fare to you, for your sense of taste, like all your other senses, will become so acute with the general improvement in your condition that you will find new delights in common things.

No glutton ever enjoyed a meal like the person who eats for hunger only, who gets the most out of every mouthful, and who stops on the instant that he feels the edge taken from his hunger. The first intimation that hunger is abating is the signal from the sub-conscious mind that it is time to quit.

The average person who takes up this plan of living will be greatly surprised to learn how little food is really required to keep the body in perfect condition.

The amount depends upon the work — upon how much muscular exercise is taken, and upon the extent to which the person is exposed to cold.

The woodchopper who goes into the forest in the winter time and swings his axe all day can eat two full meals, but the brain worker who sits all day on a chair, in a warm room, does not need one-third and often not one-tenth as much. Most woodchoppers eat two or three times as much, and most brain workers from three to ten times as much as nature calls for, and the elimination of this vast amount of surplus rubbish from their systems is a tax on vital power which in time depletes their energy and leaves them an easy prey to so-called disease.

Get all possible enjoyment out of the taste of your food, but never eat anything merely because it tastes good. And on the instant that you feel that your hunger is less keen, stop eating.

If you will consider for a moment, you will see that there is positively no other way for you to settle these various food questions than by adopting the plan here laid down for you. As to the proper time to eat, there is no other way to decide than to say that you should eat whenever you have an EARNED HUNGER. It is a self- evident proposition that that is the right time to eat, and that any other is a wrong time to eat.

As to what to eat, the Eternal Wisdom has decided that the people shall eat the best products of the zones in which they live. The staple foods of your particular zone are the right foods for you, and the Eternal Wisdom, working in and through the minds of people, has taught them how best to prepare these foods by cooking and otherwise.

And as to how to eat, you know that you must chew your food in a peaceful state of mind, and if food must be chewed, then reason tells us that the more thorough and perfect the operation the better.

I repeat that success in anything is attained by making each separate act a success in itself. If you make each action, however small and unimportant, a thoroughly successful action, your day's work as a whole cannot result in failure. If you make the actions of each day successful, the sum total of your life cannot be failure.

A great success is the result of doing a large number of little things, and doing each one in a perfectly successful way. If every thought is a healthy thought, and if every action of your life is performed in a healthy way, you must soon attain to perfect health. It is impossible to devise a way in which you can perform the act of eating more successfully, and in a manner more in accord with the laws of life, than by chewing every mouthful to a liquid, enjoying the taste fully, and keeping a cheerful confidence the while. Nothing can be added to make the process more successful, while if anything be subtracted, the process will not be a completely healthy one.

In the matter of how much to eat, you will also see that there could be no other guide so natural, so safe, and so reliable as the one I have prescribed — to stop eating on the instant you feel that your hunger begins to abate. The subconscious mind may be trusted with implicit reliance to inform us when food is needed, and it may be trusted as implicitly to inform us when the need has been supplied. If ALL food is eaten for hunger, and NO food is taken merely to gratify taste, you will never eat too much, and if you eat whenever you have an EARNED hunger, you will always eat enough.

By reading carefully the summing up in the following chapter, you will see that the requirements for eating in a perfectly healthy way are really very few and simple. The matter of drinking in a natural way may be dismissed here with a very few words. If you wish to be exactly and rigidly scientific, drink nothing but water, drink only when you are thirsty, drink whenever you are thirsty, and stop as soon as you feel that your thirst begins to abate.

But if you are living rightly in regard to eating, it will not be necessary to practice asceticism or great self-denial in the matter of drinking. You can take an occasional cup of weak coffee without harm. You can, to a reasonable extent, follow the customs of those around you. Do not get the soda fountain habit. Do not drink merely to tickle your palate with sweet liquids.

Be sure that you take a drink of water whenever you feel thirst. Never be too lazy, too indifferent, or too busy to get a drink of water when you feel the least thirst. If you obey this rule, you will have little inclination to take strange and unnatural drinks. Drink only to satisfy thirst, drink whenever you feel thirst, and stop drinking as soon as you feel thirst abating. That is the perfectly healthy way to supply the body with the necessary fluid material for its internal processes.

13. IN A NUTSHELL

There is a Cosmic Life which permeates, penetrates, and fills the interspaces of the universe, being in and through all things. This Life is not merely a vibration, or form of energy — it is a Living Substance. All things are made from it. It is All, and in all.

This Substance thinks, and it assumes the form of that which it thinks about. The thought of a form, in this substance, creates the form; the thought of a motion institutes the motion. The visible universe, with all its forms and motions, exists because it is in the thought of Original Substance.

A human being is a form of Original Substance and can think original thoughts, and within himself a person's thoughts have controlling or formative power. The thought of a condition produces that condition; the thought of a motion institutes that motion. So long as a person thinks of the conditions and motions of disease, so long will the conditions and motions of disease exist within him. If a person will think only of perfect health, the Principle of Health within him will maintain normal conditions.

To be well, a person must form a conception of perfect health, and hold thoughts harmonious with that conception as regards himself and all things. He must think only of healthy conditions and functioning. He must not permit a thought of unhealthy or abnormal conditions or functioning to find lodgment in his mind at any time.

In order to think only of healthy conditions and functioning, a person must perform the voluntary acts of life in a perfectly healthy way. He cannot think perfect health so long as he knows that he is living in a wrong or unhealthy way, or even so long as he has doubts as to whether or not he is living in a healthy way.

A person cannot think thoughts of perfect health while his voluntary functions are performed in the manner of one who is sick. The voluntary functions of life are eating, drinking, breathing, and sleeping. When a person thinks only of healthy conditions and functioning, and performs these externals in a perfectly healthy manner, he must have perfect health.

In eating, a person must learn to be guided by his hunger. He must distinguish between hunger and appetite, and between hunger and the cravings of habit. He must NEVER eat unless he feels an EARNED HUNGER.

He must learn that genuine hunger is never present after natural sleep, and that the demand for an early morning meal is purely a matter of habit and appetite; and he must not begin his day by eating in violation of natural law. He must wait until he has an Earned Hunger, which, in most cases, will make his first meal come at about the noon hour.

No matter what his condition, vocation, or circumstances, he must make it his rule not to eat until he has an EARNED HUNGER, and he may remember that it is far better to fast for several hours after he has become hungry than to eat before he begins to feel hunger. It will not hurt you to go hungry for a few hours, even though you are working hard, but it will hurt you to fill your stomach when you are not hungry, whether you are working or not. If you never eat until you have an Earned Hunger, you may be certain that in so far as the time of eating is concerned, you are proceeding in a perfectly healthy way. This is a self-evident proposition.

As to what he shall eat, a person must be guided by that Intelligence which has arranged that the people of any given portion of the earth's surface must live on the staple products of the zone which they inhabit. Have faith in God, and trust God's ability to guide your taste to that which your body requires. Do not worry over the controversies as to the relative merits of cooked and raw foods, of vegetables and meats, or as to your need for carbohydrates and proteins.

Eat only when you have an earned hunger, and then take the best foods of the healthy people in the zone in which you live, and have perfect confidence that the results will be good. They will be.

Do not seek for luxuries, or for things imported or fixed up to tempt the taste. Stick to the plain foods, and when these do not "taste good," fast until they do. Then you will be functioning in a perfectly healthy manner, so far as what to eat is concerned. I repeat, if you have no hunger or taste for the plain foods, do not eat at all. Wait until hunger comes. Go without eating until the plainest food tastes good to you, and then begin your meal with what you like best.

In deciding how to eat, a person must be guided by reason. We can see that the abnormal states of hurry and worry produced by wrong thinking about business and similar things have led us to form the habit of eating too fast, and chewing too little. We know that an angry or distracting atmosphere upsets the process of digestion. Reason tells us that food should be chewed, and that the more thoroughly it is chewed the better it is prepared for the chemistry of digestion. Furthermore, we can see that the person who eats slowly and chews his food to a liquid, keeping his mind on the process and giving it his undivided attention, will enjoy more of the pleasure of taste than he who bolts his food with his mind on something else.

To eat in a perfectly healthy manner, a person must concentrate his attention on the act with cheerful enjoyment and confidence. He must taste his food, and he must reduce each mouthful to a liquid before swallowing it. The foregoing instructions, if followed, make the function of eating completely perfect. Nothing can be added as to what, when, and how.

In the matter of how much to eat, a person must be guided by the same inward intelligence, or Principle of Health, which tells him when food is wanted. He must stop eating in the moment that he feels hunger abating; he must not eat beyond this point to gratify taste. If he ceases to eat in the instant that the inward demand for food ceases he will never overeat, and the function of supplying the body with food will be performed in a perfectly healthy manner.

The matter of eating naturally is a very simple one; there is nothing in all the foregoing that cannot be easily practiced by anyone. This method, put into practice, will infallibly result in perfect digestion and assimilation, and all anxiety and careful thought concerning the matter can at once be dropped from the mind. Whenever you have an earned hunger, eat with thankfulness from the variety of natural foods before you, chewing each mouthful to a liquid, and stopping when you feel the edge taken from your hunger.

The importance of the mental attitude is sufficient to justify an additional word. While you are eating, as at all other times, think only of healthy conditions and normal functioning. Enjoy what you eat. If you carry on a conversation at the table, talk of the goodness of the food, and of the pleasure it is giving you. Never mention that you dislike this or that. Speak only of those things which you like. Never discuss the wholesomeness or unwholesomeness of foods. Never mention or think of unwholesomeness at all.

If there is anything on the table for which you do not care, pass it by in silence, or with a word of commendation. Never criticize or object to anything. Eat your food with gladness and with singleness of heart, praising God and giving thanks. Let your watchword be perseverance. Whenever you fall into the old way of hasty eating, or of wrong thought and speech, bring yourself up short and begin again.

It is of the most vital importance to you that you should be a self-controlling and self-directing person, and you can never hope to become so unless you can master yourself in so simple and fundamental a matter as the manner and method of your eating. If you cannot control yourself in this, you cannot control yourself in anything that will be worthwhile.

On the other hand, if you carry out the foregoing instructions, you may rest in the assurance that in so far as right thinking and right eating are concerned you are living in a perfectly scientific way, and you may also be assured that if you practice what is prescribed in the following chapters you will quickly build your body into a condition of perfect health.

14. BREATHING

The function of breathing is a vital one, and it immediately concerns the continuance of life. We can live many hours without sleeping, and many days without eating or drinking, but only a few minutes without breathing.

The act of breathing is involuntary, but the manner of it and the provision of the proper conditions for its healthy performance fall within the scope of volition. A person will continue to breathe involuntarily, but he can voluntarily determine what he shall breathe, and how deeply and thoroughly he shall breathe. And he can, of his own volition, keep the physical mechanism in condition for the perfect performance of the function.

It is essential, if you wish to breathe in a perfectly healthy way, that the physical machinery used in the act should be kept in good condition. You must keep your spine moderately straight, and the muscles of your chest must be flexible and free in action. You cannot breathe in the right way if your shoulders are greatly stooped forward and your chest hollow and rigid. Sitting or standing at work in a slightly stooping position tends to produce a hollow chest. So does lifting heavy weights — or light weights.

The tendency of work, of almost all kinds, is to pull the shoulders forward, curve the spine, and flatten the chest, and if the chest is greatly flattened, full and deep breathing becomes impossible and perfect health is out of the question.

Various gymnastic exercises have been devised to counteract the effect of stooping while at work, such as hanging by the hands from a swing or trapeze bar, or sitting on a chair with the feet under some heavy article of furniture and bending backward until the head touches the floor, and so on. All these are good enough in their way, but very few people will follow them long enough and regularly enough to accomplish any real gain in physique. The taking of "health exercises" of any kind is burdensome and unnecessary.

There is a more natural, simpler, and much better way.

This better way is to keep yourself straight, and to breathe deeply. Let your mental conception of yourself be that you are a perfectly straight person, and whenever the matter comes to your mind, be sure that you instantly expand your chest, throw back your shoulders, and "straighten up."

Whenever you do this, slowly draw in your breath until you fill your lungs to their utmost capacity. "Crowd in" all the air you possibly can, and while holding it for an instant in the lungs, throw your shoulders still further back, and stretch your chest. At the same time try to pull your spine forward between the shoulders. Then let the air go easily.

This is the one great exercise for keeping the chest full, flexible, and in good condition. Straighten up, fill your lungs FULL, stretch your chest and straighten your spine, and exhale easily. And this exercise you must repeat, in season and out of season, at all times and in all places, until you form a habit of doing it. You can easily do so. Whenever you step out of doors into the fresh, pure air, BREATHE. When you are at work, and think of yourself and your position, BREATHE. When you are in company, and are reminded of the matter, BREATHE. When you are awake in the night, BREATHE. No matter where you are or what you are doing, whenever the idea comes to your mind, straighten up and BREATHE. If you walk to and from your work, take this exercise all the way. It will soon become a delight to you, and you will keep it up, not for the sake of health, but as a matter of pleasure.

Do not consider this a "health exercise." *Never take health exercises or do gymnastics to make you well. To do so is to recognize sickness as a present fact or as a possibility, which is precisely what you must not do.* The people who are always taking exercises for their health are always thinking about being sick. It ought to be a matter of pride with you to keep your spine straight and strong — as much so as it is to keep your face clean.

Keep your spine straight, and your chest full and flexible for the same reason that you keep your hands clean and your nails manicured — because it is slovenly to do otherwise. Do it without a thought of sickness, present or possible. You must either be crooked and unsightly or you must be straight, and if you are straight your breathing will take care of itself. You will find the matter of health exercises referred to again in a future chapter.

It is essential, however, that you should breathe AIR. It appears to be the intention of nature that the lungs should receive air containing its regular percentage of oxygen and not greatly contaminated by other gases, or by filth of any kind.

Do not allow yourself to think that you are compelled to live or work where the air is not fit to breathe. If your house cannot be properly ventilated, move. And if you are employed where the air is bad, get another job — you can, by practicing the methods given in the preceding volume of this series, The Science of Getting Rich.

If no one would consent to work in bad air, employers would speedily see to it that all work rooms were properly ventilated. The worst air is that filled with poisonous chemical gases. Next to that is air heavily charged with mold, or factory dust particles. After that is air from which the oxygen has been exhausted by breathing — as that of churches and theaters where crowds of people congregate, and the outlet and supply of air are poor.

Then there is air containing other natural gases than oxygen and hydrogen — sewer gas and the effluvium from decaying things. Air that contains house-hold dust or pollen may be endured better than any of these. Small particles of organic matter other than food are more easily thrown off from the lungs than gases, which go into the blood.

I speak advisedly when I say "other than food." Air is largely a food. It is the most thoroughly alive thing we take into the body. Every breath carries life. The odors from earth, grass, tree, flower, plant, and from cooking foods are foods in themselves. They are minute particles of the substances from which they come, and are often so attenuated that they pass directly from the lungs into the blood, and are assimilated without digestion. And the atmosphere is permeated with the One Original Substance, which is life itself.

Consciously recognize this whenever you think of your breathing, and think that you are breathing in life. You really are, and conscious recognition helps the process. See to it that you do not breathe air containing poisonous gases, and that you do not rebreathe the air which has been used by yourself or others.

That is all there is to the matter of breathing correctly. Keep your spine straight and your chest flexible, and breathe pure air, recognizing with thankfulness the fact that you breathe in the Eternal Life. That is not difficult, and beyond these things give little thought to your breathing except to thank God that you have learned how to do it perfectly.

15. SLEEP

Vital power is renewed in sleep. Every living thing sleeps. Humans, animals, reptiles, fish, and insects sleep, and even plants have regular periods of slumber. And this is because it is in sleep that we come into such contact with the Principle of Life in nature that our own lives may be renewed. It is in sleep that our brains are recharged with vital energy and the Principle of Health within us is given new strength. It is of the first importance, then, that we should sleep in a natural, normal, and perfectly healthy manner.

Studying sleep, we note that the breathing is much deeper and more forcible and rhythmic than in the waking state. Much more air is inspired when asleep than when awake, and this tells us that the Principle of Health requires large quantities of some element in the atmosphere for the process of renewal.

If you would surround sleep with natural conditions, then, the first step is to see that you have an unlimited supply of fresh and pure air to breathe. Physicians have found that sleeping in the pure air of out-of-doors is very effective in the treatment of pulmonary troubles, and, taken in connection with the Way of Living and Thinking prescribed in this book, you will find that it is just as effective in curing every other sort of trouble.

Do not take any half-way measures in this matter of securing pure air while you sleep. Ventilate your bedroom thoroughly — so thoroughly that it will be practically the same as sleeping out of doors. Have a door or window open wide; have one open on each side of the room, if possible. If you cannot have a good draught of air across the room, pull the head of your bed close to the open window, so that the air from without may come fully into your face. No matter how cold or unpleasant the weather, have a window open, and open wide, and try to get a circulation of pure air through the room. Pile on the bedclothes, if necessary, to keep you warm, but have an unlimited supply of fresh air from out of doors. This is the first great requisite for healthy sleep.

The brain and nerve centers cannot be thoroughly vitalized if you sleep in "dead" or stagnant air. You must have the living atmosphere, vital with nature's Principle of Life. I repeat, do not make any compromise in this matter. Ventilate your sleeping room completely, and see that there is a circulation of outdoor air through it while you sleep. You are not sleeping in a perfectly healthy way if you shut the doors and windows of your sleeping room, whether in winter or summer.

Have fresh air. If you are where there is no fresh air, move. If your bedroom cannot be ventilated, get into another house.

Next in importance is the mental attitude in which you go to sleep. It is well to sleep intelligently, purposefully, knowing what you do it for. Lie down thinking that sleep is an infallible vitalizer, and go to sleep with a confident faith that your strength is to be renewed, that you will awake full of vitality and health. Put purpose into your sleep as you do into your eating. Give the matter your attention for a few minutes, as you go to rest.

Do not seek your couch with a discouraged or depressed feeling; go there joyously, to be made whole. Do not forget the exercise of gratitude in going to sleep. Before you close your eyes, give thanks to God for having shown you the way to perfect health, and go to sleep with this grateful thought uppermost in your mind.

A bedtime prayer of thanksgiving is a mighty good thing. It puts the Principle of Health within you into communication with its source, from which it is to receive new power while you are in the silence of unconsciousness.

You may see that the requirements for perfectly healthy sleep are not difficult. First, to see that you breathe pure air from out of doors while you sleep, and, second, to put the Within into touch with the Living Substance by a few minutes of grateful meditation as you go to bed. Observe these requirements, go to sleep in a thankful and confident frame of mind, and all will be well. If you have insomnia, do not let it worry you. While you lie awake, form your conception of health. Meditate with thankfulness on the abundant life which is yours. Breathe, and feel perfectly confident that you will sleep in due time — and you will. Insomnia, like every other ailment, must give way before the Principle of Health aroused to full constructive activity by the course of thought and action herein described.

The reader will now comprehend it is not at all burdensome or disagreeable to perform the voluntary functions of life in a perfectly healthy way. The perfectly healthy way is the easiest, simplest, most natural, and most pleasant way. The cultivation of health is not a work of art, difficulty, or strenuous labor. You have only to lay aside artificial observances of every kind and eat, drink, breathe, and sleep in the most natural and delightful way, and if you do this, thinking health and only health, you will certainly be well.

16. SUPPLEMENTARY INSTRUCTIONS

In forming a conception of health, it is necessary to think of the manner in which you would live and work if you were perfectly well and very strong — to imagine yourself doing things in the way of a perfectly well and very strong person, until you have a fairly good conception of what you would be if you were well.

Then take a mental and physical attitude in harmony with this conception, and do not depart from this attitude. You must unify yourself in thought with the thing you desire, and whatever state or condition you unify with yourself in thought will soon become unified with you in body. The scientific way is to sever relations with everything you do not want, and to enter into relations with everything you do want. Form a conception of perfect health, and relate yourself to this conception in word, act, and attitude.

Guard your speech. Make every word harmonize with the conception of perfect health. Never complain. Never say things like these: "I did not sleep well last night," "I have a pain in my side," "I do not feel at all well today," and so on. Say: "I am looking forward to a good night's sleep tonight," "I can see that I progress rapidly," and things of similar meaning. As far as everything which is connected with disease is concerned, your way is to forget it; and as far as everything which is connected with health is concerned, your way is to unify yourself with it in thought and speech.

This is the whole thing in a nutshell: *make yourself one with Health in thought, word, and action, and do not connect yourself with sickness either by thought, word, or action.*

Do not read "doctor books" or medical literature, or the literature of those whose theories conflict with those herein set forth. To do so will certainly undermine your faith in the Way of Living upon which you have entered and cause you to again come into mental relations with disease. This book really gives you all that is required — nothing essential has been omitted, and practically all the superfluous has been eliminated.

The Science of Being Well is an exact science, like arithmetic. Nothing can be added to the fundamental principles, and if anything be taken from them, a failure will result. If you follow strictly the way of living prescribed in this book, you will be well. And you certainly CAN follow this way, both in thought and action.

Relate not only yourself, but so far as possible all others, in your thoughts, to perfect health. Do not sympathize with people when they complain, or even when they are sick and suffering. Turn their thoughts into a constructive channel if you can. Do all you can for their relief, but do it with the health thought in your mind.

Do not let people tell their woes and catalogue their symptoms to you. Turn the conversation to some other subject, or excuse yourself and go. Better be considered an unfeeling person than to have the disease thought forced upon you.

When you are in company of people whose conversational stock-in-trade is sickness and kindred matters, ignore what they say and fall to offering a mental prayer of gratitude for your perfect health. And if that does not enable you to shut out their thoughts, say good-by and leave them.

No matter what they think or say, politeness does not require you to permit yourself to be poisoned by diseased or perverted thought. When we have a few more hundreds of thousands of enlightened thinkers who will not stay where people complain and talk sickness, the world will advance rapidly toward health. When you let people talk to you of sickness, you assist them to increase and multiply sickness.

What shall I do when I am in pain? Can one be in actual physical suffering and still think only thoughts of health? Yes. Do not resist pain; recognize that it is a good thing. Pain is caused by an effort of the Principle of Health to overcome some unnatural condition. This you must know and feel.

When you have a pain, think that a process of healing is going on in the affected part, and mentally assist and cooperate with it. Put yourself in full mental harmony with the power which is causing the pain — assist it, help it along. Do not hesitate, when necessary, to use hot fomentations and similar means to further the good work which is going on. If the pain is severe, lie down and give your mind to the work of quietly and easily cooperating with the force which is at work for your good.

This is the time to exercise gratitude and faith. Be thankful for the power of health which is causing the pain, and be certain that the pain will cease as soon as the good work is done. Fix your thoughts, with confidence, on the Principle of Health which is making such conditions within you that pain will soon be unnecessary. You will be surprised to find how easily you can conquer pain, and after you have lived for a time in this Scientific Way, pains and aches will be things unknown to you.

What shall I do when I am too weak for my work? Shall I drive myself beyond my strength, trusting in God to support me? Shall I go on, like the runner, expecting a "second wind?" No; better not. When you begin to live in this Way, you will probably not be of normal strength, and you will gradually pass from a low physical condition to a higher one. If you relate yourself mentally with health and strength, and perform the voluntary functions of life in a perfectly healthy manner, your strength will increase from day to day, but for a time you may have days when your strength is insufficient for the work you would like to do.

At such times rest, and exercise gratitude. Recognize the fact that your strength is growing rapidly, and feel a deep thankfulness to the Living One from whom it comes. Spend an hour of weakness in thanksgiving and rest, with full faith that great strength is at hand, and then get up and go on again. While you rest do not think of your present weakness; think of the strength that is coming.

Never, at any time, allow yourself to think that you are giving way to weakness. When you rest, as when you go to sleep, fix your mind on the Principle of Health which is building you into complete strength.

What shall I do about that great bugaboo which scares millions of people to death every year — constipation? Do not worry. Read Horace Fletcher on The A.B.- Z. of Our Own Nutrition, and get the full force of his explanation of the fact that when you live on this scientific plan there will be much less matter to eliminate. The material from the plant foods you are naturally guided to eat will take care of the matter. The gross feeders who eat from three to ten times as much fat, meat, and starch as can be utilized in their systems have a great amount of waste to eliminate and not the plant materials to assist, but if you live in the manner we have described it will be otherwise with you.

If you eat only when you have an EARNED HUNGER, and chew every mouthful to a liquid, and if you stop eating the instant you BEGIN to be conscious of an abatement of your hunger, you will so perfectly prepare your food for digestion and assimilation that practically all of it will be taken up by the absorbents, and there will be little remaining in the bowels to be excreted. If you are able to entirely banish from your memory all that you have read in "doctor books" and patent medicine advertisements concerning constipation, you need give the matter no further thought at all. The Principle of Health will take care of it.

But if your mind has been filled with fear-thought in regard to constipation, it may be well in the beginning for you to occasionally flush the colon with warm water. There is not the least need of doing it, except to make the process of your mental emancipation from fear a little easier; it may be worthwhile for that. And as soon as you see that you are making good progress, and that you have cut down your quantity of food, and are really eating in the Scientific Way, dismiss constipation from your mind forever; you have nothing more to do with it. Put your trust in that Principle within you which has the power to give you perfect health. Relate to It by your reverent gratitude to the Principle of Life which is All Power, and go on your way rejoicing.

What about exercise? Everyone is the better for a little all-round use of the muscles every day, and the best way to get this is to do it by engaging in some form of play or amusement. Get your exercise in the natural way — as recreation, not as a forced stunt for health's sake alone. Ride a horse or a bicycle, play tennis or tenpins, or toss a ball. Have some avocation like gardening in which you can spend an hour every day with pleasure and profit. There are a thousand ways in which you can get exercise enough to keep your body supple and your circulation good, and yet not fall into the rut of "exercising for your health." Exercise for fun or profit. Exercise because you are too healthy to sit still, and not because you wish to become healthy, or to remain so.

Are long continued fasts necessary? Seldom, if ever. The Principle of Health does not often require 20, 30, or 40 days to get ready for action. Under normal conditions, hunger will come in much less time. In most long fasts, the reason hunger does not come sooner is because it has been inhibited by the patient himself. He begins the fast with the FEAR if not actually with the hope that it will be many days before hunger comes. The literature he has read on the subject has prepared him to expect a long fast, and he is grimly determined to go to a finish, let the time be as long as it will. And the sub-conscious mind, under the influence of powerful and positive suggestion, suspends hunger. When, for any reason, nature takes away your hunger, go cheerfully on with your usual work, and do not eat until she gives it back. No matter if it is two, three, ten days, or longer, you may be perfectly sure that when it is time for you to eat you will be hungry. And if you are cheerfully confident and keep your faith in health, you will suffer from no weakness or discomfort caused by abstinence.

When you are not hungry, you will feel stronger, happier, and more comfortable if you do not eat than you will if you do eat, no matter how long the fast. And if you live in the scientific way described in this book, you will never have to take long fasts, you will seldom miss a meal, and you will enjoy your meals more than ever before in your life. Get an earned hunger before you eat, and whenever you get an earned hunger, eat.

17. A SUMMARY OF THE SCIENCE OF BEING WELL

Health is perfectly natural functioning, normal living. There is a Principle of Life in the universe; it is the Living Substance, from which all things are made. This Living Substance permeates, penetrates, and fills the interspaces of the universe. In its invisible state it is in and through all forms, and yet all forms are made of it.

To illustrate: Suppose that a very fine and highly diffusible aqueous vapor should permeate and penetrate a block of ice. The ice is formed from living water and is living water in form, while the vapor is also living water, unformed, permeating a form made from itself. This illustration will explain how Living Substance permeates all forms made from It. All life comes from It. It is all the life there is.

This Universal Substance is a thinking substance, and takes the form of its thought. The thought of a form, held by it, creates the form; and the thought of a motion causes the motion. It cannot help thinking, and so is forever creating. And it must move on toward fuller and more complete expression of itself. This means toward more complete life and more perfect functioning — and that means toward perfect health. The power of the living substance must always be exerted toward perfect health. It is a force in all things making for perfect functioning.

All things are permeated by a power which makes for health.

A human being can relate himself to this power, and ally himself with it. He can also separate himself from it in his thoughts.

A human being is a form of this Living Substance, and has within him a Principle of Health. This Principle of Health, when in full constructive activity, causes all the involuntary functions of the human body to be perfectly performed.

A human being is a thinking substance, permeating a visible body, and the processes of his body are controlled by his thought.

When a person thinks only thoughts of perfect health, the internal processes of his body will be those of perfect health. A person's first step toward perfect health must be to form a conception of himself as perfectly healthy and as doing all things in the way and manner of a perfectly healthy person. Having formed this conception, he must relate himself to it in all his thoughts, and sever all thought relations with disease and weakness. If he does this, and thinks his thoughts of health with positive FAITH, a person will cause the Principle of Health within him to become constructively active, and to heal all his diseases. He can receive additional power from the universal Principle of Life by faith, and he can acquire faith by looking to this Principle of Life with reverent gratitude for the health it gives him. If a person will consciously accept the health which is being continually given to him by the Living Substance, and if he will be duly grateful for it, he will develop faith.

A person cannot think only thoughts of perfect health unless he performs the voluntary functions of life in a perfectly healthy manner. These voluntary functions are eating, drinking, breathing, and sleeping. If a person thinks only thoughts of health, has faith in health, and eats, drinks, breathes, and sleeps in a perfectly healthy way, he must have perfect health.

Health is the result of thinking and acting in a Certain Way, and if a sick person begins to think and act in this Way, the Principle of Health within him will come into constructive activity and heal all his diseases. This Principle of Heath is the same in all, and is related to the Life Principle of the universe. It is able to heal every disease, and will come into activity whenever a person thinks and acts in accordance with the Science of Being Well. Therefore, every person can attain perfect health. **The End**

BOOK THREE
THE SCIENCE OF
BEING GREAT

1. ANY PERSON MAY BECOME GREAT

THERE is a Principle of Power in every person. By the intelligent use and direction of this principle, a person can develop his own mental faculties. We have an inherent power by which we may grow in whatsoever direction we please, and there does not appear to be any limit to the possibilities of our growth. No person has yet become so great in any faculty but that it is possible for someone else to become greater. The possibility is in the Original Substance from which we are made. Genius is Omniscience flowing into us. Genius is more than talent. Talent may merely be one faculty developed out of proportion to other faculties, but genius is the union of man and God in the acts of the soul. Great men and women are always greater than their deeds. They are in connection with a reserve power that is without limit. We do not know where the boundary of the mental powers of a person is; we do not even know that there is a boundary.

The power of conscious growth is not given to the lower animals; it is human's alone and may be developed and increased by him. The lower animals can, to a great extent, be trained and developed by people; but we can train and develop ourselves. We alone have this power, and we have it to an apparently unlimited extent.

The purpose of life for us is growth, just as the purpose of life for trees and plants is growth. Trees and plants grow automatically and along fixed lines; we can grow as we will. Trees and plants can only develop certain possibilities and characteristics; a person can develop any power which is or has been shown by any person, anywhere. Nothing that is possible in spirit is impossible in flesh and blood. Nothing that we can think is impossible in action. Nothing that we can imagine is impossible of realization. We are formed for growth, and we are under the necessity of growing. It is essential to our happiness that we should continuously advance.

Life without progress becomes unendurable, and the person who ceases from growth must either become imbecile or insane. The greater and more harmonious and well-rounded our growth, the happier we will be.

There is no possibility in anyone that is not in every man and woman; but if they proceed naturally, no two people will grow into the same thing, or be alike.

Every man and woman comes into the world with a predisposition to grow along certain lines, and growth is easier for them along those lines than in any other way. This is a wise provision, for it gives endless variety. It is as if a gardener should throw all his bulbs into one basket; to the superficial observer they would look alike, but growth reveals a tremendous difference. So of men and women; they are like the basket of bulbs. One may be a rose and add brightness and color to some dark corner of the world; one may be a lily and teach a lesson of love and purity to every eye that sees; one may be a climbing vine and hide the rugged outlines of some dark rock; one may be a great oak among whose boughs the birds shall nest and sing, and beneath whose shade the flocks shall rest at noon, but everyone will be something worthwhile, something rare, something perfect.

There are undreamed of possibilities in the common lives all around us; in a large sense, there are no "common" people. In times of national stress and peril the cracker-box loafer of the corner store and the village drunkard become heroes and statesmen through the quickening of the Principle of Power within them. There is a genius in every man and woman, waiting to be brought forth. Every village has its great man or woman; someone to whom all go for advice in time of trouble; someone who is instinctively recognized as being great in wisdom and insight. To such a one the minds of the whole community turn in times of local crisis; they are tacitly recognized as being great. They do small things in a great way. They could do great things as well if they did but undertake them; so can anyone; so can you.

The Principle of Power gives us just what we ask of it; if we only undertake little things, it only gives us power for little things; but if we try to do great things in a great way it gives us all the power there is. But beware of undertaking great things in a small way; of that we shall speak farther on.

There are two mental attitudes a person may take. One makes him like a football. It has resilience and reacts strongly when force is applied to it, but it originates nothing; it never acts of itself. There is no power within it. People of this type are controlled by circumstances and environment; their destinies are decided by things external to themselves. The Principle of Power within them is never really active at all. They never speak or act from within. The other attitude makes people like a flowing spring. Power comes out from the center of them. They have within a well of water springing up into everlasting life. They radiate force; they are felt by their environment. The Principle of Power in them is in constant action. They are self-active. "He hath life in himself."

No greater good can come to any man or woman than to become self-active. All the experiences of life are designed by Providence to force men and women into self-activity; to compel them to cease being creatures of circumstances and master their environment. In his lowest stage, man is the child of chance and circumstance and the slave of fear. His acts are all reactions resulting from the impingement upon him of forces in his environment. He acts only as he is acted upon; he originates nothing. But the lowest savage has within him a Principle of Power sufficient to master all that he fears; and if he learns this and becomes self-active, he becomes as one of the gods.

The awakening of the Principle of Power in us is the real conversion; the passing from death to life. It is when the dead hear the voice of the Son of Man and come forth and live. It is the resurrection and the life. When we are awakened, we become sons of the Highest and all power is given to us in heaven and on earth. Nothing was ever in any man or woman that is not in you; no one ever had more spiritual or mental power than you can attain, or did greater things than you can accomplish. You can become what you want to be.

2. HEREDITY AND OPPORTUNITY

YOU are not barred from attaining greatness by heredity. No matter who or what your ancestors may have been or how unlearned or lowly their station, the upward way is open for you. There is no such thing as inheriting a fixed mental position; no matter how small the mental capital we receive from our parents, it may be increased; no person is born incapable of growth.

Heredity counts for something. We are born with subconscious mental tendencies; as, for instance, a tendency to melancholy, or cowardice, or to ill- temper; but all these subconscious tendencies may be overcome.

When the real person awakens and comes forth he can throw them off very easily. Nothing of this kind need keep you down; if you have inherited undesirable mental tendencies, you can eliminate them and put desirable tendencies in their places. An inherited mental trait is a habit of thought of your father or mother impressed upon your subconscious mind; you can substitute the opposite impression by forming the opposite habit of thought.

You can substitute a habit of cheerfulness for a tendency to despondency; you can overcome cowardice or ill-temper.

Heredity may count for something, too, in an inherited conformation of the skull. There is something in phrenology, if not so much as its exponents claim for it. It is true that the different faculties are localized in the brain, and that the power of a faculty depends upon the number of active brain cells in its area. A faculty whose brain area is large is likely to act with more power than one whose cranial section is small; hence persons with certain conformations of the skull show talent as musicians, orators, mechanics, and so on. It has been argued from this that a man's cranial formation must, to a great extent, decide his station in life, but this is an error.

It has been found that a small brain section, with many fine and active cells, gives as powerful expression to faculty as a larger brain with coarser cells; and it has been found that by turning the Principle of Power into any section of the brain, with the will and purpose to develop a particular talent, the brain cells may be multiplied indefinitely.

Any faculty, power, or talent you possess, no matter how small or rudimentary, may be increased; you can multiply the brain cells in this particular area until it acts as powerfully as you wish. It is true that you can act most easily through those faculties that are now most largely developed; you can do, with the least effort, the things which "come naturally"; but it is also true that if you will make the necessary effort you can develop any talent.

You can do what you desire to do and become what you want to be.

When you fix upon some ideal and proceed as hereinafter directed, all the power of your being is turned into the faculties required in the realization of that ideal; more blood and nerve force go to the corresponding sections of the brain, and the cells are quickened, increased, and multiplied in number.

The proper use of the mind will build a brain capable of doing what the mind wants to do.

The brain does not make the person; the person makes the brain. Your place in life is not fixed by heredity.

Nor are you condemned to the lower levels by circumstances or lack of opportunity. The Principle of Power in us is sufficient for all the requirements of our soul. No possible combination of circumstances can keep us down, if we make our personal attitude right and determine to rise.

The power which formed human beings and purposed them for growth also controls the circumstances of society, industry, and government; and this power is never divided against itself. The power which is in you is in the things around you, and when you begin to move forward, the things will arrange themselves for your advantage, as described in later chapters of this book.

Human beings were formed for growth, and all things external were designed to promote his growth. No sooner does a person awaken his soul and enter on the advancing way than he finds that not only is God for him, but nature, society, and his fellow men and women are for him also; and all things work together for his good if he obeys the law. Poverty is no bar to greatness, for poverty can always be removed.

Martin Luther, as a child, sang in the streets for bread. Linnaeus the naturalist, had only forty dollars with which to educate himself; he mended his own shoes and often had to beg meals from his friends. Hugh Miller, apprenticed to a stone mason, began to study geology in a quarry. George Stephenson, inventor of the locomotive engine, and one of the greatest of civil engineers, was a coal miner, working in a mine, when he awakened and began to think. James Watt was a sickly child, and was not strong enough to be sent to school. Abraham Lincoln was a poor boy. In each of these cases we see a Principle of Power in the man which lifts him above all opposition and adversity.

There is a Principle of Power in you; if you use it and apply it in a certain way you can overcome all heredity, and master all circumstances and conditions and become a great and powerful personality.

3. THE SOURCE OF POWER

Our brain, body, mind, faculties, and talents are the mere instruments we use in demonstrating greatness; in themselves they do not make us great. We may have a large brain and a good mind, strong faculties, and brilliant talents, and yet we are not a great person unless we use all these in a great way. That quality which enables us to use our abilities in a great way makes us great; and to that quality we give the name of wisdom. Wisdom is the essential basis of greatness.

Wisdom is the power to perceive the best ends to aim at and the best means for reaching those ends. It is the power to perceive the right thing to do. Someone who is wise enough to know the right thing to do, who is good enough to wish to do only the right thing, and who is able and strong enough to do the right thing is a truly great person.

He will instantly become marked as a personality of power in any community and men and women will delight to do him honor. Wisdom is dependent upon knowledge. Where there is complete ignorance there can be no wisdom, no knowledge of the right thing to do.

Our knowledge is comparatively limited and so our wisdom must be small, unless we can connect our mind with a knowledge greater than our own and draw from it, by inspiration, the wisdom that our own limitations deny us. This we can do; this is what the really great men and women have done.

Our knowledge is limited and uncertain; therefore we cannot have wisdom in ourselves. Only God knows all truth; therefore only God can have real wisdom or know the right thing to do at all times, and man can receive wisdom from God. I proceed to give an illustration: Abraham Lincoln had limited education; but he had the power to perceive truth. In Lincoln we see preeminently apparent the fact that real wisdom consists in knowing the right thing to do at all times and under all circumstances; in having the will to do the right thing, and in having talent and ability enough to be competent and able to do the right thing. Back in the days of the abolition agitation, and during the compromise period, when all other men were more or less confused as to what was right or as to what ought to be done, Lincoln was never uncertain. He saw through the superficial arguments of the pro-slavery; he saw, also, the impracticability and fanaticism of the abolitionists; he saw the right ends to aim at and he saw the best means to attain those ends. It was because men recognized that he perceived truth and knew the right thing to do that they made him president. Anyone who develops the power to perceive truth, and who can show that he always knows the right thing to do and that he can be trusted to do the right thing, will be honored and advanced; the whole world is looking eagerly for such men and women.

When Lincoln became president he was surrounded by a multitude of so-called able advisers, hardly any two of whom were agreed. At times they were all opposed to his policies; at times almost the whole North was opposed to what he proposed to do. But he saw the truth when others were misled by appearances; his judgment was seldom or never wrong. He was at once the ablest statesman and the best soldier of the period. Where did he, a comparatively unlearned man, get this wisdom? It was not due to some peculiar formation of his skull or to some fineness of texture of his brain. It was not due to some physical characteristic. It was not even a quality of mind due to superior reasoning power. Knowledge of truth is not often reached by the processes of reason. It was due to a spiritual insight. He perceived truth, but where did he perceive it and whence did the perception come?

We see something similar in Washington, whose faith and courage, due to his perception of truth, held the colonies together during the long and often apparently hopeless struggle of the Revolution.

We see something of the same thing in the phenomenal genius of Napoleon, who always knew, in military matters, the best means to adopt. We see that the greatness of Napoleon was in nature rather than in Napoleon, and we discover back of Washington and Lincoln something greater than either Washington or Lincoln. We see the same thing in all great men and women.

They perceive truth; but truth cannot be perceived until it exists; and there can be no truth until there is a mind to perceive it. Truth does not exist apart from mind. Washington and Lincoln were in touch and communication with a mind which knew all knowledge and contained all truth. So of all who manifest wisdom.

Wisdom is obtained by reading the mind of God.

4. THE MIND OF GOD

There is a Cosmic Intelligence which is in all things and through all things. This is the one real substance. From it all things proceed. It is Intelligent Substance or Mind Stuff. It is God.

Where there is no substance there can be no intelligence; for where there is no substance there is nothing. Where there is thought there must be a substance which thinks.

Thought cannot be function, for function is motion, and it is inconceivable that mere motion should think. Thought cannot be vibration, for vibration is motion, and that motion should be intelligent is not thinkable.

Motion is nothing but the moving of substance; if there be intelligence shown it must be in the substance and not in the motion. Thought cannot be the result of motions in the brain; if thought is in the brain it must be in the brain's substance and not in the motions which brain substance makes.

But thought is not in the brain substance, for brain substance, without life, is quite unintelligent and dead. Thought is in the life-principle which animates the brain; in the spirit substance, which is the real person. The brain does not think, the person thinks and expresses his thought through the brain.

There is a spirit substance which thinks. Just as the spirit substance of a person permeates his body, and thinks and knows in the body, so the Original Spirit Substance, God, permeates all nature and thinks and knows in nature.

Nature is as intelligent as humans, and knows more than us; nature knows all things. The All-Mind has been in touch with all things from the beginning; and it contains all knowledge. Our experience cover a few things, and these things we know; but God's experience covers all the things that have happened since the creation, from the wreck of a planet or the passing of a comet to the fall of a sparrow. All that is and all that has been are present in the Intelligence which is wrapped about us and enfolds us and presses upon us from every side.

All the encyclopedias written are but trivial affairs compared to the vast knowledge held by the mind in which humans live, move, and have their being.

The truths we perceive by inspiration are thoughts held in this mind. If they were not thoughts we could not perceive them, for they would have no existence; and they could not exist as thoughts unless there is a mind for them to exist in; and a mind can be nothing else than a substance which thinks.

We are thinking substance, a portion of the Cosmic Substance; but are limited, while the Cosmic Intelligence from which he sprang, which Jesus calls the Father, is unlimited. All intelligence, power, and force come from the Father. Jesus recognized this and stated it very plainly. Over and over again he ascribed all his wisdom and power to his unity with the Father, and to his perceiving the thoughts of God. "My Father and I are one."

This was the foundation of his knowledge and power. He showed the people the necessity of becoming spiritually awakened; of hearing his voice and becoming like him. He compared the unthinking person who is the prey and sport of circumstances to the dead man in a tomb, and besought him to hear and come forth. "God is spirit," he said; "be born again, become spiritually awake, and you may see his kingdom. Hear my voice; see what I am and what I do, and come forth and live. The words I speak are spirit and life; accept them and they will cause a well of water to spring up within you. Then you will have life within yourself."

"I do what I see the Father do," he said, meaning that he read the thoughts of God. "The Father showeth all things to the son." "If any man has the will to do the will of God, he shall know truth." "My teaching is not my own, but his that sent me." "You shall know the truth and the truth shall make you free." "The spirit shall guide you into all truth."

We are immersed in mind and that mind contains all knowledge and all truth. It is seeking to give us this knowledge, for our Father delights to give good gifts to his children.

The prophets and seers and great men and women, past and present, were made great by what they received from God, not by what they were taught by men. This limitless reservoir of wisdom and power is open to you; you can draw upon it as you will, according to your needs. You can make yourself what you desire to be; you can do what you wish to do; you can have what you want.

To accomplish this you must learn to become one with the Father so that you may perceive truth; so that you may have wisdom and know the right ends to seek and the right means to use to attain those ends, and so that you may secure power and ability to use the means. In closing this chapter resolve that you will now lay aside all else and concentrate upon the attainment of conscious unity with God.

"Oh, when I am safe in my sylvan home,

I tread on the pride of Greece and Rome;

And when I am stretched beneath the pines,

Where the evening star so holy shines,

I laugh at the lore and pride of man,

At the Sophist schools and the learned clan;

For what are they all in their high conceit,

When man in the bush with God may meet?"

5. PREPARATION

DRAW nigh to God and He will draw nigh to you."

If you become like God you can read his thoughts; and if you do not you will find the inspirational perception of truth impossible.

You can never become a great person until you have overcome anxiety, worry, and fear. It is impossible for an anxious person, a worried one, or a fearful one to perceive truth; all things are distorted and thrown out of their proper relations by such mental states, and those who are in them cannot read the thoughts of God. If you are poor, or if you are anxious about business or financial matters, you are recommended to study carefully the first volume of this series, "The Science of Getting Rich." That will present to you a solution for your problems of this nature, no matter how large or how complicated they may seem to be. There is not the least cause for worry about financial affairs; every person who wills to do so may rise above want, have all he needs, and become rich. The same source upon which you propose to draw for mental unfoldment and spiritual power is at your service for the supply of all your material wants. Study this truth until it is fixed in your thoughts and until anxiety is banished from your mind; enter the Certain Way, which leads to material riches.

Again, if you are anxious or worried about your health, realize it is possible for you to attain perfect health so that you may have strength sufficient for all that you wish to do and more. That Intelligence which stands ready to give you wealth and mental and spiritual power will rejoice to give you health also. Perfect health is yours for the asking, if you will only obey the simple laws of life and live aright. Conquer ill-health and cast out fear.

But it is not enough to rise above financial and physical anxiety and worry; you must rise above moral evil-doing as well. Sound your inner consciousness now for the motives which actuate you and make sure they are right. You must cast out lust, and cease to be ruled by appetite, and you must begin to govern appetite. You must eat only to satisfy hunger, never for gluttonous pleasure, and in all things you must make the flesh obey the spirit.

You must lay aside greed; have no unworthy motive in your desire to become rich and powerful. It is legitimate and right to desire riches, if you want them for the sake of the soul, but not if you desire them for the lusts of the flesh.

Cast out pride and vanity; have no thought of trying to rule over others or of outdoing them. This is a vital point; there is no temptation so insidious as the selfish desire to rule over others. Nothing so appeals to the average man or woman as to sit in the uppermost places at feasts, to be respectfully saluted in the market place, and to be called Rabbi, Master.

To exercise some sort of control over others is the secret motive of every selfish person. The struggle for power over others is the battle of the competitive world, and you must rise above that world and its motives and aspirations and seek only for life. Cast out envy; you can have all that you want, and you need not envy any man what he has. Above all things, see to it that you do not hold malice or enmity toward any one; to do so cuts you off from the mind whose treasures you seek to make your own. "He that loveth not his brother, loveth not God." Lay aside all narrow personal ambition and determine to seek the highest good and to be swayed by no unworthy selfishness.

Go over all the foregoing and set these moral temptations out of your heart one by one; determine to keep them out. Then resolve that you will not only abandon all evil thought but that you will forsake all deeds, habits, and courses of action which do not commend themselves to your noblest ideals. This is supremely important; make this resolution with all the power of your soul, and you are ready for the next step toward greatness, which you will find explained in the following chapter.

6. THE SOCIAL POINT OF VIEW

WITHOUT faith it is impossible to please God," and without faith it is impossible for you to become great. The distinguishing characteristic of all really great men and women is an unwavering faith. We see this in Lincoln during the dark days of the war; we see it in Washington at Valley Forge; we see it in Livingstone, the crippled missionary, threading the mazes of the dark continent, his soul aflame with the determination to let in the light upon the accursed slave trade, which his soul abhorred; we see it in Luther, and in Frances Willard, in every man and woman who has attained a place on the muster roll of the great ones of the world.

Faith—not a faith in one's self or in one's own powers but faith in principle; in the Something Great which upholds right, and which may be relied upon to give us the victory in due time. Without this faith it is not possible for anyone to rise to real greatness. The person who has no faith in principle will always be small. Whether you have this faith or not depends upon your point of view. You must learn to see the world as being produced by evolution; as a something which is evolving and becoming, not as a finished work. Millions of years ago God worked with very low and crude forms of life; low and crude, yet each perfect after its kind. Higher and more complex organisms, animal and vegetable, appeared through the successive ages; the earth passed through stage after stage in its unfoldment, each stage perfect in itself, and to be succeeded by a higher one. What I wish you to note is that the so-called "lower organisms" are as perfect after their kind as the higher ones; that the world in the Eocene period was perfect for that period; it was perfect, but God's work was not finished. This is true of the world to-day. Physically, socially, and industrially it is all good, and it is all perfect. It is not complete anywhere or in any part, but so far as the handiwork of God has gone it is perfect. **This must be your point of view: that the world and all it contains is perfect, though not completed.**

"All's right with the world." That is the great fact. There is nothing wrong with anything; there is nothing wrong with anybody. All the facts of life you must contemplate from this standpoint. There is nothing wrong with nature. Nature is a great advancing presence, working beneficently for the happiness of all. All things in Nature are good; she has no evil. She is not complete, for creation is still unfinished, but she is going on to give to man even more bountifully than she has given to him in the past. Nature is a partial expression of God, and God is love. She is perfect but not complete.

So of human society and government. What though there are trusts and combinations of capital and strikes and lockouts and so on. All these things are part of the forward movement; they are incidental to the evolutionary process of completing society. When it is complete there will be no more of these inharmonies; but it cannot be completed without them. J. P. Morgan is as necessary to the coming social order as the strange animals of the age of reptiles were to the life of the succeeding period, and just as these animals were perfect after their kind, so Morgan is perfect after his kind. Behold it is all very good. See society, government, and industry as being perfect now, and as advancing rapidly toward being complete; then you will understand that there is nothing to fear, no cause for anxiety, nothing to worry about. Never complain of any of these things. They are perfect; this is the very best possible world for the stage of development man has reached.

This will sound like rank folly to many, perhaps to most people. "What!" they will say, "are not child labor and the exploitation of men and women in filthy and unsanitary factories evil things? Are not saloons evil? Do you mean to say that we shall accept all these and call them good?"

Child labor and similar things are no more evil than the way of living and the habits and practices of the cave dweller were evil. His ways were those of the savage stage of man's growth, and for that stage they were perfect. Our industrial practices are those of the savage stage of industrial development, and they are also perfect. Nothing better is possible until we cease to be mental savages in industry and business, and become men and women. This can only come about by the rise of the whole race to a higher viewpoint. And this can only come about by the rise of such individuals here and there as are ready for the higher viewpoint. The cure for all these inharmonies lies not with the masters or employers but with the workers themselves.

Whenever they reach a higher viewpoint, whenever they shall desire to do so, they can establish complete brotherhood and harmony in industry; they have the numbers and the power. They are getting now what they desire. Whenever they desire more in the way of a higher, purer, more harmonious life, they will receive more. True, they want more now, but they only want more of the things that make for animal enjoyment, and so industry remains in the savage, brutal, animal stage; when the workers begin to rise to the mental plane of living and ask for more of the things that make for the life of the mind and soul, industry will at once be raised above the plane of savagery and brutality. But it is perfect now upon its plane; behold, it is all very good.

So of saloons and dens of vice. If a majority of the people desire these things, it is right and necessary that they should have them. When a majority desire a world without such discords, they will create such a world. So long as men and women are on the plane of bestial thought, so long the social order will be in part disorder, and will show bestial manifestations. The people make society what it is, and as the people rise above the bestial thought, society will rise above the beastly in its manifestations. But a society which thinks in a bestial way must have saloons and dives; it is perfect after its kind, as the world was in the Eocene period, and very good.

All this does not prevent you from working for better things. You can work to complete an unfinished society, instead of to renovate a decaying one; and you can work with a better heart and a more hopeful spirit. It will make an immense difference with your faith and spirit whether you look upon civilization as a good thing which is becoming better or as a bad and evil thing which is decaying. One viewpoint gives you an advancing and expanding mind and the other gives you a descending and decreasing mind. One viewpoint will make you grow greater and the other will inevitably cause you to grow smaller. One will enable you to work for the eternal things; to do large works in a great way toward the completing of all that is incomplete and inharmonious; and the other will make you a mere patchwork reformer, working almost without hope to save a few lost souls from what you will grow to consider a lost and doomed world. So you see it makes a vast difference to you, this matter of the social viewpoint. "All's right with the world. Nothing can possibly be wrong but my personal attitude, and I will make that right. I will see the facts of nature and all the events, circumstances, and conditions of society, politics, government, and industry from the highest viewpoint. It is all perfect, though incomplete. It is all the handiwork of God; behold, it is all very good."

7. THE INDIVIDUAL POINT OF VIEW

IMPORTANT as the matter of your point of view for the facts of social life is, it is of less moment than your viewpoint for your fellow men, for your acquaintances, friends, relatives, your immediate family, and, most of all, yourself. You must learn not to look upon the world as a lost and decaying thing but as a something perfect and glorious which is going on to a most beautiful completeness; and you must learn to see men and women not as lost and accursed things, but as perfect beings advancing to become complete. There are no "bad" or "evil" people. An engine which is on the rails pulling a heavy train is perfect after its kind, and it is good.

The power of steam which drives it is good. Let a broken rail throw the engine into the ditch, and it does not become bad or evil by being so displaced; it is a perfectly good engine, but off the track. The power of steam which drives it into the ditch and wrecks it is not evil, but a perfectly good power. So that which is misplaced or applied in an incomplete or partial way is not evil. There are no evil people; there are perfectly good people who are off the track, but they do not need condemnation or punishment; they only need to get upon the rails again.

That which is undeveloped or incomplete often appears to us as evil because of the way we have trained ourselves to think. The root of a bulb which shall produce a white lily is an unsightly thing; one might look upon it with disgust. But how foolish we should be to condemn the bulb for its appearance when we know the lily is within it. The root is perfect after its kind; it is a perfect but incomplete lily, and so we must learn to look upon every man and woman, no matter how unlovely in outward manifestation; they are perfect in their stage of being and they are becoming complete. Behold, it is all very good.

Once we come into a comprehension of this fact and arrive at this point of view, we lose all desire to find fault with people, to judge them, criticize them, or condemn them. We no longer work as those who are saving lost souls, but as those who are among the angels, working out the completion of a glorious heaven.

We are born of the spirit and we see the kingdom of God. We no longer see people as trees walking, but our vision is complete. We have nothing but good words to say. It is all good; a great and glorious humanity coming to completeness. And in our association with people this puts us into an expansive and enlarging attitude of mind; we see them as great beings and we begin to deal with them and their affairs in a great way.

But if we fall to the other point of view and see a lost and degenerate race we shrink into the contracting mind; and our dealings with people and their affairs will be in a small and contracted way. Remember to hold steadily to this point of view; if you do you cannot fail to begin at once to deal with your acquaintances and neighbors and with your own family as a great personality deals with people. This same viewpoint must be the one from which you regard yourself. You must always see yourself as a great advancing soul. Learn to say: "There is THAT in me of which I am made, which knows no imperfection, weakness, or sickness. The world is incomplete, but God in my own consciousness is both perfect and complete. Nothing can be wrong but my own personal attitude, and my own personal attitude can be wrong only when I disobey THAT which is within. I am a perfect manifestation of God so far as I have gone, and I will press on to be complete. I will trust and not be afraid." When you are able to say this understandingly you will have lost all fear and you will be far advanced upon the road to develop a great and powerful personality.

8. CONSECRATION

HAVING attained to the viewpoint which puts you into the right relations with the world and with your fellow men, the next step is consecration; and consecration in its true sense simply means obedience to the soul. You have that within you which is ever impelling you toward the upward and advancing way; and that impelling something is the divine Principle of Power; you must obey it without question. No one will deny the statement that if you are to be great, the greatness must be a manifestation of something within; nor can you question that this something must be the very greatest and highest that is within.

It is not the mind, or the intellect, or the reason.

You cannot be great if you go no farther back for principle than to your reasoning power. Reason knows neither principle nor morality. Your reason is like a lawyer in that it will argue for either side. The intellect of a thief will plan robbery and murder as readily as the intellect of a saint will plan a great philanthropy. Intellect helps us to see the best means and manner of doing the right thing, but intellect never shows us the right thing. Intellect and reason serve the selfish man for his selfish ends as readily as they serve the unselfish man for his unselfish ends. Use intellect and reason without regard to principle, and you may become known as a very able person, but you will never become known as a person whose life shows the power of real greatness. There is too much training of the intellect and reasoning powers and too little training in obedience to the soul. This is the only thing that can be wrong with your personal attitude—when it fails to be one of obedience to the Principle of Power.

By going back to your own center you can always find the pure idea of right for every relationship. To be great and to have power it is only necessary to conform your life to the pure idea as you find it in the GREAT WITHIN. Every compromise on this point is made at the expense of a loss of power. You *must* remember this.

There are many ideas in your mind which you have outgrown, and which, from force of habit, you still permit to dictate the actions of your life. Cease all this; abandon everything you have outgrown. There are many ignoble customs, social and other, which you still follow, although you know they tend to dwarf and belittle you and keep you acting in a small way. Rise above all this.

I do not say that you should absolutely disregard conventionalities, or the commonly accepted standards of right and wrong. You cannot do this; but you can deliver your soul from most of the narrow restrictions which bind the majority of your fellow human beings. Do not give your time and strength to the support of obsolete institutions, religious or otherwise; do not be bound by creeds in which you do not believe. Be free.

You have perhaps formed some sensual habits of mind or body; abandon them. You still indulge in distrustful fears that things will go wrong, or that people will betray you, or mistreat you; get above all of them. You still act selfishly in many ways and on many occasions; cease to do so.

Abandon all these, and in place of them put the best actions you can form a conception of in your mind. If you desire to advance, and you are not doing so, remember that it can be only because your thought is better than your practice. You must do as well as you think. Let your thoughts be ruled by principle, and then live up to your thoughts.

Let your attitude in business, in politics, in neighborhood affairs, and in your own home be the expression of the best thoughts you can think. Let your manner toward all, great and small, and especially to your own family circle, always be the most kindly, gracious, and courteous you can picture in your imagination. Remember your viewpoint: you are a god in the company of gods and must conduct yourself accordingly.

The steps to complete consecration are few and simple. You cannot be ruled from below if you are to be great; you must rule from above. Therefore you cannot be governed by physical impulses; you must bring your body into subjection to the mind; but your mind, without principle, may lead you into selfishness and immoral ways.

You must put the mind into subjection to the soul, and your soul is limited by the boundaries of your knowledge; you must put it into subjection to that Oversoul which needeth no searching of the understanding but before whose eye all things are spread. That constitutes consecration. Say: "I surrender my body to be ruled by my mind; I surrender my mind to be governed by my soul, and I surrender my soul to the guidance of God."

Make this consecration complete and thorough, and you have taken the second great step in the way of greatness and power.

9. IDENTIFICATION

HAVING recognized God as the advancing presence in nature, society, and your fellow human beings, and harmonized yourself with all these, and having consecrated yourself to that within you which impels toward the greatest and the highest, the next step is to become aware of and recognize fully the fact that the Principle of Power within you is God Himself. You must consciously identify yourself with the Highest. This is not some false or untrue position to be assumed; it is a fact to be recognized. You are already one with God; you want to become consciously aware of it.

There is one substance, the source of all things, and this substance has within itself the power which creates all things; all power is inherent in it. This substance is conscious and thinks; it works with perfect understanding and intelligence. You know that this is so, because you know that substance exists and that consciousness exists; and that it must be substance which is conscious. We are conscious and think; we are substance. We must be substance, else we are nothing and do not exist at all. If we are substance and think, and are conscious, then we are Conscious Substance.

It is not conceivable that there should be more than one Conscious Substance; so we are the original substance, the source of all life and power embodied in a physical form. We cannot be something different from God. Intelligence is one and the same everywhere, and must be everywhere an attribute of the same substance.

There cannot be one kind of intelligence in God and another kind of intelligence in us; intelligence can only be in intelligent substance, and Intelligent Substance is God. We are of one stuff with God, and so all the talents, powers, and possibilities that are in God are in us; not in a few exceptional people but in everyone. "All power is given to man, in heaven and on earth." "Is it not written, ye are gods?" The Principle of Power in us is us ourselves, and us ourselves are God. But while we are original substance, and have within us all power and possibilities, our consciousness is limited. We don't know all there is to know, and so we are liable to error and mistake. To save ourselves from these we must unite our mind to That outside us which does know all; we must become consciously one with God.

There is a Mind surrounding us on every side, closer than breathing, nearer than hands and feet, and in this mind is the memory of all that has ever happened, from the greatest convulsions of nature in prehistoric days to the fall of a sparrow in this present time; and all that is in existence now as well.

Held in this Mind is the great purpose which is behind all nature, and so it knows what is going to be. We are surrounded by a Mind which knows all there is to know, past, present, and to come. Everything that men have said or done or written is present there.

We are of one identical stuff with this Mind; we proceeded from it; and we can so identify ourselves with it that we may know what it knows. "My Father is greater than I," said Jesus, "I come from him." "I and my Father are one. He showeth the son all things." "The spirit shall guide you into all truth."

Your identification of yourself with the Infinite must be accomplished by conscious recognition on your part. Recognizing it as a fact, that there is only God, and that all intelligence is in the one substance, you must affirm somewhat after this wise:

"There is only one and that one is everywhere. I surrender myself to conscious unity with the highest. Not I, but the Father. I will to be one with the Supreme and to lead the divine life. I am one with infinite consciousness; there is but one mind, and I am that mind. I that speak unto you am he."

If you have been thorough in the work as outlined in the preceding chapters; if you have attained to the true viewpoint, and if your consecration is complete, you will not find conscious identification hard to attain; and once it is attained, the power you seek is yours, for you have made yourself one with all the power there is.

10. IDEALIZATION

YOU are a thinking center in original substance, and the thoughts of original substance have creative power; whatever is formed in its thought and held as a thought-form must come into existence as a visible and so-called material form, and a thought-form held in thinking substance is a reality; it is a real thing, whether it has yet become visible to mortal eye or not. This is a fact that you should impress upon your understanding—that a thought held in thinking substance is a real thing; a form, and has actual existence, although it is not visible to you. You internally take the form in which you think of yourself; and you surround yourself with the invisible forms of those things with which you associate in your thoughts.

If you desire a thing, picture it clearly and hold the picture steadily in mind until it becomes a definite thought-form; and if your practices are not such as to separate you from God, the thing you want will come to you in material form. It must do so in obedience to the law by which the universe was created.

Make no thought-form of yourself in connection with disease or sickness, but form a conception of health. Make a thought-form of yourself as strong and hearty and perfectly well; impress this thought- form on creative intelligence, and if your practices are not in violation of the laws by which the physical body is built, your thought-form will become manifest in your flesh. This also is certain; it comes by obedience to law.

Make a thought-form of yourself as you desire to be, and set your ideal as near to perfection as your imagination is capable of forming the conception. Let me illustrate: If a young law student wishes to become great, let him picture himself (while attending to the viewpoint, consecration, and identification, as previously directed) as a great lawyer, pleading his case with matchless eloquence and power before the judge and jury; as having an unlimited command of truth, of knowledge, and of wisdom. Let him picture himself as the great lawyer in every possible situation and contingency; while he is still only the student in all circumstances, let him never forget or fail to be the great lawyer in his thought-form of himself. As the thought-form grows more definite and habitual in his mind, the creative energies, both within and without, are set at work. He begins to manifest the form from within; and all the essentials without, which go into the picture, begin to be impelled toward him. He makes himself into the image and God works with him; nothing can prevent him from becoming what he wishes to be.

In the same general way the musical student pictures himself as performing perfect harmonies and as delighting vast audiences; the actor forms the highest conception he is capable of in regard to his art, and applies this conception to himself. The farmer and the mechanic do exactly the same thing.

Fix upon your ideal of what you wish to make of yourself; consider well and be sure that you make the right choice; that is, the one which will be the most satisfactory to you in a general way. Do not pay too much attention to the advice or suggestions of those around you; do not believe that any one can know, better than yourself, what is right for you. Listen to what others have to say, but always form your own conclusions. **Do not let other people decide what you are to be. Be what you feel that you want to be.**

Do not be misled by a false notion of obligation or duty. You can owe no possible obligation or duty to others which should prevent you from making the most of yourself. Be true to yourself, and you cannot then be false to anybody. When you have fully decided what thing you want to be, form the highest conception of that thing that you are capable of imagining, and make that conception a thought-form. Hold that thought-form as a fact, as the real truth about yourself, and believe in it.

Close your ears to all adverse suggestions. Never mind if people call you a fool and a dreamer. Dream on. Remember that Bonaparte, the half-starved lieutenant, always saw himself as the general of armies and the master of France, and he became in outward realization what he held himself to be in mind. So likewise will you. Attend carefully to all that has been said in the preceding chapters, and act as directed in the following ones, and you will become what you want to be.

11. REALIZATION

IF you were to stop with the close of the last chapter, however, you would never become great; you would be indeed a mere dreamer of dreams, a castle- builder. Too many do stop there; they do not understand the necessity for present action in realizing the vision and bringing the thought-form into manifestation. Two things are necessary. First, the making of the thought-form, and, second, the actual appropriation to yourself of all that goes into and around the thought-form. We have discussed the first, now we will proceed to give directions for the second. When you have made your thought-form, you are already, in your interior, what you want to be; next you must become externally what you want to be. You are already great within, but you are not yet doing the great things without. You cannot begin, on the instant, to do the great things; you cannot be before the world the great actor, or lawyer, or musician, or personality you know yourself to be; no one will intrust great things to you as yet for you have not made yourself known. But you can always begin to do small things in a great way.

Here lies the whole secret. You can begin to be great to-day in your own home, in your store or office, on the street, everywhere; you can begin to make yourself known as great, and you can do this by doing everything you do in a great way. You must put the whole power of your great soul into every act, however small and commonplace, and so reveal to your family, your friends, and neighbors what you really are. Do not brag or boast of yourself; do not go about telling people what a great personage you are; simply live in a great way. No one will believe you if you tell him you are a great man, but no one can doubt your greatness if you show it in your actions. In your domestic circle be so just, so generous, so courteous, and kindly that your family, your wife, husband, children, brothers, and sisters shall know that you are a great and noble soul. In all your relations with men be great, just, generous, courteous, and kindly. The great are never otherwise.

This for your attitude.

Next, and most important, you must have absolute faith in your own perceptions of truth. Never act in haste or hurry; be deliberate in everything; wait until you feel that you know the true way. And when you do feel that you know the true way, be guided by your own faith though all the world shall disagree with you. If you do not believe what God tells you in little things, you will never draw upon his wisdom and knowledge in larger things. When you feel deeply that a certain act is the right act, do it and have perfect faith that the consequences will be good.

When you are deeply impressed that a certain thing is true, no matter what the appearances to the contrary may be, accept that thing as true and act accordingly. The one way to develop a perception of truth in large things is to trust absolutely to your present perception of truth in small things. Remember that you are seeking to develop this very power or faculty—the perception of truth; you are learning to read the thoughts of God. Nothing is great and nothing is small in the sight of Omnipotence; he holds the sun in its place, but he also notes a sparrow's fall, and numbers the hairs of your head. God is as much interested in the little matters of everyday life as he is in the affairs of nations. You can perceive truth about family and neighborhood affairs as well as about matters of statecraft. And the way to begin is to have perfect faith in the truth in these small matters, as it is revealed to you from day to day. When you feel deeply impelled to take a course which seems contrary to all reason and worldly judgment, take that course.

Listen to the suggestions and advice of others, but always do what you feel deeply in the within to be the true thing to do. Rely with absolute faith, at all times, on your own perception of truth; but be sure that you listen to God—that you do not act in haste, fear, or anxiety. Rely upon your perception of truth in all the facts and circumstances of life. If you deeply feel that a certain man will be in a certain place on a certain day, go there with perfect faith to meet him; he will be there, no matter how unlikely it may seem. If you feel sure that certain people are making certain combinations, or doing certain things, act in the faith that they are doing those things.

If you feel sure of the truth of any circumstance or happening, near or distant, past, present, or to come, trust in your perception. You may make occasional mistakes at first because of your imperfect understanding of the within; but you will soon be guided almost invariably right. Soon your family and friends will begin to defer, more and more, to your judgment and to be guided by you. Soon your neighbors and townsmen will be coming to you for counsel and advice; soon you will be recognized as one who is great in small things, and you will be called upon more and more to take charge of larger things.

All that is necessary is to be guided absolutely, in all things, by your inner light, your perception of truth. Obey your soul, have perfect faith in yourself. Never think of yourself with doubt or distrust, or as one who makes mistakes. "If I judge, my judgment is just, for I seek not honor from men, but from the Father only."

12. HURRY AND HABIT

No doubt you have many problems, domestic, social, physical, and financial, which seem to you to be pressing for instant solution. You have debts which must be paid, or other obligations which must be met; you are unhappily or inharmoniously placed, and feel that something must be done at once. Do not get into a hurry and act from superficial impulses. You can trust God for the solution of all your personal riddles. There is no hurry. There is only God, and all is well with the world.

There is an invincible power in you, and the same power is in the things you want. It is bringing them to you and bringing you to them. This is a thought that you must grasp, and hold continuously— that the same intelligence which is in you is in the things you desire.

They are impelled toward you as strongly and decidedly as your desire impels you toward them. The tendency, therefore, of a steadily held thought must be to bring the things you desire to you and to group them around you. So long as you hold your thought and your faith right all must go well. *Nothing can be wrong but your own personal attitude, and that will not be wrong if you trust and are not afraid.*

Hurry is a manifestation of fear; he who fears not has plenty of time. If you act with perfect faith in your own perceptions of truth, you will never be too late or too early; and nothing will go wrong. If things appear to be going wrong, do not get disturbed in mind; it is only in appearance.

Nothing can go wrong in this world but yourself; and you can go wrong only by getting into the wrong mental attitude. Whenever you find yourself getting excited, worried, or into the mental attitude of hurry, sit down and think it over; play a game of some kind, or take a vacation. Go on a trip, and all will be right when you return. So surely as you find yourself in the mental attitude of haste, just so surely may you know that you are out of the mental attitude of greatness.

Hurry and fear will instantly cut your connection with the universal mind; you will get no power, no wisdom, and no information until you are calm. And to fall into the attitude of hurry will check the action of the Principle of Power within you. Fear turns strength to weakness.

Remember that poise and power are inseparably associated. The calm and balanced mind is the strong and great mind; the hurried and agitated mind is the weak one. Whenever you fall into the mental state of hurry you may know that you have lost the right viewpoint; you are beginning to look upon the world, or some part of it, as going wrong.

At such times read Chapter Six of this book; consider the fact that this world is perfect, now, with all that it contains. Nothing is going wrong; nothing can be wrong; be poised, be calm, be cheerful; have faith in God.

Next, as to habit. It is probable that your greatest difficulty will be to overcome your old habitual ways of thought, and to form new habits. The world is ruled by habit. Kings, tyrants, masters, and plutocrats hold their positions solely because the people have come to habitually accept them. Things are as they are only because people have formed the habit of accepting them as they are. When the people change their habitual thought about governmental, social, and industrial institutions, they will change the institutions.

Habit rules us all. You have formed, perhaps, the habit of thinking of yourself as a common person, as one of a limited ability, or as being more or less of a failure. Whatever you habitually think yourself to be, that you are.

You must form, now, a greater and better habit; you must form a conception of yourself as a being of limitless power, and habitually think that you are that being. It is the habitual, not the periodical thought that decides your destiny. It will avail you nothing to sit apart for a few moments several times a day to affirm that you are great, if during all the balance of the day, while you are about your regular vocation, you think of yourself as not great.

No amount of praying or affirmation will make you great if you still habitually regard yourself as being small. The use of prayer and affirmation is to change your habit of thought. Any act, mental or physical, often repeated, becomes a habit. The purpose of mental exercises is to repeat certain thoughts over and over until the thinking of those thoughts becomes constant and habitual.

The thoughts we continually repeat become convictions. What you must do is to repeat the new thought of yourself until it is the only way in which you think of yourself. Habitual thought, and not environment or circumstance, has made you what you are. Every person has some central idea or thought-form of himself, and by this idea he classifies and arranges all his facts and external relationships.

You are classifying your facts either according to the idea that you are a great and strong personality, or according to the idea that you are limited, common, or weak. If the latter is the case you must change your central idea. Get a new mental picture of yourself.

Do not try to become great by repeating mere strings of words or superficial formulae; but repeat over and over the THOUGHT of your own power and ability until you classify external facts, and decide your place everywhere by this idea.

In another chapter will be found an illustrative mental exercise and further directions on this point.

13. THOUGHT

GREATNESS is attained only by the thinking of great thoughts. No one can become great in outward personality until he is great internally; and no one can be great internally until he THINKS. No amount of education, reading, or study can make you great without thought; but thought can make you great with very little study.

There are altogether too many people who are trying to make something of themselves by reading books without thinking; all such will fail.

You are not mentally developed by what you read, but by what you think about what you read.

Thinking is the hardest and most exhausting of all labor; and hence many people shrink from it. God has so formed us that we are continuously impelled to thought; we must either think or engage in some activity to escape thought. The headlong, continuous chase for pleasure in which most people spend all their leisure time is only an effort to escape thought. If they are alone, or if they have nothing amusing to take their attention, as a novel to read or a show to see, they must think; and to escape from thinking they resort to novels, shows, and all the endless devices of the purveyors of amusement.

Most people spend the greater part of their leisure time running away from thought, hence they are where they are. We never move forward until we begin to think.

Read less and think more. Read about great things and think about great questions and issues. We have at the present time few really great figures in the political life of our country; our politicians are a petty lot. There is no Lincoln, no Webster, no Clay, Calhoun, or Jackson. Why? Because our present statesmen deal only with sordid and petty issues— questions of dollars and cents, of expediency and party success, of material prosperity without regard to ethical right. Thinking along these lines does not call forth great souls.

The statesmen of Lincoln's time and previous times dealt with questions of eternal truth; of human rights and justice. They thought upon great themes; they thought great thoughts, and they became great.

Thinking, not mere knowledge or information, makes personality. Thinking is growth; you cannot think without growing. Every thought engenders another thought. Write one idea and others will follow until you have written a page.

You cannot fathom your own mind; it has neither bottom nor boundaries. Your first thoughts may be crude; but as you go on thinking you will use more and more of yourself; you will quicken new brain cells into activity and you will develop new faculties. Heredity, environment, circumstances,—all things must give way before you if you practice sustained and continuous thought. But, on the other hand, if you neglect to think for yourself and only use other people's thought, you will never know what you are capable of; and you will end by being incapable of anything.

There can be no real greatness without original thought. All that a person does outwardly is the expression and completion of his inward thinking. No action is possible without thought, and no great action is possible until a great thought has preceded it. Action is the second form of thought, and personality is the materialization of thought. Environment is the result of thought;

things group themselves or arrange themselves around you according to your thought.

There is, as Emerson says, some central idea or conception of yourself by which all the facts of your life are arranged and classified. Change this central idea and you change the arrangement or classification of all the facts and circumstances of your life.

You are what you are because you think as you do; you are where you are because you think as you do.

You see then the immense importance of thinking about the great essentials set forth in the preceding chapters. You must not accept them in any superficial way; you must think about them until they are a part of your central idea. Go back to the matter of the point of view and consider, in all its bearings, the tremendous thought that you live in a perfect world among perfect people, and that nothing can possibly be wrong with you but your own personal attitude. Think about all this until you fully realize all that it means to you.

Consider that this is God's world and that it is the best of all possible worlds; that He has brought it thus far toward completion by the processes of organic, social, and industrial evolution, and that it is going on to greater completeness and harmony. Consider that there is one great, perfect, intelligent Principle of Life and Power, causing all the changing phenomena of the cosmos. Think about all this until you see that it is true, and until you comprehend how you should live and act as a citizen of such a perfect whole.

Next, think of the wonderful truth that this great Intelligence is in you; it is your own intelligence. It is an Inner Light impelling you toward the right thing and the best thing, the greatest act, and the highest happiness. It is a Principle of Power in you, giving you all the ability and genius there is. It will infallibly guide you to the best if you will submit to it and walk in the light. Consider what is meant by your consecration of yourself when you say: "I will obey my soul." This is a sentence of tremendous meaning; it must revolutionize the attitude and behavior of the average person.

Then think of your identification with this Great Supreme; that all its knowledge is yours, and all its wisdom is yours, for the asking. You are a god if you think like a god. If you think like a god you cannot fail to act like a god. Divine thoughts will surely externalize themselves in a divine life. Thoughts of power will end in a life of power. Great thoughts will manifest in a great personality. Think well of all this, and then you are ready to act.

14. ACTION AT HOME

Do not merely think that you are going to become great; think *that you are great now.* Do not think that you will begin to act in a great way at some future time; begin now. Do not think that you will act in a great way when you reach a different environment; act in a great way where you are now. Do not think that you will begin to act in a great way when you begin to deal with great things; begin to deal in a great way with small things. Do not think that you will begin to be great when you get among more intelligent people, or among people who understand you better; begin now to deal in a great way with the people around you.

If you are not in an environment where there is scope for your best powers and talents you can move in due time; but meanwhile you can be great where you are. Lincoln was as great when he was a backwoods lawyer as when he was President; as a backwoods lawyer he did common things in a great way, and that made him President. Had he waited until he reached Washington to begin to be great, he would have remained unknown. You are not made great by the location in which you happen to be, nor by the things with which you may surround yourself. You are not made great by what you receive from others, and you can never manifest greatness so long as you depend on others. You will manifest greatness only when you begin to stand alone. Dismiss all thought of reliance on externals, whether things, books, or people. As Emerson said, "Shakespeare will never be made by the study of

Shakespeare." Shakespeare will be made by the thinking of Shakespearean thoughts.

Never mind how the people around you, including those of your own household, may treat you. That has nothing at all to do with your being great; that is, it cannot hinder you from being great. People may neglect you and be unthankful and unkind in their attitude toward you; does that prevent you from being great in your manner and attitude toward them? "Your Father," said Jesus, "is kind to the unthankful and the evil." Would God be great if he should go away and sulk because people were unthankful and did not appreciate him ? Treat the unthankful and the evil in a great and perfectly kind way, just as God does.

Do not talk about your greatness; you are really, in essential nature, no greater than those around you.

You may have entered upon a way of living and thinking which they have not yet found, but they are perfect on their own plane of thought and action. You are entitled to no special honor or consideration for your greatness. You are a god, but you are among gods. You will fall into the boastful attitude if you see other people's shortcomings and failures and compare them with your own virtues and successes; and if you fall into the boastful attitude of mind, you will cease to be great, and become small. Think of yourself as a perfect being among perfect beings, and meet every person as an equal, not as either a superior or an inferior. Give yourself no airs; great people never do. Ask no honors and seek for no recognition; honors and recognition will come fast enough if you are entitled to them.

Begin at home. It is a great person who can always be poised, assured, calm, and perfectly kind and considerate at home. If your manner and attitude in your own family are always the best you can think, you will soon become the one on whom all the others will rely. You will be a tower of strength and a support in time of trouble. You will be loved and appreciated. At the same time do not make the mistake of throwing yourself away in the service of others. The great person respects himself; he serves and helps, but he is never slavishly servile. You cannot help your family by being a slave to them, or by doing for them those things which by right they should do for themselves. You do a person an injury when you wait on him too much. The selfish and exacting are a great deal better off if their exactions are denied. The ideal world is not one where there are a lot of people being waited on by other people; it is a world where everybody waits on himself. Meet all demands, selfish and otherwise, with perfect kindness and consideration; but do not allow yourself to be made a slave to the whims, caprices, exactions, or slavish desires of any member of your family. To do so is not great, and it works an injury to the other party.

Do not become uneasy over the failures or mistakes of any member of your family, and feel that you must interfere. Do not be disturbed if others seem to be going wrong, and feel that you must step in and set them right. Remember that every person is perfect on his own plane; you cannot improve on the work of God. Do not meddle with the personal habits and practices of others, though they are your nearest and dearest; these things are none of your business. Nothing can be wrong but your own personal attitude; make that right and you will know that all else is right. You are a truly great soul when you can live with those who do things which you do not do, and yet refrain from either criticism or interference. Do the things which are right for you to do, and believe that every member of your family is doing the things which are right for him. Nothing is wrong with anybody or anything; behold, it is all very good.

Do not be enslaved by anyone else, but be just as careful that you do not enslave anyone else to your own notions of what is right.

Think, and think deeply and continuously; be perfect in your kindness and consideration; let your attitude be that of a god among gods, and not that of a god among inferior beings. This is the way to be great in your own home.

15. ACTION ABROAD

THE rules which apply to your action at home must apply to your action everywhere. Never forget for an instant that this is a perfect world, and that you are a god among gods. You are as great as the greatest, but all are your equals.

Rely absolutely on your perception of truth. Trust to the inner light rather than to reason, but be sure that your perception comes from the inner light; act in poise and calmness; be still and attend on God. Your identification of yourself with the All-Mind will give you all the knowledge you need for guidance in any contingency which may arise in your own life or in the lives of others. It is only necessary that you should be supremely calm, and rely upon the eternal wisdom which is within you. If you act in poise and faith, your judgment will always be right, and you will always know exactly what to do. Do not hurry or worry; remember Lincoln in the dark days of the war. James Freeman Clarke relates that after the battle of Fredericksburg, Lincoln alone furnished a supply of faith and hope for the nation. Hundreds of leading men, from all parts of the country, went sadly into his room and came out cheerful and hopeful. They had stood face to face with the Highest, and had seen God in this lank, ungainly, patient man, although they knew it not.

Have perfect faith in yourself and in your own ability to cope with any combination of circumstances that may arise. Do not be disturbed if you are alone; if you need friends they will be brought to you at the right time. Do not be disturbed if you feel that you are ignorant; the information that you need will be furnished you when it is time for you to have it. That which is in you impelling you forward is in the things and people you need, impelling them toward you.

If there is a particular person you need to know, he will be introduced to you; if there is a particular book you need to read it will be placed in your hands at the right time. All the knowledge you need will come to you from both external and internal sources.

Your information and your talents will always be equal to the requirements of the occasion. Remember that Jesus told his disciples not to worry as to what they should say when brought before the judges; he knew that the power in them would be sufficient for the needs of the hour. As soon as you awaken and begin to use your faculties in a great way you will apply power to the development of your brain; new cells will be created and dormant cells quickened into activity, and your brain will be qualified as a perfect instrument for your mind.

Do not try to do great things until you are ready to go about them in a great way. If you undertake to deal with great matters in a small way— that is, from a low viewpoint or with incomplete consecration and wavering faith and courage—you will fail. Do not be in a hurry to get to the great things. Doing great things will not make you great, but becoming great will certainly lead you to the doing of great things.

Begin to be great where you are and in the things you do every day. Do not be in haste to be found out or recognized as a great personality. Do not be disappointed if men do not nominate you for office within a month after you begin to practice what you read in this book. Great people never seek for recognition or applause; they are not great because they want to be paid for being so. Greatness is reward enough for itself; the joy of being something and of knowing that you are advancing is the greatest of all joys possible to man.

If you begin in your own family, as described in the preceding chapter, and then assume the same mental attitude with your neighbors, friends, and those you meet in business, you will soon find that people are beginning to depend on you. Your advice will be sought, and a constantly increasing number of people will look to you for strength and inspiration, and rely upon your judgment.

Here, as in the home, you must avoid meddling with other people's affairs. Help all who come to you, but do not go about officiously endeavoring to set other people right. Mind your own business. It is no part of your mission in life to correct people's morals, habits, or practices. Lead a great life, doing all things with a great spirit and in a great way; give to him that asketh of thee as freely as ye have received, but do not force your help or your opinions upon any man.

If your neighbor wishes to smoke or drink, it is his business; it is none of yours until he consults you about it.

If you lead a great life and do no preaching, you will save a thousand times as many souls as one who leads a small life and preaches continuously.

If you hold the right viewpoint of the world, others will find it out and be impressed by it through your daily conversation and practice.

Do not try to convert others to your point of view, except by holding it and living accordingly. If your consecration is perfect you do not need to tell anyone; it will speedily become apparent to all that you are guided by a higher principle than the average man or woman.

If your identification with God is complete, you do not need to explain the fact to others; it will become self-evident. To become known as a great personality, you have nothing to do but to live.

Do not imagine that you must go charging about the world like Don Quixote, tilting at windmills, and overturning things in general, in order to demonstrate that you are somebody. Do not go hunting for big things to do. Live a great life where you are, and in the daily work you have to do, and greater works will surely find you out. Big things will come to you, asking to be done.

Be so impressed with the value of a man that you treat even a beggar or the tramp with the most distinguished consideration. All is God. Every man and woman is perfect. Let your manner be that of a god addressing other gods.

Do not save all your consideration for the poor; the millionaire is as good as the tramp. This is a perfectly good world, and there is not a person or thing in it but is exactly right; be sure that you keep this in mind in dealing with things and men.

Form your mental vision of yourself with care. Make the thought-form of yourself as you wish to be, and hold this with the faith that it is being realized, and with the purpose to realize it completely. Do every common act as a god should do it; speak every word as a god should speak it; meet men and women of both low and high estate as a god meets other divine beings. Begin thus and continue thus, and your unfoldment in ability and power will be great and rapid.

16. SOME FURTHER EXPLANATIONS

We go back here to the matter of the point of view, for, besides being vitally important, it is the one which is likely *to give the student the most trouble. We have been* trained, partly by mistaken religious teachers, to look upon the world as being like a wrecked ship, storm-driven upon a rocky coast; utter destruction is inevitable at the end, and the most that can be done is to rescue, perhaps, a few of the crew. This view teaches us to consider the world as essentially bad and growing worse; and to believe that existing discords and inharmonies must continue and intensify until the end. It robs us of hope for society, government, and humanity, and gives us a decreasing outlook and contracting mind.

This is all wrong. The world is not wrecked. It is like a magnificent steamer with the engines in place and the machinery in perfect order. The bunkers are full of coal, and the ship is amply provisioned for the cruise; there is no lack of any good thing.

Every provision Omniscience could devise has been made for the safety, comfort, and happiness of the crew; the steamer is out on the high seas tacking hither and thither because no one has yet learned the right course to steer. We are learning to steer, and in due time will come grandly into the harbor of perfect harmony.

The world is good, and growing better. Existing discords and inharmonies are but the rollings of the ship incidental to our own imperfect steering; they will all be removed in due time. This view gives us an increasing outlook and an expanding mind; it enables us to think largely of society and of ourselves, and to do things in a great way. Furthermore, we see that nothing can be wrong with such a world or with any part of it, including our own affairs. If it is all moving on toward completion, then it is not going wrong; and as our own personal affairs are a part of the whole, they are not going wrong. You and all that you are concerned with are moving on toward completeness. Nothing can check this forward movement but yourself; and you can only check it by assuming a mental attitude which is at cross purposes with the mind of God.

You have nothing to keep right but yourself; if you keep yourself right, nothing can possibly go wrong with you, and you can have nothing to fear. No business or other disaster can come upon you if your personal attitude is right, for you are a part of that which is increasing and advancing, and you must increase and advance with it.

Moreover your thought-form will be mostly shaped according to your viewpoint of the cosmos. If you see the world as a lost and ruined thing you will see yourself as a part of it, and as partaking of its sins and weaknesses. If your outlook for the world as a whole is hopeless, your outlook for yourself cannot be hopeful.

If you see the world as declining toward its end, you cannot see yourself as advancing. Unless you think well of all the works of God you cannot really think well of yourself, and unless you think well of yourself you can never become great.

I repeat that your place in life, including your material environment, is determined by the thought- form you habitually hold of yourself. When you make a thought-form of yourself you can hardly fail to form in your mind a corresponding environment. If you think of yourself as an incapable, inefficient person, you will think of yourself with poor or cheap surroundings.

Unless you think well of yourself you will be sure to picture yourself in a more or less poverty stricken environment. These thoughts, habitually held, become invisible forms in the surrounding mind-stuff, and are with you continually. In due time, by the regular action of the eternal creative energy, the invisible thought-forms are produced in material stuff, and you are surrounded by your own thoughts made into material things.

See nature as a great living and advancing presence, and see human society in exactly the same way.

It is all one, coming from one source, and it is all good. You yourself are made of the same stuff as God. All the constituents of God are parts of yourself; every power that God has is a constituent of man. You can move forward as you see God doing. You have within yourself the source of every power.

17. MORE ABOUT THOUGHT

GIVE place here to some further consideration of thought. You will never become great until your own thoughts make you great, and therefore it is of the first importance that you should THINK.

You will never do great things in the external world until you think great things in the internal world; and you will never think great things until you think about *truth;* about the verities. To think great things you must be absolutely sincere; and to be sincere you must know that your intentions are right. Insincere or false thinking is never great, however logical and brilliant it may be.

The first and most important step is to seek the truth about human relations; to know what you ought to be to other people, and what they ought to be to you.

This brings you back to the search for a right viewpoint. You should study organic and social evolution. Read Darwin and Walter Thomas Mills, and when you read, THINK; think the whole matter over until you see the world of things and people in the right way. THINK about what God is doing until you can SEE what he is doing.

Your next step is to think yourself into the right personal attitude. Your viewpoint tells you what the right attitude is, and obedience to the soul puts you into it. It is only by making a complete consecration of yourself to the highest that is within you that you can attain to sincere thinking.

So long as you know you are selfish in your aims, or dishonest or crooked in any way in your intentions or practices, your thinking will be false and your thoughts will have no power. THINK about the way you are doing things; about all your intentions, purposes, and practices, until you know that they are right.

The fact of his own complete unity with God is one that no person can grasp without deep and sustained thinking. Anyone can accept the proposition in a superficial way, but to feel and realize a vital comprehension of it is another matter.

It is easy to think of going outside of yourself to meet God, but it is not so easy to think of going inside yourself to meet God. But God is there, and in the holy of holies of your own soul you may meet him face to face. It is a tremendous thing, this fact that all you need is already within you; that you do not have to consider how to get the power to do what you want to do or to make yourself what you want to be. You have only to consider how to use the power you have in the right way. And there is nothing to do but to begin. Use your perception of truth; you can see some truth today; live fully up to that and you will see more truth tomorrow.

To rid yourself of the old false ideas you will have to think a great deal about the value of people— the greatness and worth of a human soul. You must cease from looking at human mistakes and look at successes; cease from seeing faults and see virtues. You can no longer look upon men and women as lost and ruined beings who are descending into hell; you must come to regard them as shining souls who are ascending toward heaven.

It will require some exercise of will power to do this, but this is the legitimate use of the will—to decide what you will think about and how you will think. The function of the will is to direct thought. Think about the good side of people; the lovely, attractive part, and exert your will in refusing to think of anything else in connection with them.

I know of no one who has attained to so much on this one point as Eugene V. Debs, twice the Socialist candidate for president of the United States. Mr. Debs reverences humanity. No appeal for help is ever made to him in vain. No one receives from him an unkind or censorious word. You cannot come into his presence without being made sensible of his deep and kindly personal interest in you. No one, whether millionaire, grimy workingman, or toil worn woman, meets him without receiving the radiant warmth of a brotherly affection that is sincere and true. No ragged child speaks to him on the street without receiving instant and tender recognition. Debs loves people. This has made him the leading figure in a great movement, the beloved hero of a million hearts, and will give him a deathless name. It is a great thing to love people so and it is only achieved by thought. Nothing can make you great but thought.

"We may divide thinkers into those who think for themselves and those who think through others. The latter are the rule and the former the exception. The first are original thinkers in a double sense, and egotists in the noblest meaning of the word."—*Schopenhauer*.

"The key to every man is his thought. Sturdy and defiant though he look he has a helm which he obeys, which is the idea after which all his facts are classified. He can only be reformed by showing him a new idea which commands his own." —*Emerson*.

"All truly wise thoughts have been thought already thousands of times; but to make them really ours we must think them over again honestly till they take root in our personal expression." —*Goethe*.

"All that a man is outwardly is but the expression and completion of his inward thought. To work effectively he must think clearly. To act nobly he must think nobly." —*Charming*.

"Great men are they who see that spirituality is stronger than any material force; that thoughts rule the world." —*Emerson*.

"Some people study all their lives, and at their death they have learned everything except to think." —*Domergue*.

"It is the habitual thought that frames itself into our life. It affects us even more than our intimate social relations do. Our confidential friends have not so much to do in shaping our lives as the thoughts have which we harbor." —*J. W. Teal*

"When God lets loose a great thinker on this planet, then all things are at risk. There is not a piece of science but its flank may be turned to-morrow; nor any literary reputation or the so-called eternal names of fame that may not be refused and condemned."— *Emerson,*

Think! *Think!!* THINK!!!

18. JESUS' IDEA OF GREATNESS.

IN the twenty-third chapter of Matthew Jesus makes a very plain distinction between true and false greatness ; and also points out the one great danger to all who wish to become great—the most insidious of temptations which all must avoid and fight unceasingly who desire to really climb in the world. Speaking to the multitude and to his disciples he bids them beware of adopting the principle of the Pharisees. He points out that while the Pharisees are just and righteous men, honorable judges, true lawgivers and upright in their dealings with men, they "love the uppermost seats at feasts and greetings in the market place, and to be called Master, Master"; and in comparison with this principle, he says: "He that will be great among you let him serve."

The average person's idea of a great man, rather than of one who serves, is of one who succeeds in getting himself served. He gets himself in a position to command men; to exercise power over them, making them obey his will. The exercise of dominion over other people, to most persons, is a great thing. Nothing seems to be sweeter to the selfish soul than this.

You will always find every selfish and undeveloped person trying to domineer over others, to exercise control over other men. Savage men were no sooner placed upon the earth than they began to enslave one another. For ages the struggle in war, diplomacy, politics, and government has been aimed at the securing of control over other men. Kings and princes have drenched the soil of the earth in blood and tears in the effort to extend their dominions and their power,—to rule more people.

The struggle of the business world to-day is the same as that on the battlefields of Europe a century ago so far as the ruling principle is concerned. Robert G. Ingersoll could not understand why men like Rockefeller and Carnegie seek for more money and make themselves slaves to the business struggle when they already have more than they can possibly use. He thought it a kind of madness and illustrated it as follows: "Suppose a man had fifty thousand pairs of pants, seventy-five thousand vests, one hundred thousand coats, and one hundred and fifty thousand neckties, what would you think of him if he arose in the morning before light and worked until after it was dark every day, rain or shine, in all kinds of weather, merely to get another necktie?"

But it is not a good simile. The possession of neckties gives a man no power over other men, while the possession of dollars does. Rockefeller, Carnegie, and their kind are not after dollars but power. It is the principle of the Pharisee; it is the struggle for the high place. It develops able men, cunning men, resourceful men, but not great men.

I want you to contrast these two ideas of greatness sharply in your minds. "He that will be great among you let him serve." Let me stand before the average American audience and ask the name of the greatest American and the majority will think of Abraham Lincoln; and is this not because in Lincoln above all the other men who have served us in public life we recognize the spirit of service? Not servility, but service. Lincoln was a great man because he knew how to be a great servant. Napoleon, able, cold, selfish, seeking the high places, was a brilliant man. Lincoln was great, Napoleon was not.

The very moment you begin to advance and are recognized as one who is doing things in a great way you will find yourself in danger. The temptation to patronize, advise, or take upon yourself the direction of other people's affairs is sometimes almost irresistible.

Avoid, however, the opposite danger of falling into servility, or of completely throwing yourself away in the service of others. To do this has been the ideal of a great many people. The completely self-sacrificing life has been thought to be the Christ-like life, because, as I think, of a complete misconception of the character and teachings of Jesus. I have explained this misconception in a little book which I hope you may all sometime read, *A New Christ*.

Thousands of people imitating Jesus, as they suppose, have belittled themselves and given up all else to go about doing good; practicing an altruism that is really as morbid and as far from great as the rankest selfishness. The finer instincts which respond to the cry of trouble or distress are not by any means all of you; they are not necessarily the best part of you.

There are other things you must do besides helping the unfortunate, although it is true that a large part of the life and activities of every great person must be given to helping other people. As you begin to advance they will come to you. Do not turn them away. But do not make the fatal error of supposing that the life of complete self-abnegation is the way of greatness.

To make another point here, let me refer to the fact that Swedenborg's classification of fundamental motives is exactly the same as that of Jesus. He divides all men into two groups: those who live in pure love, and those who live in what he, calls the love of ruling for the love of self.

It will be seen that this is exactly the same as the lust for place and power of the Pharisees. Swedenborg saw this selfish love of power as the cause of all sin. It was the only evil desire of the human heart, from which all other evil desires sprang. Over against this he places pure love. He does not say love of God or love of man, but merely love. Nearly all religionists make more of love and service to God than they do of love and service to man. But it is a fact that love to God is not sufficient to save a man from the lust for power, for some of the most ardent lovers of the Deity have been the worst of tyrants. Lovers of God are often tyrants, and lovers of men are often meddlesome and officious.

19. A VIEW OF EVOLUTION.

BUT how shall we avoid throwing ourselves into altruistic work if we are surrounded by poverty, ignorance, suffering, and every appearance of misery as very many people are? Those who live where the withered hand of want is thrust upon them from every side appealingly for aid must find it hard to refrain from continuous giving. Again, there are social and other irregularities, injustices done to the weak, which fire generous souls with an almost irresistible desire to set things right. We want to start a crusade; we feel that the wrongs will never be righted until we give ourselves wholly to the task. In all this we must fall back upon the point of view. We must remember that this is not a bad world but a good world in the process of becoming.

Beyond all doubt there was a time when there was no life upon this earth. The testimony of geology to the fact that the globe was once a ball of burning gas and molten rock, clothed about with boiling vapors, is indisputable. And we do not know how life could have existed under such conditions; that seems impossible. Geology tells us that later on a crust formed, the globe cooled and hardened, the vapors condensed and became mist or fell in rain. The cooled surface crumbled into soil; moisture accumulated, ponds and seas were gathered together, and at last somewhere in the water or on the land appeared something that was alive.

It is reasonable to suppose that this first life was in single-celled organisms, but behind these cells was the insistent urge of Spirit, the Great One Life seeking expression. And soon organisms having too much life to express themselves with one cell had two cells and then many, and still more life was poured into them. Multiple-celled organisms were formed; plants, trees, vertebrates, and mammals, many of them with strange shapes, but all were perfect after their kind as everything is that God makes. No doubt there were crude and almost monstrous forms of both animal and plant life; but everything filled its purpose in its day and it was all very good. Then another day came, the great day of the evolutionary process, a day when the morning stars sang together and the sons of God shouted for joy to behold the beginning of the end, for man, the object aimed at from the beginning, had appeared upon the scene.

An ape-like being, little different from the beasts around him in appearance but infinitely different in his capacity for growth and thought. Art and beauty, architecture and song, poetry and music, all these were unrealized possibilities in that ape man's soul. And for his time and kind he was very good.

"It is God that worketh in you to will and to do of his good pleasure," says St. Paul. From the day the first man appeared God began to work IN men, putting more and more of himself into each succeeding generation, urging them on to larger achievements and to better conditions, social, governmental, and domestic. Those who looking back into ancient history see the awful conditions which existed, the barbarities, idolatries, and sufferings, and reading about God in connection with these things are disposed to feel that he was cruel and unjust to man, should pause to think. From the ape man to the coming Christ man the race has had to rise. And it could only be accomplished by the successive unfoldments of the various powers and possibilities latent in the human brain. Naturally the cruder and more animal-like part of man came to its full development first; for ages men were brutal; their governments were brutal, their religions were brutal, their domestic institutions were brutal, and what appears to be an immense amount of suffering resulted from this brutality. But God never delighted in suffering, and in every age he has given men a message, telling them how to avoid it. And all the while the urge of life, insistent, powerful, compelling, made the race keep moving forward; a little less brutality in each age and a little more spirituality in each age.

And God kept on working in man. In every age there have been some individuals who were in advance of the mass and who heard and understood God better than their fellows. Upon these the inspiring hand of Spirit was laid and they were compelled to become interpreters. These were the prophets and seers, sometimes the priests and kings, and oftener still they were martyrs driven to the stake, the block, or the cross. It is to these who have heard God, spoken his word, and demonstrated his truth in their lives that all progress is really due.

Again, considering for a moment the presence of what is called evil in the world, we see that that which appears to us to be Evil is only undeveloped; and that the undeveloped is perfectly good in its own stage and place. Because all things are necessary to man's complete unfoldment, all things in human life are the work of God. The graft rings in our cities, the red-light districts and their unfortunate inmates, these he consciously and voluntarily produced. Their part in the plan of unfoldment must be played. And when their part has been played he will sweep them off the stage as he did the strange and poisonous monsters which filled the swamps of the past ages.

In concluding this vision of evolution we might ask why it was all done, what is it for? This question should be easy for the thoughtful mind to answer. God desired to express himself, to live in form, and not only that, but to live in a form through which he could express himself on the highest moral and spiritual plane.

God wanted to evolve a form in which he could live as a god and manifest himself as a god. This was the aim of the evolutionary force. The ages of warfare, bloodshed, suffering, injustice, and cruelty were tempered in many ways with love and justice as time advanced. And this was developing the brain of man to a point where it should be capable of giving full expression to the love and justice of God.

The end is not yet; God aims not at the perfection of a few choice specimens for exhibition, like the large berries at the top of the box, but at the glorification of the race. The time will come when the Kingdom of God shall be established on earth; the time foreseen by the dreamer of the Isle of Patmos, when there shall be no more crying, neither shall there be any more pain, for the former things are all passed away, and there shall be no night there.

20. SERVING GOD.

I HAVE brought you thus far through the two preceding chapters with a view to finally settling the question of duty. This is one that puzzles and perplexes very many people who are earnest and sincere, and gives them a great deal of difficulty in its solution. When they start out to make something of themselves and to practice the science of being great, they find themselves necessarily compelled to rearrange many of their relationships. There are friends who perhaps must be alienated, there are relatives who misunderstand and who feel that they are in some way being slighted; the really great man is often considered selfish by a large circle of people who are connected with him and who feel that he might bestow upon them more benefits than he, does. The question at the outset is: Is it my duty to make the most of myself regardless of everything else? Or shall I wait until I can do so without any friction or without causing loss to any one?

This is the question of duty to self, versus duty to others.

One's duty to the world has been thoroughly discussed in the preceding pages and I give some consideration now to the idea of duty to God. An immense number of people have a great deal of uncertainty, not to say anxiety, as to what they ought to do for God. The amount of work and service that is done for him in these United States in the way of church work and so on is enormous. An immense amount of human energy is expended in what is called serving God. I propose to consider briefly what serving God is and how a man may serve God best, and I think I shall be able to make plain that the conventional idea as to what constitutes service to God is all wrong.

When Moses went down into Egypt to bring out the Hebrews from bondage, his demand upon Pharaoh, in the name of the Deity, was, "Let the people go that they may serve me." He led them out into the wilderness and there instituted a new form of worship which has led many people to suppose that worship constitutes the service of God, although later God himself distinctly declared that he cared nothing for ceremonies, burned offerings, or oblation, and the teaching of Jesus, if rightly understood, would do away with organized temple worship altogether. God does not lack anything that men may do for him with their hands or bodies or voices. Saint Paul points out that man can do nothing for God, for God does not need anything.

The view of evolution which we have taken shows God seeking expression through man. Through all the successive ages in which his spirit has urged man up the height, God has gone on seeking expression. Every generation of men is more Godlike than the preceding generation. Every generation of men demands more in the way of fine homes, pleasant surroundings, congenial work, rest, travel, and opportunity for study than the preceding generation.

I have heard some shortsighted economists argue that the working people of today ought surely to be fully contented because their condition is so much better than that of the working-man two hundred years ago who slept in a windowless hut on a floor covered with rushes in company with his pigs. If that man had all that he was able to use for the living of all the life he knew how to live, he was perfectly content, and if he had lack he was not contented. The person of today has a comfortable home and very many things, indeed, that were unknown a short period back in the past, and if he has all that he can use for the living of all the life he can imagine, he will be content. But he is not content.

God has lifted the race so far that any common person can picture a better and more desirable life than he is able to live under existing conditions. And so long as this is true, so long as a person can think and clearly picture to himself a more desirable life, he will be discontented with the life he has to live, and rightly so. That discontent is the Spirit of God urging men on to more desirable conditions. It is God who seeks expression in the race. "He worketh in us to will and to do."

The only service you can render God is to give expression to what he is trying to give the world, through you. The only service you can render God is to make the very most of yourself in order that God may live in you to the utmost of your possibilities. In a former work of this series, The Science of Getting Rich, I refer to the little boy at the piano, the music in whose soul could not find expression through his untrained hands. This is a good illustration of the way the Spirit of God is over, about, around, and in all of us, seeking to do great things with us, so soon as we will train our hands and feet, our minds, brains, and bodies to do his service.

Your first duty to God, to yourself, and to the world is to make yourself as great a personality, in every way, as you possibly can. And that, it seems to me, disposes of the question of duty.

There are one or two other things which might be disposed of in closing this chapter. I have written of opportunity in a preceding chapter. I have said, in a general way, that it is within the power of every man to become great, just as in "The Science of Getting Rich" I declared that it is within the power of every man to become rich. But these sweeping generalizations need qualifying. There are men who have such materialistic minds that they are absolutely incapable of comprehending the philosophy set forth in these books.

There is a great mass of men and women who have lived and worked until they are practically incapable of thought along these lines; and they cannot receive the message. Something may be done for them by demonstration, that is, by living the life before them. But that is the only way they can be aroused. The world needs demonstration more than it needs teaching. For this mass of people our duty is to become as great in personality as possible in order that they may see and desire to do likewise. It is our duty to make ourselves great for their sakes, so that we may help prepare the world that the next generation shall have better conditions for thought. One other point. I am frequently written to by people who wish to make something of themselves and to move out into the world, but who are hampered by home ties, having others more or less dependent upon them, whom they fear would suffer if left alone. In general I advise such people to move out fearlessly, and to make the most of themselves. If there is a loss at home it will be only temporary and apparent, for in a little while, if you follow the leading of Spirit, you will be able to take better care of your dependents than you have ever done before.

21. A MENTAL EXERCISE.

THE purpose of mental exercises must not be misunderstood. There is no virtue in charms or formulated strings of words; there is no short cut to development by repeating prayers or incantations. A mental exercise is an exercise, not in repeating words, but in the thinking of certain thoughts. The phrases that we repeatedly hear become convictions, as Goethe says; and the thoughts that we repeatedly think become habitual, and make us what we are. The purpose in taking a mental exercise is that you may think certain thoughts repeatedly until you form a habit of thinking them; then they will be your thoughts all the time. Taken in the right way and with an understanding of their purpose, mental exercises are of great value; but taken as most people take them they are worse than useless.

The thoughts embodied in the following exercise are the ones you want to think. You should take the exercise once or twice daily, but you should think the thoughts continuously. That is, do not think them twice a day for a stated time and then forget them until it is time to take the exercise again. The exercise is to impress you with the material for continuous thought.

Take a time when you can have from twenty minutes to half an hour secure from interruption, and proceed first to make yourself physically comfortable. Lie at ease in a Morris chair, or on a couch, or in bed; it is best to lie flat on your back. If you have no other time, take the exercise on going to bed at night and before rising in the morning.

First let your attention travel over your body from the crown of your head to the soles of your feet, relaxing every muscle as you go. Relax completely. And next, get physical and other ills off your mind. Let the attention pass down the spinal cord and out over the nerves to the extremities, and as you do so think:—

"My nerves are in perfect order all over my body. They obey my will, and I have great nerve force." Next, bring your attention to the lungs and think:—

"I am breathing deeply and quietly, and the air goes into every cell of my lungs, which are in perfect condition. My blood is purified and made clean."

Next, to the heart:— "My heart is beating strongly and steadily, and my circulation is perfect, even to the extremities." Next, to the digestive system:— "My stomach and bowels perform their work perfectly. My food is digested and assimilated and my body rebuilt and nourished. My liver, kidneys, and bladder each perform their several functions without pain or strain; I am perfectly well. My body is resting, my mind is quiet, and my soul is at peace. "I have no anxiety about financial or other matters. God, who is within me, is also in all things I want, impelling them toward me; all that I want is already given to me. I have no anxiety about my health, for I am perfectly well. I have no worry or fear whatever.

"I rise above all temptation to moral evil. I cast out all greed, selfishness, and narrow personal ambition; I do not hold envy, malice, or enmity toward any living soul. I will follow no course of action which is not in accord with my highest ideals. I am right and I will do right."

VIEWPOINT.

All is right with the world. It is perfect and advancing to completion. I will contemplate the facts of social, political, and industrial life only from this high viewpoint. Behold, it is all very good. I will see all human beings, all my acquaintances, friends, neighbors, and the members of my own household in the same way. They are all good. Nothing is wrong with the universe; nothing can be wrong but my own personal attitude, and henceforth I keep that right. My whole trust is in God.

CONSECRATION.

I will obey my soul and be true to that within me which is highest. I will search within for the pure idea of right in all things, and when I find it I will express it in my outward life. I will abandon everything I have outgrown for the best I can think. I will have the highest thoughts concerning all my relationships, and my manner and action shall express these thoughts. I surrender my body to be ruled by my mind; I yield my mind to the dominion of my soul, and I give my soul to the guidance of God.

IDENTIFICATION.

There is but one substance and source, and of that I am made and with it I am one. It is my Father; I proceeded forth and came from it. My Father and I are one, and my Father is greater than I, and I do His will. I surrender myself to conscious unity with Pure Spirit; there is but one and that one is everywhere. I am one with the Eternal Consciousness.

IDEALIZATION.

Form a mental picture of yourself as you want to be, and at the greatest height your imagination can picture. Dwell upon this for some little time, holding the thought: "This is what I really am; it is a picture of my own soul. I am this now in soul, and I am becoming this in outward manifestation."

REALIZATION.

I appropriate to myself the power to become what I want to be, and to do what I want to do. I exercise creative energy; all the power there is mine. I will arise and go forth with power and perfect confidence; I will do mighty works in the strength of the Lord, my God. I will trust and not fear, for God is with me.

22. A SUMMARY OF THE SCIENCE OF BEING GREAT

We ALL are made of the one intelligent substance, and therefore all contain the same essential powers and possibilities. Greatness is equally inherent in all, and may be manifested by all. Every person may become great. Every constituent of God is a constituent of man.

We may overcome both heredity and circumstances by exercising the inherent creative power of the soul. If we are to become great, the soul must act, and must rule the mind and the body. Our knowledge is limited, and we fall into error through ignorance; to avoid this we must connect our soul with Universal Spirit. Universal Spirit is the intelligent substance from which all things come; it is in and through all things. All things are known to this universal mind, and we can so unite ourselves with it as to enter into all knowledge.

To do this we must cast out of ourselves everything which separates us from God. We must will to live the divine life, and we must rise above all moral temptations; we must forsake every course of action that is not in accord with our highest ideals.

We must reach the right viewpoint, recognizing that God is all, in all, and that there is nothing wrong. We must see that nature, society, government, and industry are perfect in their present stage, and advancing toward completion; and that all men and women everywhere are good and perfect. We must know that all is right with the world, and unite with God for the completion of the perfect work. It is only as we see God as the Great Advancing Presence in all, and good in all, that we can rise to real greatness.

We must consecrate ourselves to the service of the highest that is within ourselves, obeying the voice of the soul. There is an Inner Light in every one which continuously impels us toward the highest, and we must be guided by this light if we would become great.

We must recognize the fact that we are one with the Father, and consciously affirm this unity for ourselves and for all others. We must know ourselves to be a god among gods, and act accordingly. We must have absolute faith in our own perceptions of truth, and begin at home to act upon these perceptions. As we see the true and right course in small things, we must take that course. We must cease to act unthinkingly, and begin to think; and we must be sincere in our thought.

We must form a mental conception of ourselves at the highest, and hold this conception until it is our habitual thought-form of ourselves. This thought-form we must keep continuously in view. We must outwardly realize and express that thought-form in our actions. We must do everything that we do in a great way. In dealing with family, neighbors, acquaintances, and friends, we must make every act an expression of our ideal.

Whoever reaches the right viewpoint and makes full consecration, and who fully idealizes itself as great, and who makes every act, however trivial, an expression of the ideal, has already attained to greatness.

Everything we do will be done in a great way; will make us known, and we will be recognized as personalities of power. We will receive knowledge by inspiration, and will know all that we need to know. We will receive all the material wealth we form in our thoughts, and will not lack for any good thing. We will be given ability to deal with any combination of circumstances which may arise, and our growth and progress will be continuous and rapid. Great works will seek us out, and all people will delight to do us honor. Because of its peculiar value to the student of the Science of Being Great, I close this book by giving a portion of Emerson's essay on the "Oversoul." This great essay is fundamental, showing the foundation principles of monism and the science of greatness. I recommend the student to study it most carefully in connection with this book.

***

What is the universal sense of want and ignorance, but the fine innuendo by which the great soul makes its enormous claim? Why do men feel that the natural history of man has never been written, but always he is leaving behind what you have said of him, and it becomes old, and books of metaphysics worthless? The philosophy of six thousand years has not searched the chambers and magazines of the soul. In its experiments there has always remained, in the last analysis, a residuum it could not resolve. Man is a stream whose source is hidden. Always our being is descending into us from we know not whence. The most exact calculator has no prescience that somewhat incalculable may not balk the very next moment. I am constrained every moment to acknowledge a higher origin for events than the will I call mine.

As with events, so it is with thoughts. When I watch that flowing river, which, out of regions I see not, pours for a season its streams into me,—I see that I am a pensioner,—not a cause, but a surprised spectator of this ethereal water; that I desire and look up, and put myself in the attitude for reception, but from some alien energy the visions come.

The Supreme Critic on all the errors of the past and present, and the only prophet of that which must be, is that great nature in which we rest, as the earth lies in the soft arms of the atmosphere; that Unity, that Oversoul, with which every man's particular being is contained and made one with all other; that common heart, of which all sincere conversation is the worship, to which all right action is submission; that overpowering reality which confutes our tricks and talents, and constrains every one to pass for what he is, and to speak from his character and not from his tongue; and which evermore tends and aims to pass into our thought and hand, and become wisdom, and virtue, and power, and beauty. We live in succession, in division, in parts, in particles. Meantime within man is the soul of the whole; the wise silence; the universal beauty, to which every part and particle is equally related; the eternal One. And this deep power in which we exist, and whose beatitude is all accessible to us, is not only self- sufficing and perfect in every hour, but the act of seeing, and the thing seen, the seer and the spectacle, the subject and the object, are one. We see the world piece by piece, as the sun, the moon, the animal, the tree; but the whole, of which these are the shining parts, is the soul. It is only by the vision of that Wisdom, that the horoscope of the ages can be read, and it is only by falling back on our better thoughts, by yielding to the spirit of prophecy which is innate in every man, that we know what it saith. Every man's words, who speaks from that life, must sound vain to those who do not dwell in the same thought on their own part. I dare not speak for it. My words do not carry its august sense; they fall short and cold. Only itself can inspire whom it will, and behold! Their speech shall be lyrical and sweet, and universal as the rising of the wind. Yet I desire, even by profane words, if sacred I may not use, to indicate the heaven of this deity, and to report what hints I have collected of the transcendent simplicity and energy of the Highest Law. If we consider what happens in conversation, in reveries, in remorse, in times of passion, in surprises, in the instruction of dreams wherein often we see ourselves in masquerade,—the droll disguises only magnifying and enhancing a real element, and forcing it on our distinct notice,—we shall catch many hints that will broaden and lighten into knowledge of the secret of nature. All goes to show that the soul in man is not an organ, but animates and exercises all the organs; is not a function, like the power of memory, of calculation, of comparison,—but uses these as hands and feet; is not a faculty, but a light; is not the intellect or the will, but the master of the intellect and the will;—is the vast background of our being, in which they lie,—an immensity not possessed and that cannot be possessed. From within or from behind, a light shines through us upon things, and makes us aware that we are nothing, but the light is all. A man is the façade of a temple wherein all wisdom and all good abide.

What we commonly call man, the eating, drinking, planting, counting man, does not, as we know him, represent ourselves, but misrepresents ourselves. Him we do not respect, but the soul, whose organ he is, would he let it appear through his action, would make our knees bend. When it breathes through his intellect, it is genius; when it flows through his affection it is love. * * * *

After its own law and not by arithmetic is the rate of its progress to be computed. The soul's advances are not made by gradation, such as can be represented by motion in a straight line; but rather by ascension of state, such as can be represented by metamorphosis,— from the *egg* to the worm, from the worm to the fly. The growths of genius are of a certain total character, that does not advance the elect individual first over John, then Adam, then Richard, and give to each the pain of discovered inferiority, but by every throe of growth the man expands there where he works, passing, at each pulsation, classes, populations of men. With each divine impulse the mind rends the thin rinds of the visible and finite, and comes out into eternity, and inspires and expires its air. It converses with truths that have always been spoken in the world, and becomes conscious of a closer sympathy with Zeno and Arrian, than with persons in the house.

This is the law of moral and of mental gain. The simple rise as by specific levity, not into a particular virtue, but into the region of all the virtues. They are in the spirit which contains them all. The soul is superior to all the particulars of merit. The soul requires purity, but purity is not it; requires justice, but justice is not that; requires beneficence, but is somewhat better: so that there is a kind of descent and accommodation felt when we leave speaking of moral nature, to urge a virtue which it enjoins. For, to the soul in her pure action, all the virtues are natural, and not painfully acquired. Speak to his heart, and the man becomes suddenly virtuous.

Within the same sentiment is the germ of intellectual growth, which obeys the same law. Those who are capable of humility, of justice, of love, of aspiration, are already on a platform that commands the sciences and arts, speech and poetry, action and grace. For whoso dwells in this mortal beatitude, does already anticipate those special powers which men prize so highly; just as love does justice to all the gifts of the object beloved.

The lover has no talent, no skill, which passes for quite nothing with his enamored maiden, however little she may possess of related faculty. And the heart which abandons itself to the Supreme Mind finds itself related to all its works and will travel a royal road to particular knowledge and powers. For, in ascending to this primary and aboriginal sentiment, we have come from our remote station on the circumference instantaneously to the center of the world, where, as in the closet of God, we see causes, and anticipate the universe, which is but a slow effect.

THE END.

BOOK FOUR
HOW TO GET WHAT
YOU WANT

1. DEFINITION OF SUCCESS

Getting what you want is success; and success is an effect, coming from the application of a cause. ***Success is essentially the same in all cases; the difference is in the things the successful people want, but not in the success.***

Success is essentially the same, whether it results in the attainment of health, wealth, development or position; success is attainment, without regard to the things attained. And it is a law in nature that like causes always produce like effects; therefore, since success is the same in all cases, the cause of success must be the same in all cases.

The cause of success is always in the person who succeeds; you will see that this must be true, because if the cause of success were in nature, outside the person, then all persons similarly situated would succeed.

The cause of success is not in the environment of the individual, because if it were, all persons within a given radius would be successful, and success would be wholly a matter of neighborhood; and we see that people whose environments are practically the same, and who live in the same neighborhood show us all degrees of success and failure; therefore, we know that the cause of success must be in the individual, and nowhere else.

It is, therefore, mathematically certain that you can succeed if you will find out the cause of success, and develop it to sufficient strength, and apply it properly to your work; for the application of a sufficient cause cannot fail to produce a given effect. If there is a failure anywhere, of any kind, it is because the cause was either not sufficient or was not properly applied.

The cause of success is some power within you; you have the power to develop any power to a limitless extent; for there is no end to mental growth; you can increase the strength of this power indefinitely, and so you can make it strong enough to do what you want to do, and to get what you want to get; when it is strong enough you can learn how to apply it to the work, and there-fore, you can certainly succeed. All you have to learn is what is the cause of success and how it must be applied.

The development of the special faculties to be used in your work is essential. We do not expect anyone to succeed as a musician without developing the musical faculty; and it would be absurd to expect a machinist to succeed without developing the mechanical faculty, a clergyman to succeed without developing spiritual understanding and the use of words, or a banker to succeed without developing the faculty of finance. And in choosing a business, you should choose the one which will call for the use of your strongest faculties.

If you have good mechanical ability, and are not spiritually minded and have no command of language, do not try to preach; and if you have the taste and talent to combine colors and fabrics into beautiful creation in millinery and dress, do not learn typewriting or stenography; get into a business which will use your strongest faculties, and develop these faculties all you can; and even this is not enough to insure success.

There are people with fine musical talent who fail as musicians; people with good mechanical ability who fail as carpenters, blacksmiths and machinists; people with deep spirituality and fluent use of language who fail as clergymen; or with keen and logical minds who fail as lawyers, and so on. The special faculties used in your work are the tools you use, but success does not depend alone on having good tools; it depends more on the power which uses and applies the tools. Be sure that your tools are the best and kept in the best condition; you can cultivate any faculty to any desired extent.

The application of the musical faculty causes success in music; that of the mechanical faculty causes success in mechanical pursuits; that of the financial faculty causes success in banking, and so on; and the something which applies these faculties, or causes them to be applied is the cause of success. The faculties are tools; the user of the tools is you, yourself; that in you which can cause you to use the tools in the right way, at the right time and in the right place is the cause of success. What is this something in the person which causes him to use his faculties successfully?

What it is and how to develop it will be fully explained in the next section; but before taking that up you should read this section over several times, so as to fix upon your mind the impregnable logic of the statement that you can succeed. You can -and if you study the foregoing argument well you will- be convinced that you can; and to become convinced that you can succeed is the first requisite to success.

2. THE SOMETHING OF THOSE WHO SUCCEED

The faculties of the human mind are the tools with which success is attained, and the right application of these tools to your work or business will do it successfully and get what you want. A few people succeed because they use their faculties successfully, and the majority, who have equally good faculties, fail because they use them unsuccessfully.

There is something in the person who succeeds which enables him to use his faculties successfully, and this something must be cultivated by all who succeed; the question is: What is it? It is hard to find a word which shall express it, and not be misleading.

This *something* is Poise; and poise is peace and power combined; but it is more than poise, for poise is a condition, and this something is an action as well as a condition. This something is Faith; but it is more than faith, as faith is commonly understood: As commonly understood, faith consists in the action of believing things which cannot be proved; and the something which causes success is more than that. It is Conscious Power in Action. It is ACTIVE POWER- CONSCIOUSNESS.

Power-Consciousness is what you feel when you know that you can do a thing; and you know HOW to do the thing. If I can cause you to KNOW that you can succeed, and to know that you know HOW to succeed, I have placed success within your grasp; for if you know that you can do a thing and know that you know how to do it, it is impossible that you should fail to do it, if you really try. When you are in full Power-Consciousness, you will approach the task in an absolutely successful frame of mind. Every thought will be a successful thought, every action a successful action; and if every thought and action is successful, the sum-total of all your actions cannot be failure.

What I have to do in these lessons, then, is to teach you how to create Power-Consciousness in yourself, so that you will know that you can do what you want to do and then to teach you how to do what you want todo. Read again the preceding section; it proves by unanswerable logic that you CAN succeed. It shows that all that is in any mind is in your mind; the difference, if any, being in development. It is a fact in nature that the undeveloped is always capable of development; we see then that the cause of success is in you, and is capable of full development.

Having read this you must believe that it is possible for you to succeed; but it is not enough for you to believe that you can; you must know that you can; and the sub-conscious mind must know it as well as the objective mind.

People have a way of saying, *"he can who thinks he can"*; but this is not true. It is not even true that he can who knows he can, if only the objective mind is spoken of; for the sub-conscious mind will often completely set aside and overcome what is positively known by the objective mind. It is a true statement, however, that he can whose sub-conscious mind knows that he can; and it is especially true if his objective mind has been trained to do the work. People fail because they think, objectively, that they can do things, but do not know, sub-consciously, that they can do them. It is more than likely that your sub-conscious mind is even now impressed with doubts of your ability to succeed; and these must be removed, or it will withhold its power when you need it most.

The sub-conscious mind is the source from which power comes in the action of any faculty; and a doubt will cause this power to be withheld, and the action will be weak; therefore, your first step must be to impress your sub-conscious mind with that fact that you CAN. This must be done by repeated suggestions. Practice the following mental exercise several times a day, and especially just before going to sleep; think quietly about the sub-conscious mentality, which permeates your whole body as water permeates a sponge; as you think of this mind, try to feel it; you will soon be able to become conscious of it.

Hold this consciousness, and say with deep, earnest feeling: "I CAN succeed! All that is possible to any one is possible to me. I AM successful. I do succeed, for I am full of the Power of Success."

This is the simple truth. Realize that it is true, and repeat it over and over until your mentality is saturated through and through with the knowledge that YOU CAN DO WHAT YOU WANT TO DO. *You can; other people have, and you can do more than any one has ever done, for no one has ever yet used all the power that is capable of being used. It is within your power to make a greater success in your business than any one has ever made before you.*

Practice the above autosuggestion for a month with persistence, and you will begin to KNOW that you have within you that which CAN do what you want to do; and then you will be ready for the next section which will tell you how to proceed in doing what you want to do. But remember that it is absolutely essential that you should first impress upon the sub-conscious mind the knowledge that you CAN.

3. THE RIGHT WAY TO GET WHAT YOU WANT

Having filled your mentality, conscious and sub-conscious, with the faith that you CAN get what you want, the next question is one of the methods.

You know that you can do it if you proceed in the right way; but, which is the right way?

This much is certain: to get more, you must make constructive use of what you have.

You cannot use what you have not; therefore, your problem is how to make the most constructive use of what you already have.

Do not waste any time considering how you would use certain things if you had them; consider, simply, how to use what you have.

It is also certain that you will progress more rapidly if you make the most perfect use of what you have. In fact, the degree of rapidity with which you attain what you want will depend upon the perfection with which you use what you have. Many people are at a standstill, or find things coming their way very slowly because they are making only partial use of present means, power and opportunities.

You may see this point more plainly by considering an analogy in nature. In the process of evolution, the squirrels developed their leaping power to its fullest extent; then a continuous effort to advance brought forth the flying squirrel, which has a membrane uniting the legs in such a way as to form a parachute and enable the animal to sail some distance beyond an ordinary leap. A little extension of the parachute jump of the flying squirrel produced the bat, which as membranous wings and can fly; and continuous flight produced the bird with feathered wings.

The transition from one plane to another was accomplished simply by perfecting and extending functions. If the squirrels had not kept leaping further and further, there would have been no flying squirrel, and no power of flight. Making constructive use of the leaping power produced flight. *If you are only jumping half as far as you can, you will never fly.*

In nature we see that life advances from one plane to another by perfecting functions on the lower plane. Whenever an organism contains more life than it can express by functioning perfectly on its own plane, it begins to perform the functions of the next higher or larger plane. The first squirrel which began to develop the parachute membrane must have been a very perfect leaper. This is the fundamental principle of evolution, and of all attainment.

In accordance with this principle, then, you can advance only by more than filling your present place. You must do, perfectly, all that you can do now; and it is the law that by doing perfectly all that you can do now you will become able to do later things which you cannot do now.

The doing to perfection of one thing invariably provides us with the equipment for doing the next larger thing, because it is a principle inherent in nature that life continuously advances.

Every person who does one thing perfect is instantly presented with an opportunity to begin doing the next larger thing. This is the universal law of all life, and is unfailing.

First, do perfectly all that you can do now; keep on doing it perfectly until the doing of it becomes so easy that you have surplus power left after doing it; then by this surplus power you will get a hold on the work of a higher plane, and begin to extend your correspondence with environment.

Get into a business which will use your strongest faculties, even if you must commence at the bottom; then develop those faculties to the utmost. Cultivate power-consciousness, so that you can apply your faculties successfully, and apply them in doing perfectly everything you can do now, where you are now.

Do not wait for a change of environment; it may never come. Your only way of reaching a better environment is by making constructive use of your present environment.

Only the most complete use of your present environment will place you in a more desirable one.

If you wish to extend your present business, remember that you can only do it by doing in the most perfect manner the business you already have. When you put life enough into your business to more than fill it, the surplus will get you more business. Do not reach out after more until you have life to spare after doing perfectly all that you have to do now. It is of no advantage to have more work or more business than you have life to do perfectly; if that is the case, increase your vital power first. And remember, it is the perfection with which you do what you have to do now that extends your field and brings you in touch with a larger environment.

Bear in mind that the motive force which gets you what you want is life; and that what you want, in the last analysis, is only an opportunity to live more; and that, therefore, you can get what you want only through the operation of that universal law by which all life advances continuously into fuller expression.

That law is that whenever an organism has more life than can find expression by functioning perfectly on a given plane, its surplus life lifts it to the next higher plane. When you put enough of yourself into your present work to do it perfectly, your surplus power will extend your work into a larger field. It is also essential that you should have in mind what you want, so that your surplus power may be turned in the right direction. Form a clear conception of what you seek to accomplish, but do not let what you seek to accomplish interfere with doing perfectly what you have to do now.

Your concept of what you want is a guide to your energies, and an inspiration to cause you to apply them to the utmost to your present work. Live for the future now. Suppose that your desire is to have a department store, and you have only capital enough to start a peanut stand. Do not try to start a department store today, on a peanut stand capital; but start the peanut stand in the full faith and confidence that you will be able to develop it into a department store. Look upon the peanut stand merely as the beginning of the department store, and make it grow; you can.

Get more business by using constructively the business you have now; get more friends by using constructively the friends you already have; get a better position by using constructively the one you now have; get more domestic happiness by the constructive use of the love that already exists in your home.

4. BE THE BEST IN EVERY THING YOU DO

You can obtain what you want only by applying your faculties to your work and your environment. You become able to apply your faculties successfully by acquiring Power-Consciousness; and you go forward by a concentration on today's work, and by doing perfectly everything that can be done at the present time. You can get what you want in the future only by concentrating all your energies upon the constructive use of whatever you are in relation with today. An indifferent or half-hearted use of the elements in today's environment will be fatal to tomorrow's attainment.

Do not desire for today what is beyond your ability to get today; but be sure you get today the very best that can be had. Never take less than the very best that can be had at the present time; but do not waste energy by desiring what cannot be had at the present time. If you always have the best that can be had, you will continue to have better and better things, because it is a fundamental principle in the universe that life shall continually advance into more life, and into the use of more and better things; this is the principle which causes evolution. But if you are satisfied with less than the best that can be had, you will cease to move forward.

Every transaction and relation of today whether it be business, domestic or social, must be made a stepping stone to what you want in the future; and to accomplish this you must put into each more than enough life to fill it. There must be surplus power in everything you do. It is this surplus power which causes advancement and gets you what you want; where there is no surplus power there is no advancement and no attainment. It is the surplus of life above and beyond the functions of present environment which causes evolution; and evolution is advancing into more life, or getting what you want.

Suppose, for instance, you are in trade or a profession, and wish to increase your business; it will not do, when you sell goods or service to make the matter a merely perfunctory transaction, taking the customer's money, giving him good value, and letting him go away feeling that you had no interest in the matter beyond giving him a fair deal and profiting thereby. Unless he feels that you have a personal interest in him and his needs, and that you are honestly desirous to increase his welfare, you have made a failure and are losing ground. When you can make every customer feel that you are really trying to advance his interests as well as your own, your business will grow. It is not necessary to give premiums, or heavier weights or better values than others give to accomplish this; it is done by putting life and interest into every transaction, however small.

If you desire to change your avocation, make your present business a stepping-stone to the one you want. As long as you are in your present business, fill it with life; the surplus will tend toward what you want. Take a live interest in every man, woman and child you meet in either a business or social way, and sincerely desire the best for them; they will soon begin to feel that your advancement is a matter of interest to them and they will unite their thoughts for your good. This will form a battery of power in your favor and will open ways of advancement for you.

If you are an employee and desire promotion, put life into everything you do; put in more than enough life and interest to fill each piece of work. But do not be servile; never be a flunkey; and above all things avoid the intellectual prostitution which is the vice of our times in many trades and most professions.

I mean by this the being a mere hired apologist for and defender of immorality, graft, dishonesty, or vice in any form. The intellectual prostitute may rise in the service, but he is a lost soul.

Respect yourself; be absolutely just to all; put LIFE into every act and thought and fix Power-Conscious thought upon the fact that you are entitled to promotion; it will come as soon as you can more than fill your present place in every day. If it does not come from you present employer it will come from another; it is the law that whosoever more than fills his present place must be advanced. But for this law there could be no evolution, and no progress; but mark well what follows: It is not enough that you should merely put surplus life into your business relations. You will not advance far if you are a good business person or employee, but a bad husband or wife, an unjust parent, or, an untrustworthy friend. Your failure in these respects will make you incapable of using your success for the advancement of life, and so you will not come under the operation of the constructive law.

Many people who fulfill the law in business are prevented from progressing because they are unkind to their spouses, or deficient in some other relation of life. To come under the operation of the evolutionary force you must more than fill EVERY present relation. A telegraph operator desired to get away from the key, and get onto a small farm; and he began to move in that direction by being "good" to his wife. He "courted" her, without any reference to his desire; and from being half indifferent she became interested and eager to help; soon they had a little piece of ground in the edge of the town, and she raised poultry and superintended a garden while he "pounded the key"; now they have a farm and he has obtained his desire. You can secure the cooperation, not only of your wife but of all the people around you by putting life and interest into all your relations with them.

Put into every relation, business, domestic or social, more than enough life to fill that relation; have faith, which is Power-Consciousness; know what you want in the future, but have today the very best that can be obtained today; never be satisfied at any time with less than the best that can be had at that time, but never waste energy in desiring what is not to be had now; use all things for the advancement of life for yourself and for all with whom you are related in any way. Follow out these principles of action and you cannot fail to get what you want; for the universe is so constructed that all things must work together for your good.

5. FINAL CONSIDERATIONS

Wealth-culture consists in making constructive use of the people and things in your environment.

First, get a clear mental picture of what you want. If your present business or profession is not the one most suitable to your talents and tastes, decide upon the one which is most suitable; and determine to get into that business or profession, and to achieve the very greatest success in it. Get a clear idea of what you want to do, and get a mental concept of the utmost success in that business or profession; and determine that you will attain to that. Give a great deal of time to forming this concept or mental picture; the more clear and definite it is, the easier will be your work. The man who is not quite sure what he wants to build will put up a wobbling and shaky structure.

Know what you want, and keep the picture of it in the background of your mind night and day; let it be like a picture on the wall of your room, always in your consciousness, night and day. And then begin to move toward it. Remember that if you have not the fully developed talent now, you can develop it as you go along; you can surely do what you want to do.

It is quite likely that at present you cannot do the thing you want to do because you are not in the right environment, and have not the necessary capital; but this does not hinder you from the beginning to move toward the right environment, and from beginning to acquire capital. Remember that you move forward only by doing what you can in your present environment. Suppose that you have only capital enough to operate a newsstand, and your great desire is to own a department store; do not get the idea that there is some magical method by which you can successfully operate a department store on a newsstand capital.

There is, however, a mental science method by which you can so operate a newsstand as to certainly cause it to grow into a department store. Consider that your newsstand is one department of the store you are going to have; fix your mind on the department store, and begin to assimilate the rest of it. You will get it, if you make every act and thought constructive. *To make every act and thought constructive, everyone must convey the idea of increase.*

Steadily hold in mind the thought of advancement for yourself; know that you are advancing toward what you want, and act and speak in this faith. Then every word and act will convey the idea of advancement and increase to others, and they will be drawn to you. Always remember that what all people are seeking for is increase.

First, study over the facts in regard to the great abundance until you know that there is wealth for you, and that you do not have to take this wealth from anyone else. Avoid the competitive spirit. You can readily see that if there is limitless abundance there is enough for you, without robbing anyone else. Then, knowing that it is the purpose of nature that you should have what you want, reflect upon the fact that you can get it only by acting. Consider that you can act only upon your present environment; and do not try to act now upon environment of the future. Then remember that in acting upon your present environment, you must make every act a success in itself; and that in doing this you must hold the purpose to get what you want. You can hold this purpose only as you get a clear mental picture of what you want; be sure that you have that. Also, remember that your actions will not have dynamic moving power unless you have an unwavering faith that you get what you want.

Form a clear mental picture of what you want; hold the purpose to get it; do everything perfectly, not in a servile spirit, but because you are a master mind; keep unwavering faith in your ultimate attainment of your goal, and you cannot fail to move forward.

BOOK FIVE.
A NEW CHRIST

1. HIS PERSONALITY

This series will not be an attempt to prove something about Christ; it will be an effort to ascertain by scientific study, what He was, how He lived, and what He taught. Too many people have studied Jesus from the standpoint of some preconceived notion of Him or His mission, such an attitude always leads to erroneous conclusions.

The common concept of Christ was given to the church by the priests of the dark ages, at a time when a religious ideal was wanted which should induce men to be content with slavery, and to bow their necks to every kind of wrong and oppression; and this concept was drawn almost wholly from the poetry of Isaiah; the Christ of the churches is the Christ of Isaiah, and our ideas of Him are not drawn at all from an impartial study of the history of His life.

Such passages in the prophecies as; "He is despised and rejected of men; a man of sorrows and acquainted with grief; and we hid, as it were, our faces from him; he is brought as a lamb to the slaughter, and as a sheep before her shearers is dumb, so he opened not his mouth," have been quoted to show His character, and the meekness and humbly submissive spirit with which He endured wrong and injustice; and we have had held up as the ideal man a despised, friendless, poverty-stricken laborer whom the upper classes regarded with scorn because of his lowly origin and station; who had no friends save fishermen, laborers, outcasts and sinners; who was often shirtless and hungry, and who bore insults and persecutions with meek submission, and walked about in a scornful world with his hands always uplifted in loving benediction.

This character has too long been offered as the Christian ideal; Be meek, Be submissive, Be lamb-like or sheep-like. Bow your head before the persecutor, and offer your back to the shearer. Rejoice when you are fleeced; it is for the glory of God. It is a good religion for the man with the shears.

The Christ who was held up in the old fashioned orthodox pulpit is a weak character. He is not the kind of a man we would nominate for president, and his followers have very little faith in him as an organizer.

No railroad magnate of today would make him foreman of a section; and if it were broadcast over the country tonight that the president of the United States had resigned and that Jesus would be inaugurated tomorrow, 95 percent of the Christians there would draw their money out of the banks for fear Jesus might start a panic. What we propose to do now is to ascertain by a study of the four gospels in the light of history whether this is the real Christ; and if not, to find what the real Christ was like.

The Real Jesus Christ

In the first place, then, Jesus could not have been despised because He was a carpenter, or the reputed son of a carpenter. Custom required every Jewish Rabbi or teacher to have a trade. We read in the Talmud of Rabbi Johanan, the blacksmith, and of Rabbi Isaac, the shoemaker, learned and highly honored men. Rabbi Jesus, the carpenter, would be spoken of in the same way. St. Paul, a very learned man, was a tent-maker by trade. At that time, and among that people, Jesus could not have been despised for His birth and station. And He was popularly supposed to be of royal blood, being saluted as the son of David; His lineage was well known. The people who cried "Hosannah to the son of David" knew that He was an aristocrat of the aristocrats; a prince of the royal house. He was not "lowly" in birth, nor was He supposed to be so. On this point I refer you to Matthew 9:27; Matthew 15:22; Matthew 20:30; Matthew 21:9; Mark 10:47.

He Was Educated

Second, He could not have been despised for His ignorance, for He was a very learned man. Whenever He went into a synagogue He was selected to read the law and teach the congregation, as the one best qualified for that work. Luke says; "There went a fame of Him through all the region round about, and He taught in their synagogues, being glorified of all." In those times of fierce religious disputation, no unlearned man could have held his own in such fashion. He must have been letter-perfect in the books of the Jewish law, for He was always able to rout His adversaries by making apt quotations from their own books. Even His enemies always addressed Him as Master, or Teacher, acknowledging His profound learning. On this point, read Matthew 13:54; Mark 12:24-34; Luke 4:14-15; John 7:19-23; John 10:34.

Jesus Had Plenty

Third, He was not despised for His poverty, for He had many wealthy and influential friends, and knew no lack of anything. Lazarus and his sisters, whose home was always open to Him, were people of consequence; for we are told that "many of the Jews" came to comfort the sisters when Lazarus died.

Luke says that Joanna, the wife of Chuza, the king's steward, and other women "ministered unto him of their substance"; that is, they were supporters of His work. The king's steward was a high official, and his wife would be a prominent lady.

Joseph of Arimathea, who came to get the body of Jesus, was a well- to-do man. So, probably was Nicodemus. Jesus healed the sick in the families of rulers and high officials, and they appear to have responded liberally in supplying His financial needs. True, He held no property and bought no real estate; but He dressed expensively, lived well and never lacked for money. When He was crucified the soldiers cast lots for His clothing because it was too fine to cut up, as they would have done with the garments of an ordinary man; and on the night of His betrayal, when Judas went out, it was supposed by the others that he had gone to give something to the poor. It must have been their custom to give away money, or how could such a supposition have arisen?

In that country and climate, the wants of Jesus and His disciples were few and simple, and they seem to have been fully supplied. He wore fine clothes, had plenty to eat and drink, and had money to give away. Read Luke 8:1-3; Luke 5:33; Luke 23:50; John 11:19; John 12:2; John 19:23.

Jesus Was Not Humble

Fourth, Jesus was not humble, in the commonly accepted meaning of the word. He was a man of the most impressive, commanding and powerful personal appearance. He "spoke as one having authority" and "his word was with power."

Frequently, we are told, great fear and awe fell upon the people at His mighty words and works. In one place they were so frightened that they besought Him to leave; and John tells how certain officers sent to arrest Him in the market place lost their nerve in His commanding presence, and went back, saying "Surely, never man spoke like this man."

On the night of His arrest a band of soldiers approached Him in the grove and asked for Jesus of Nazareth; and when He answered "I am he," such was His majesty and psychic power that they prostrated themselves; "they went backward," the account says, "and fell to the ground" (John 18:6).

To be like the Christ of the four Gospels, one must be learned, well dressed, well supplied with money, and of noble and commanding appearance, speaking with authority, and having tremendous magnetic power. And now, what was His attitude toward His fellow men?

2. HIS ATTITUDE

One of the very best ways to reach an understanding of Jesus is by studying His reasons for taking the title He assumed - the Son of Man. He rarely spoke of Himself in any other way. This term, Son of Man, was common in the Jewish prophecies, and in the current conversation of the times, and it was simply an emphatic way of saying "Man." If you wished to emphasize your fealty to democracy, you might say "I am a son of Thomas Jefferson"; and if you wished to emphasize your fealty to humanity, you would say as Jesus did. "I am a son of man."

The World Jesus Lived In

The Roman empire was a great taxing machine. In its conquered provinces, the people were left, as far as possible, with their own local government and institutions of justice, the function of the Roman officials being to extort tribute, or collect taxes. Every form of extortion and oppression was practiced by the governors, procurators and tax collectors upon those who had property. Open robbery, torture, kidnapping, false accusation and imprisonment might be visited upon the man who had money to tempt the cupidity of the higher powers; and as the oppressed property owners had no way of meeting the exactions of the government but by exploiting the poor, the condition of the masses was pitiful indeed.

You will readily see that the business, and property-owning class had to get the money to pay their taxes by exploiting the multitude in some way. It is an economic axiom which is indisputable that all taxation of whatever kind, upon whomsoever levied, must at last be wrung from the hard hands of the producers; no one, however, seems to comprehend this fact as little as the producers themselves. They strenuously eject all offers of deliverance, and generally kill those who try to help them.

Jesus received His only real and permanent following from among the middle class, as we shall see, and was crucified by the workers, whom He was trying to deliver from oppression. It was no middle class mob which demanded the liberation of Barabbas and howled for the blood of Christ.

To give you an idea as to how oppressive the Roman taxation was, we may estimate from certain passages in Josephus that the private income of Herod the Great was three and one-half millions of dollars a year (**N.E. Around $90 million of today**).

That is vastly less, of course, than the income of our John D. Rockefeller; but our Herods have a much larger, richer, and more populous country to levy taxes on, and they have discovered methods of extortion which lay the crude ways of the monarchs of antiquity very far in the shade. The enormous sums which were collected from the little province of Galilee brought the unhappy workers down to the last extremity of destitution; they could go no lower and live.

The Sects of Jesus' Day

In Judea at this time were several religious sects, which were also, in a way, political parties, scheming for prestige and power, and for influence with Rome. The Pharisees, Sadducees, Essenes, Samaritans, etc., disagreed upon various questions, as the existence or non-existence of angels, the resurrection of the dead, baptism, and so on. The strife between these parties was desperately acrimonious and bitter, often to the point of open violence. You will notice as you read that they were always ready to "take up stones" to end a dispute; riots were of daily occurrence in the streets of Jerusalem, and only the psychic power and commanding personality of Jesus saved Him from being stoned by these religious mobs. Read Luke 4:28-30; Luke 20:6; John 8:59.

The leaders of these sects were, of course, of the middle, or property-owning class; but the rank and file were the common masses, sunk in the most abject poverty - taxed, beaten, robbed, outraged, slaughtered, with no voice lifted anywhere in their behalf. No one, Jew or Gentile, thought for a moment of demanding justice for the mongrel multitude.

It is said of Jesus that He 'had compassion on the multitude, because they fainted, and were amazed, and were like sheep without a shepherd' Matthew 9:36 They had then, as now, plenty of shepherds to baptize them, to interpret prophecy for them, to instruct them in "spiritual" things; but none to demand a lightening of their burdens; none to cry out in their behalf for justice. The principal care of the shepherds was that the flock should be so doctrinally correct that they would never, never consent to be sheared by the opposing party.

The New Thought of Jesus' Time

Into this maze of oppression, taxation, murder, outrage and theological discussion comes the grand, strong figure of this young prince and scholar, saying; *'The Spirit of the Lord is upon me, for he hath anointed me to preach good news to the poor. I am no Pharisee; I am no Sadducee, Essene, or Samaritan; I am a man. I come, not in behalf of Pharisaism or Samaritanism, but in behalf of humanity.'*

Here was an altogether different religious attitude; He had no 'ism' to build up; His only creed was justice, His only doctrine the square deal. No wonder they were *amazed at his doctrine.*

No wonder His *'word was with power.'* No wonder they said *'he speaketh as one having authority.'* Jesus said of Himself that the father had given Him authority to execute judgment because He was man (John 5:27). That is the only reason God could possibly have for giving authority to any man; if there is a man anywhere today upon whom the divine sanction rests, it is not because he is a Pharisee, a Methodist, Presbyterian, Republican or Democrat, but because he is a MAN.

And it is further true that amongst all those who claim leadership by virtue of divine authority we may apply this test with certainty - that the man who stands for humanity, first, last and all the time, against all vested interests, religious and economic, is the man who stands as Jesus stood.

The man who stands for humanity against the vested religious interests of his time frequently is called an infidel; and the man who stands for the propertyless against the vested political and economic interests of his time is called a traitor. Jesus was crucified on the charges of infidelity and treason, and He was guilty on both counts.

Let no one be too horrified here to proceed further; for there are no prouder titles when justly held than the terms Infidel and Traitor. It was a grand saying of Wendell Phillips 'Write upon my grave Infidel-Traitor; infidel to every church that compromises with wrong; traitor to every government that oppresses the poor'

The most sinful infidelity is not being unfaithful to some church, but being unfaithful to the truth; and the vilest treason is not turning against some government, but turning against the weak and helpless. This was the attitude which Jesus took; He gave expression to all this when He took the title which made Him the champion of humanity when He said, "I am the Son of Man." We will now take up the consideration of His teachings.

3. HIS TEACHINGS ABOUT MAN

If Jesus was a Savior, He came to save mankind, collectively and individually, from sin, from Error; for there is nothing but error to be saved from. That is what He says of Himself, in John 18:37; "To this end was I born, and for this cause came I into the world, that I should bear witness to the truth."

A lost world is a world which has lost the truth about life; and a lost man or woman is simply one who has lost the truth about life; and there is no other way under heaven to save the lost but by telling them the truth about life.

This simple sentence in which He concisely states His mission lets in a flood of light upon His theory of life; He came to save from sin, disease and poverty by telling the truth. Then sin, disease and poverty are untruths; that is, they are wrong ways of living. We will consider first His broader and more generic application of truth, and later, His application of it to the individual.

In the sermon on the mount, He says (Matthew 5:21-22); "Ye have heard that it was said by them of old time, thou shalt not kill; and whosoever shall kill shall be in danger of the judgment; but I say unto you, that whosoever is angry with his brother without a cause shall be in danger of the judgment; and whosoever shall say to his brother Raca, shall be in danger of the council; but whosoever shall say Thou fool, shall be in danger of hell fire." The phrase, "thou fool," as we understand it now, does not give the meaning of the original at all; it would be better rendered by some such phrase as "you are of no value" or "you are good for nothing."

I can make His meaning clear, I think, by an illustration. I was sitting in a hotel lobby, once, when the news came of a coalmine horror in which a number of poor fellows lost their lives. Two well-dressed men near me were discussing the affair, and one said; "Oh, well, it's only a couple of Huniaks less. A million more are ready to step into their shoes tomorrow; the world hasn't lost anything."

Jesus says whosoever shall speak of a man as that man spoke, is in danger of hell fire. That man, and those who think and speak as he does, are the real murderers of all who die in mine and mill and under rolling wheels; they make the slaughter possible by cheapening the estimate that is put on the value of a human life. Whosoever talks of "cheap" people, and of "lower" classes, and insists that some are especially valuable to God, and that others are their "inferiors," will go to hell, said Jesus; and I think He was right. A little farther on in His life, we shall see how He proved it, and on what great natural fact He based His assertion. I have given you the exact meaning of the quoted passage, and the only meaning which may legitimately be drawn from it. Turn now to the 12th chapter of Matthew and read the first eight verses.

The Sabbath

There you find that the disciples were crossing the fields on the Sabbath day, and that they plucked the ears of corn, and ate as they went. This gave great offence to the Pharisees. They were not offended because they took the grain, for, under the Jewish law, the right of the hungry wayfarer to life transcended the property rights of the owner of the field; none might say the famished man nay, if he chose to pluck and eat. It was not to a theft of grain that the Pharisees objected, but to the fact that the plucking and eating were done on the Sabbath day. The Pharisees believed that the one thing most valuable to God was their church with its institutions and observances. They would not break the Sabbath to feed a hungry man, or to heal a sick man, because they thought the Sabbath was more valuable to God than the man.

And so they complained to Jesus, and He answered them, "Have ye not heard what David did, when he was hungry; he and they that were with him?" and He went on to tell them from their own scriptures, in which, as I have said, He was letter-perfect, how David and his followers went into the temple and took the sacred shew bread and ate it - and God approved. "One standeth here," said Jesus, "greater than the temple." "The (son of) man is lord of the Sabbath day." That is, God cares more for a hungry man than He does for a holy day or house. In the second chapter of Mark, where the same story is told, He adds, "The Sabbath was made for man, and not man for the Sabbath."

Organizations

Here is brought out and sharply defined the issue between Jesus and His opponents. They were exalting the temple, the worship, the Sabbath, the ceremonial; He exalted the man. They declared that God was working through humanity to build systems and institutions; He declared that God was working through systems and institutions to build humanity. And I, for one, agree with Jesus. I feel no reverence for buildings; even though they are magnificent structures, where the dim light falls through stained glass windows upon the sculptured forms of saints and angels, where robed priests chant in solemn cadence; these things move me little.

But when I stand in a schoolroom and look into the bright faces of a hundred, boys and girls - when I stand in the crowded marketplace, or in a mill or factory where my brothers and sisters toil to supply the needs of the world, and I remember that every soul before me contains possibilities as boundless as the universe itself; when I stand in the presence of this toiling, seeking, loving, suffering, glorious, common humanity, I bare my head and bow in reverence, for here, indeed, I am in the presence of Almighty God. One is here greater than the temple, greater than the Sabbath, greater than the system, greater than the institution, the Church or State. *God has a higher call for man than the keeping of certain days and places holy. This whole earth is a holy place, because it is consecrated by the love of God to fulfill His purpose in unfolding the high destiny of man.*

Little Children

In the 18th chapter of Matthew you will read how Jesus took a little child and set him in the midst, of them, and said; "Whosoever shall humble himself as this little child, the same shall be greatest in the kingdom of heaven"; and He went on to assert that whatsoever should offend the child had better be cast into the sea.

You will get a good idea of the prevailing misconception concerning Jesus and His times if you study the pictures you commonly see of the scene where He blessed the little children. He is always shown to us surrounded by prettily dressed women, who are bringing nice clean babies for Him to love and bless; and it looks very easy for one to humble himself as one of those.

But turn back to our description of the condition of the masses in His day, and you will get a different idea. That was a slave child that He set in the midst of them; unwashed, uncombed, covered with vermin and noisome sores repulsive to every sense; a child of the abyss, in the darkest period of the world's history. And what could He mean by telling us to humble ourselves as such a child? Is it that we should be childlike in spirit, teachable, credulous? No; there is only one way. Stand beside that child of the gutter, and say; "Before God he is as good as I. He is entitled to everything that I claim for myself and for my children, and I will not rest until all that I demand for my own is his also." Then you will have humbled yourself as the little child by acknowledging his equality with you, and then you will begin to be great in the kingdom of heaven.

"Whosoever shall offend one of these little (slaves?) ones, it is better that a millstone shall be hanged about his neck, and he were cast into the sea." Yes, any man, or woman, or railroad system, or financial system, or industrial order or disorder that stands between the poor man's child and life, is under the curse of God. It is better that all the corn crops of a thousand years be lost, than that the least injustice shall be done to one such little child. That is what Jesus taught; and it is not to be wondered at that He was crucified.

4. HIS TEACHINGS ABOUT WEALTH

One day Jesus was teaching the people, and He said, in substance; "Why are you worried about things to eat, and to wear". Look at the birds; they have not a fraction of your intelligence; they do not know enough to sow, or reap, or gather provision for the future; and yet they have no famine. You, with your great intelligence, surely ought to be able to live with more ease and safety than the lower orders of life; yet the only fear and anxiety are to be found among men. Seek the kind of kingdom your Father wants; a perfectly righteous order of things, and you will have plenty of everything." This is a rather free translation of Matthew 6:25-34, but it is a very accurate rendering of the meaning of the original; much more accurate than that given by the King James version.

And I wish here to give you a word of caution. I frequently receive letters from people who lay great stress on the interpretation of some particular passage from the New Testament, and even on that of some single word; as if the letter of it was a perfect and infallible guide. Now, remember that Jesus taught and spoke in the Aramaic, a dialect which had entirely supplanted the Hebrew among the Jews of Palestine, and that His sayings, in that language, were held in memory about seventy years before they appeared in the Greek, written in the manuscripts of the gospels; and that from the Greek they were translated into the English of 500 years ago, in our King James version. Five hundred years ago many words in our language carried meanings which are lost now; and so you will see how foolish it is to pin so much faith on single detached sayings and passages, which may not at all convey the meaning He gave to them. We never can understand him until we study his teachings as a connected whole.

Wealth for All

On the face of things it would look as if He told the truth when He said that there was no need for worry. There is no lack of the things needed, and where there is no lack there is no necessity for worry. This world would produce food, under intensive cultivation, for more than ten times its present population. It would produce the fabrics wherewith to clothe ten times its present population finer than Solomon was arrayed in all his glory. It would furnish building material sufficient to erect a palace larger than the Capitol at Washington for every family now living, and there would be material enough left over to house another generation.

Our Father has provided the raw material for all the things essential to life, and He has provided a thousandfold more than we can use. The race, taken as a whole, is rich; immensely rich; it is only individuals within the race who are poor.

The satisfaction of human needs is a problem of machinery and organization, and the machinery is pretty well perfected; it is now, then, a matter of organization. Seek the Father's Kingdom, says Jesus, and you solve the bread and butter problem. Does that sound like a rational interpretation of the passage we are speaking of? Turn to the 12th chapter of Luke, and read the parallel passage.

The Kingdom of God

Now, what did He mean by the kingdom of God? Practically all commentators agree, now, that He did not mean a distinct Heaven, which we cannot enter until we die; and they agree, also that He did not mean a church like the one we have now.

If you can conceive of the church as expanded until it filled the whole earth; all the people united in one, and all practicing what the churches preach now, that would be very like a Kingdom of God as Jesus describes it.

He illustrates it by showing that the birds know no anxiety; they live in the Father's kingdom. They all, alike, have access to the Supply. There is no bug trust, and no shrewd bird has, as yet, cornered the worm market. When, instead of going freely to the Great Supply, the birds begin to compete for the limited portions of it, there will begin to be an anxiety among them. There can be no Father's kingdom unless all can have equal access to the Great Supply.

Equality and Democracy

You will find this confirmed in the twenty-third chapter of Matthew, in the first twelve verses. Here He lays the foundation of the kingdom in the fact of the Fatherhood of God, and I will call the attention of the literalists especially to the fact that the sayings were addressed "to the multitude" as well as to His disciples.

He assures them all that God is their Father, and that they are brethren; and that hence, they should not compete for the best place at the feast. If, instead of struggling with each other, you will go lovingly to the feast together, is there not enough for all? Let there be no striving for mastery, or power over one another; just plain equality and democracy, says Jesus, and no one will have to bear a heavy burden anymore.

Suppose the father of a family should see his children gather around a table, where he had provided for them as bountifully as our Father has for us; and suppose that the largest boy should get to the table first and gather all the best food around his plate. When his little sister reaches for a nice piece of cake he slaps her; he strikes back the out stretched hands of the others, and says:

Get away! Our father put this here, and I am the first one to get to it; so it is mine. Get away" (strike, push, shove) and, looking up to his parent, he addresses him thus: "Our father (biff), thy kingdom come (bang), thy will be done (whack)." Would not that father say, "My will will not be done until you, with your brothers and sisters, go together to the Supply I have provided."

And if the large boy should say then: "Well, father, I will hold it as your trustee, giving to the others as I think it best for them, and seeing that all is done decently and in order," would not the father say, "I do not want benevolence, or charity, or self-denial, or Sabbath observance, but that each one shall go freed to the Supply for all that he needs."

The idea of Jesus appears to be that if each one will go freely to the Supply, there can be no poverty or lack of any kind; and His idea appears to be sound. If the supply is super-abundant, and all go freely to it, how can anybody have lack? The trouble is that we have our eyes fixed, not on the Abundance, but on the Uppermost Place.

It is as if there were a mountain of gold, to which we might go for wealth, but on our way thither we find a few scattering nuggets which have been washed down by the rains, and we stop to fight for the possession of these fragments, and so lose the whole.

In this connection, look up the parallel passages in Luke, and note the one in the twenty-second chapter, where He cautions them against that most insidious of temptations, the desire to pose as a "benefactor." No benefactors are needed where all may go to the Supply. You are to serve by inviting men to the feast, not by handing them a few crumbs from your own plate. It is not possible that there should be benefactions, benefactors or charity in the kingdom of God; so long as there is need for these things we are not in His kingdom.

And how can we hope to establish the kingdom by practicing things which do notbelong to it?

"Love Thy Neighbor"

It is in this light that we must consider His command to love one's neighbor as one's self. What does it mean, this loving one's neighbor as himself? Suppose my wife and I sit down to lunch; and there is nothing on the table but a crust of bread and a piece of pie. And suppose that I hastily grasp the pie, and say; "My dear, I certainly love you devotedly; I do wish you had some pie, also," and I swallow it, and leave her the crust; have I loved her as myself? If I love her as myself, I will desire pie for her as intensely as for myself, and I will try as hard to get it for her as for myself.

If I love you as myself, what I try to get for myself I will try to get for you, and what I try to get for my children I will try to get for your children, and I will no more rest under an injustice done to you or yours than if it had been done to me or mine.

And when we all desire for everybody all that we desire for ourselves, what is there for us to do but to stop competing for a part and turn to the abundance of the Great Whole, which is the Kingdom of God.

5. THE APOSTOLS AND THEIR FAILURE

No one who studies carefully the teachings of Jesus can doubt that by the phrases, *Kingdom of Heaven* and *Kingdom of God,* He meant such a righteous adjustment of social relations as would have revolutionized the Society of His day; or which, if applied in our time, would revolutionize the society of this day.

You will get this idea pretty clearly if you study His use of the term "this world," and His comparison of the "world" with the kingdom. When He speaks of the "world" He never means the earth; He always refers to the existing social and governmental order; the world of men; organized society. He speaks of this world as a living, sentient thing; as loving, hating, etc.; and it can hardly be that He refers to the senseless clods and stones composing the material planet on which we live.

Thus in John 17:14, He says: "The world hath hated them, because they are not of the world." In the same chapter He speaks of His disciples as being in the world, but not of the world; as being sent into the world; and He prays that the world may believe, and that the world may know. In the two preceding chapters He speaks of the world as being overcome. Follow this clue through all His teachings, and you must conclude that by the "world" He means the existing order of human relationships.

The World and the Kingdom

Having come to an understanding of this, we can appreciate the contrast He draws between the world and the Kingdom. His Kingdom, He says, is "not of this world"; that is, it is not on the same basis as the world's kingdoms. "If My kingdom were of this world, then would My servants fight" (John 18:36).

In the world's kingdoms they fight; in His Kingdom they co-operate. In the world's kingdoms they sustain the relationship of master and servant; in His Kingdom, they are 'friends' (John 15:15) (Matthew 23:10).

The world's kingdoms are divided against them-selves (Matthew 12:25), but in God's Kingdom they do not try to conquer or master one another. That is the essential thought of the life of the Kingdom - that there shall be no seeking for power over other men; over against it He places the essential thought of the world-life, which is the strife for power, and for the uppermost place.

So, when they sought to make Him king by force (John 6:15), He refused, because that would have been placing His Kingdom on the world basis of strife and competition, and a kingdom over which Jesus ruled by force of arms would, after all, differ from the world kingdoms only in degree, and not in principle. The only kingdom in the establishment of which He could assist was the Father's Kingdom; a co-operative commonwealth, in which all should have access on equal terms to God, and to the Great Supply.

So He sends His followers out, not to fight or conquer, but to go as lambs among wolves, and by teaching and living to transform the insane and struggling world into a vast brotherhood. He believed that He had overcome the world by His demonstration, and that it must soon come to its end.

The End of the World

This brings up another point for our consideration. When He speaks of the "end of the world" it is apparent that He is not referring to some tremendous cataclysm which shall destroy the planet, but to a social change; a world revolution. In the twenty-fourth chapter of Matthew, He does, indeed, give some symbolical pictures of the darkness of the sun and moon, etc., which He quotes from the prophecies; but as we shall see in a future chapter, the "coming of the son of man" meant to Him, not His own personal return to establish a spiritual force-kingdom, but the awakening of racial Man, and his entrance into his heritage. When Man awakes and enters into his own, the world will be ended and the Kingdom will begin; that is the Coming of Man, which the prophets foretold.

That is the way Jesus interpreted them, as you will see if you study Him carefully and without prejudice. He does not appear to have had any idea that the planet would *come to an end;* or that He would actually come in personal presence to do what He steadfastly refused to do while here: set up a kingdom based on force. The apostles caught this concept of the Kingdom, and they set forth with joyous confidence to build a united and harmonious world.

Read the second and fourth chapters of the Acts, and read the writings of the early Christian fathers and you will see that their idea was not to build an institution for worship, in a bad world, but to build the world itself into a righteous, united and orderly society. Property was held in common, and there was no poverty among them which was not shared by all, and no riches which were not enjoyed by all.

The early Christian societies were little commonwealths, and the inspiring purpose to which they held with intense enthusiasm was the building of the world into one great commonwealth.

The apostles were communist organizers, and the purpose of Jesus as understood by them was the establishment of a communistic state which should grow up within the kingdoms of the World, and absorb them all, not by force, but by conquest of truth; by evangelizing the world, by educating it to the brotherhood ideals and methods.

Their dream was a world of Man, where the united efforts of all should center in the development of the little child; it was this glorious vision which gave virility and power to their preaching, and it was the loss of this vision which cost the church its spiritual power. The church of today is alive in proportion as it receives this world-vision; as it sees the kingdom and helps reorganize society.

Why Communism Fails

We may here consider for a moment why the communistic experiment failed, and we shall find the reason easy to get at. Communism has always failed, and always will fail, because it interferes with the Great Purpose, which is the complete development of the individual soul. It extinguishes the individual in the mass, and takes all initiative from him. Seeking to prevent him from gaining power over other men, it robs him of power over himself. It destroys individuality for man can develop only by the free proprietary use of everything he is individually capable of using.

Capitalism robs the majority of men of the opportunity to make proprietary use of the things necessary for their individual development; Communism would rob all men of this opportunity. In this, both are the opposites of Christian socialism.

Christian Socialism

Socialism would tremendously extend private property. Its cardinal doctrine is that the individual should own, absolutely and without question, everything which they need or can use individually; and that the right to hold private property should be limited only when we come to those things which a man cannot operate without exploiting other men. Man, under socialism, may acquire and hold all that he can use for his own development; but he may not own that which makes him master of another man.

As we approach socialism, the millions of families who are now propertyless will acquire and own beautiful homes, with the gardens and the land upon which to raise their food; they will own horses and carriages, automobiles and pleasure yachts; their houses will contain libraries, musical instruments, paintings and statuary, all that a person may need for the soul-growth of themselves and theirs, they shall own and use as they will.

But highways, railroads, natural resources, and the great machines will be owned and operated by organized society, so that all who will may purchase the product upon equal terms. Socialism, when properly understood, offers us the most complete individualism, while communism would submerge the individual in the mass.

The apostles failed because communism is a failure in the nature of things, while the world, at that time, had not evolved far enough to make socialism possible. They tried to establish for all a life which was only possible to a few.

6. THE SOURCE OF POWER

Jesus ascribed all His marvelous power to the mental relationship which existed between Himself and the Father. He uses the terms Father and God interchangeable, and says: "My father, of whom ye say that he is your God" (John 8:54).

And in His talk with the Samaritan woman, He explains clearly His conception of God, declaring that "God is Spirit" (Not A Spirit, as the King James version has it), and that He is not to be worshipped in some particular place like Jerusalem, or on some specially consecrated mountain, but may be approached, or worshipped in spirit and in truth, anywhere.

The Father, as described by Jesus, is Universal Spirit, working in all, through all, and FOR ALL. He describes this spirit as making the sun to shine, and causing the rain to fall, and so as being the POWER behind nature; as clothing the lilies of the field, and causing the hair to grow on man's heads, and so as being the one and only LIFE; as quickening and leading men to truth and so as being the one and only INTELLIGENCE.

Every man is a God, according to Jesus, because it is Spirit which lives in man; He said to them: "Ye are Gods" (John 10:34). Spirit holds the earth in its orbit, makes the sun rise, sends the rain, and causes the coming of seedtime and harvest; Spirit lives in the lily and clothes it finer than Solomon was arrayed in all his glory; Spirit lives in man.

There is only one power, only one life, only one intelligence.

Unity of Man in God

As I have said, Jesus ascribed all His power to His conscious unity of mind with this One Intelligence. "I and my father are one," said He. 'I do always his will.'

And He went on to declare that because He always did the will of Spirit, Universal Spirit worked in and through Him. "I do always those things that please him," said he (John 8:29). "I come, not to do mine own will, but the will of him that sent me." "I seek not mine own will, but the will of him" - and so on.

He made it perfectly plain that it was because of this unity of mind with the Father -which we call cosmic consciousness– that the Father could work through Him.

Because I will to do his will, said Jesus, my father and I act as one; and so it is not I that do the works, but the Father that worketh in me. He was consciously one with the one Spirit, and so all power in heaven and earth was at His service; He was consciously one with the one Life, and so He could transfigure His body, and heal others; "there went out from him a virtue (a realization of truth) that healed them all"; He was consciously one with the one Intelligence, and so all knowledge and all wisdom were His.

This is a point we must not lose sight of; that all that there is in the life of Jesus which transcends the ordinary, He positively declares to be due to His cosmic consciousness; to unity of mind and will with the All-Spirit.

Cosmic Consciousness

I will quote you a few more passages on this point; "He that sent me is true, whom ye know not; but I know him" (John 7:28-29). "I know him, and keep his saying" (John 8:55). "The son can do nothing of himself, but what he seeth the father do" (John 5:19). "As the father knoweth me, even so know I the father" (John 10:15). To "know" the father can have but one meaning; and that is to be conscious of Spirit; to have my own consciousness so unified with the consciousness of Spirit that what Spirit knows I know; what Spirit sees I see; and what Spirit does, I do.

My father is greater than I; I proceeded forth and came from Him; but if I unite with Him in consciousness, He is in me and I in Him, and He and I are one.

Jesus declares that this cosmic consciousness is the source of all power; He demonstrates that it is perfect health, both in His own person, and by healing others; "and this is life eternal to KNOW thee" (John 17:3). He asserts that it gives perfect wisdom - "The father loveth the son, and showeth him all things." "My judgment is true; for I am not alone, but I and the father" (John 8:16). And He asserts that it is wealth; "All things that the father hath are mine" (John 16:15).

Christ's Brothers

He does not trace His power to something peculiar about His birth, but to His conscious unity with Spirit.

He does not say that God is His father alone, but that He is our father. He says; "One is your father, and all ye are brethren."

He says in the sermon on the mount; "It is your father who feeds and cares for you; be his children in mind and will, as you are in fact."

He does not assert that He is a demi-god, and that we are men; but that He is God, and we may be God, too, if we will; "He that willeth to do the will of God, shall know"; "shall enter the kingdom," and so on.

"The works that I do, ye shall do also; and greater works than these shall ye do."

The consciousness that He had, He seems to think quite possible for all of us; "That they may all be one," he prays, in the seventeenth chapter of John, "as thou, Father, art in me, and I in thee, that they may be one in us." "I in them, and thou in me, that they may be made perfect in one." What He is, we can any or all of us become, He says.

Jesus' Relationship to God

It is not within the scope of this little book to study whether Jesus really was born in a different way from other people; that inquiry must be reserved for a more pretentious work. But this is quite certain, that He Himself made no claim to being different from the rest of us, except as to the extent of His consciousness.

He was conscious of a relationship with Spirit which the world knew nothing about; this relationship existed for the world as well as for Himself, whenever the world would recognize it, and enter into it. And for all to enter into this conscious unity with Spirit would save the world from sin, sickness, ignorance and poverty; it would establish the Kingdom of God. He could pray for no greater good than that they might be "one with the Father," even as He was one with the Father. To be one with the Father is to be one with Spirit; and to be one with Spirit is to so harmonize with it that thought, life, power, and wisdom shall come in a continuous inflow from Spirit into our minds and bodies.

Man's Relationship to God

There is, according to Jesus, one Spirit who is all the power there is, all the life there is, and all the intelligence there is; and this Spirit has children, who are of the same substances as

Himself, and who have power to think independently, and to separate themselves in consciousness from Him. And the power to think independently implies the possibility of thinking erroneously; if man separates himself in consciousness from God, he is sure to fall into error, for he can see only an infinitesimal portion of the truth.

Man's life, man's power, and man's wisdom decrease in exact proportion to the extent of his separation in consciousness from God.

Jesus found a world of men who had lost the consciousness of God, and because of doing so had become afflicted with the most horrible diseases; had fallen into the vilest depths of sin and debauchery; had sunk to the lowest levels of poverty and misery, and were in danger of losing life itself. To this lost and struggling world, He gave a demonstration of the possibilities of a life of cosmic consciousness -of conscious unity with Spirit. He demonstrated power over nature by calming the storm, and precipitating the food elements from the atmosphere to feed the hungry multitude; He demonstrated the power of Life to heal the sick; He demonstrated the Wisdom which is beyond the limited consciousness of Man, and He demonstrated wealth; and finally, He demonstrated power over death.

And He told them how He did what He did, and how any other man might do the same, and even greater works.

The method of attaining cosmic consciousness we will consider in the next chapter.

7. ATTAINING COSMIC CONSCIOUSNESS

"And this is Life Eternal: to know God."

Cosmic consciousness or conscious unity with Eternal Spirit can only be attained by a continuous and sustained effort on the part of man. The extension of consciousness always requires a mental effort; and this mental effort, when it is a seeking for unity with Spirit, constitutes prayer.

Prayer is an effort of the human mind to become acquainted with God. It is not an effort to establish a relationship which does not exist, but to fully comprehend and recognize a relationship which already exists. Prayer can have but one object, and that is unity with Spirit; for all other things are included in that.

We do not really seek, through prayer, to get health, peace, power or wealth; we seek to get unity with God; and when we get unity with God, health, peace, power and wealth are ours without asking. Study the intercessory prayer, as it is called, in the seventeenth chapter of John, and you will see that Jesus asks nothing for men except that they may be one in mind with God. This is the one thing needful; all other things are contained in it.

Whoever has full spiritual consciousness has health, peace, power and wealth.

Oneness Through Prayer and Will

Jesus laid great stress on prayer in His teachings, and demonstrated His reliance upon it in His daily practice. The gospels abound with references to His praying; to His going apart to pray, continuing all night in prayer, and so on. It is evident that His consciousness that He and the Father were one was only retained by persistently and continuously affirming and reaffirming the fact. This fact, it must be remembered, is in direct contradiction to our objective consciousness.

We appear to think, live, move and have our being entirely in ourselves and of ourselves; our physical senses deny the existence of a God. God is not found by extending the outward or objective consciousness. 'God is Spirit,' said Jesus, 'and they who approach Him must approach Him through their own spirits.'

To attain cosmic consciousness, the effort of prayer must be, first to arouse to activity the spirit in man and second, to unite that spirit in conscious union with God. The spirit of man -the ego- the man himself, is aroused whenever the will acts. Only the man himself can will; and when he wills it is his whole personality which comes into action.

We see, then, that Jesus was perfectly scientific in laying down His first requirement for attaining cosmic consciousness-that one must will to do the will of God. He plainly ascribes His own power to His setting His will to do the will of Cosmic Spirit; and He says;

"He that willeth to do the will of God shall know."

To will to do the will of the Father, to keep His sayings, to do His works; this was the first step toward unity. And the next was the prayer of faith.

The Prayer of Faith

The prayer of faith is clearly described in Mark 11:23-24.

"Whosoever shall say unto this mountain, Be thou removed, and be thou cast into the sea; and shall not doubt in his heart, but shall believe that those things which he saith shall come to pass; he shall have whatsoever he saith. "Therefore, I say unto you, what things soever ye desire when ye pray, believe that ye receive them (now), and ye shall have them."

We see, here, that the prayer of faith cannot be offered twice for the same thing. As soon as you have asked, if you have real faith, your prayer changes to an affirmation of possession. Having willed to do the will of God, and having asked God to receive you into Himself, nothing is left you but to declare, "I and my Father are one."

This is the point which has been missed by most commentators - that the prayer of faith, when uttered, becomes an affirmation of possession. You cannot continue to pray for a thing when you believe that you receive it; you can only return thanks and assert that it is yours.

The Process of Receiving

First, will to do the will of God, and then (2) pray that you may be one with Him; and then (3) affirm, "I and my father are one." And when you have definitely established in your consciousness the fact of your unity with Spirit, then draw your deductions of health, peace, power and wealth from this fact, and affirm them; otherwise you may not demonstrate them, for while they are all included in the fact of your unity with God, the mere assertion of that may not bring all the corollaries to your consciousness.

When the disciples came to Jesus asking Him to teach them to pray, He gave them the Lord's prayer; and it begins; "Thy kingdom come." When one has said that, he has asked for all there is; in the Kingdom of God no one would be without daily bread, or suffer evil; but these things are included in the prayer in order to make the thing prayed for more definite to the understanding.

So, the general affirmation of unity with God is not sufficiently definite to bring us health, peace, power and wealth; we do not clearly understand that these are included, and it is better to affirm them. But we must be definite and specific in our understanding of the fact of our unity with God.

"That Mind Which Was in Christ Jesus"

"I and my Father are one." That is good, but it does not convey the idea to the modern mind with sufficient distinctness.

"There is one Intelligence, and I am one with that Intelligence." Better, but somewhat clumsy.

"There is one MIND, and I am that MIND." That is a most clear-cut and concise statement of the fact; it would be hard to put it more tersely.

"There is ONE MIND." When you say that, think of the one Intelligence, permeating all things, vitalizing all things, giving coherence and purpose to all things. Get your thought fixed on this MIND, so that it seems to you that you can see and feel it! Then say: "I AM that MIND."

It is that MIND which is speaking, when I speak; which is acting when I act.

I-AM-that-MIND.

It takes affirming and reaffirming to get this fact fixed in consciousness, but all the time you put into the work is most profitably spent. You can well afford to go, as Jesus did, into the desert to fast and meditate for forty days; you can well afford to spend whole nights in prayer, if by doing so you can arrive at a full consciousness of your unity with God.

For then you will have entered the Kingdom.

"There is one MIND, and I am that MIND." Say it continuously, and always when you say it, try to comprehend all that it means. You; you who speak, are eternal mind; eternal power; eternal life.

All things are yours, and all things are possible unto you, when once you have banished the false idea of separateness from your consciousness.

Your word will be with power, and you will speak as one having authority; you will demonstrate health, power, wealth and wisdom, when the consciousness that you are the ETERNAL ONE has obtained complete possession of your mind, objective and subjective. And you can bring this about; only faith and continuing in affirmation while you will to do the will of God, are required.

8. DEMONSTRATION AND ATTAINMENT

After you have affirmed and reaffirmed your unity with the One Mind until that unity has become a fact present to your consciousness, the next step is to become Life-conscious.

Understand that the Mind is a living mind; that it is life, itself. If yu are Mind, you are also Life. There is only one Life, which is in all, and through all; and you are that Life.

So, follow your first affirmation with this; "That MIND is eternal, and it is LIFE; I am that MIND, and I am ETERNAL LIFE."

Repeat this until you have thoroughly stamped it upon your mentality, both conscious and subconscious; until you habitually think of yourself as life, and as eternal life. Now, you habitually think of yourself as a dying being, or as one moving on toward age and decay; this is an error, born of holding separate consciousness. Meet every suggestion of age, decay or death with the positive assertion: "I am ETERNAL LIFE."

Jesus said: "And this is life eternal; to know thee, the LIVING God." To know God is to be conscious of your unity with Him; how else can you know him?"

Health Consciousness

After Life-consciousness is attained, the step to Health-consciousness is easy. The One Mind is the living stuff from which you are made; and it is Pure Life. Life must be Health; it is inconceivable that an inflow of pure life should carry with it anything but health. A fountain cannot send forth sweet and bitter at the same time. A good tree cannot bring forth corrupt fruit. Light hath no fellowship with darkness. The One Mind cannot know disease; can have no consciousness of disease.

The consciousness of disease is an error, the result of judging by appearances; and we judge by appearances only so long as we retain the separate consciousness. One cannot be Life-conscious and conscious of disease at the same time; when we become fully life- conscious we lose the disease-consciousness. So, the next affirmation is; "That Mind knows no disease; I am that Mind and I am HEALTH." Affirm it with faith; it will cure every sickness, if the affirmation is made in the consciousness that you and your Father are one.

Power Consciousness

Next comes power-consciousness; and the affirmation for this is: "That Mind is the source of all POWER, and cannot know doubt nor fear; I am that Mind, and I am PEACE and POWER."

It needs no argument to show that the source of all power cannot be afraid of anything; what could there be for it to be afraid of? Nor can the source of all power have doubts as to its being able to do any conceivable thing, or to cope with any possible combination of circumstances; what is there that all the power there is cannot do?

It is only when you conceive of yourself as separate from this power that you begin to have doubts as to your ability to do things; it is only as you hold this separate consciousness that you can be afraid.

Jesus never showed any doubt; nor did He ever manifest fear. He knew that no harm could come to Him, against His will; and none did. He was not crucified because His enemies gained a victory over Him; He went voluntarily to the cross, to make a demonstration which should finally show the truth to His disciples. "No man takes my life," said He, "I lay it down of myself; I have power to lay it down, and I have power to take it again" (John 10:18).

To have power-consciousness gives poise; poise is the peaceful consciousness of power and is the result of affirming unity with power until it becomes a present fact in consciousness. "Peace I leave with you; my peace I give unto you. Let not your heart be troubled; neither let it be afraid."

You cannot keep your heart from being afraid if you retain consciousness of yourself as something apart from Power. So, understand and affirm that you are one with Power.

Wisdom Consciousness

Wisdom-consciousness is next. Power without wisdom may be a dreadful and destructive thing, like the strength of the runaway horse; and power can be constructive only when wisely applied. So we must affirm the fact of our wisdom. The One Mind, being the source of all things, must know all things from the beginning; must know all truth.

The mind which knows all truth cannot be mistaken; mistakes are caused by a partial knowledge of the truth. Such a mind cannot know error. Knowing ALL truth, it can only act along the lines of perfect truth; it can only entertain in consciousness the idea of perfect truth.

It cannot know good from evil; it can know only the good. To recognize anything as evil, a mind must have only a partial knowledge, and a limited consciousness. What seems to be evil is always the result of partial knowledge. Where knowledge is perfect, there is no evil; and no one can be conscious of that which does not exist.

"God is light and in him is no darkness at all." "God is of too pure eyes to behold evil, and cannot look upon iniquity."

When we become conscious of ALL truth, we lose the consciousness of evil.

With complete consciousness judgment becomes impossible, for there is nothing to judge. You do not have to exercise judgment when you know the right way; you do not sit in judgment on others where there is no evil.

So Jesus said; "Ye judge after the flesh; I judge no man." "I am come, not to judge the world, but to save the world." "The Father judgeth no man."

Where evil and error are non-existent, there can be no judgment. To rise above the error of belief in evil, use this affirmation; "That Mind knows only TRUTH, and knows ALL truth; I am that Mind, and I am KNOWLEDGE and WISDOM."

Wealth Consciousness

Having attained consciousness of eternal life, of health, power, and wisdom, what else do you need? Wealth-consciousness; the assurance of affluence and abundance.

The one Mind is the original substance, from which all things proceed forth. There is only one element; all things are formed of one stuff.

Science is now precipitating sugar, coloring matter, and other substances from the atmosphere; that seems to be akin to what Jesus did when He fed the multitude, in the so-called miracles of the loaves and fishes. The elements which compose all visible nature are in the atmosphere, waiting to be organized into form;

and the atmosphere itself is only a condensed and palpable form of the one original substance - Spirit - God.

All things are made from, and made of, one living intelligent substance; One Mind, and you are that Mind. Therefore, you are the substance from which all things are made, and you are also the Power which makes and forms; you are wealth and abundance, for you are all there is.

So, affirm; "All things, created and uncreated, are in that Mind; I am that Mind, and I am WEALTH and PLENTY."

I Am the Way, Truth, Life

Lastly, say; "I am the WAY, and the TRUTH, and the LIFE; the LIGHT in me shines out to bless the world."

This will give you love-consciousness: the will to bless, and the will to love. Eternal life; health; power and peace; wisdom; wealth; and love; when you are conscious of all these, you have attained cosmic consciousness; you are in Christ and Christ is in you.

Statement of Being

There is one Mind, and I AM that Mind. That Mind is eternal, and it is Life.

I am that Mind, and I am ETERNAL LIFE.

That Mind knows no disease; I am that Mind, and I am HEALTH. That Mind is the source of all Power, and cannot know doubt nor fear; I am that Mind, and I am POWER and PEACE.

That Mind knows only Truth and knows ALL truth; I am that Mind, and I am KNOWLEDGE and WISDOM.

All things created and uncreated, are in that Mind; I am that Mind, and I am WEALTH and PLENTY.

I am the WAY, and the TRUTH, and the LIFE; the LIGHT in me shines out to bless the world.

BOOK SIX
JESUS, THE MAN AND HIS WORK*

* This booklet is a lecture delivered at the Auditorium, Cincinnati, November 11, 1905, under the auspices of the local branch of the Socialist Party. It made so favorable an impression on certain listeners that they determined to have it printed. Years later, the author developed "A New Christ" based on these ideas.

Jesus: The Man and His Work

It is doubtful if any man was ever more misunderstood by the people of His own time than Jesus of Nazareth. Certainly no man was ever more grossly misrepresented by succeeding generations, and especially by those who professed to be His friends and followers.

The Christian religion was first recognized by the powers of the state at an era when the interests of the ruling class demanded the utmost submission and conformity on the part of the people; and out of the needs of the kingly and priestly classes for a religious ideal which should induce men to be contented with slavery, to bow their necks to the yoke of taxation, and to submit to every form of economic evil without protest, was born the concept of the message, and of the personal character of Jesus which is accepted as orthodox today.

The picture of the man Jesus which you hold in your minds has been drawn far more from the poetry of Isaiah, written 700 years before He was born, than from the four gospels, which purport to be narratives of eye witnesses of His life and works. Such passages in Isaiah as: "He is despised and rejected of men; a man of sorrows and acquainted with grief: and we hid as it were our faces from him; he was oppressed, and he was afflicted and he opened not his mouth; he is brought as a lamb to the slaughter, and as a sheep before her shearers is dumb, so he opened not his mouth," have been quoted to show the meekness and the humility, the submissive spirit with which Christ endured wrong and injustice; and we have had held up as the saviour of the world a despised, friendless, poverty-stricken laborer whom the upper classes regarded with scorn because of his lowly origin and station; who had no friends save fisherman, laborers, outcasts and sinners; who was often shelterless and hungry, and who bore insults and persecutions with meek submission and walked about a scornful world with his hands always uplifted in loving benediction.

And this character is held up to us as the Christian ideal. Be meek. Be submissive. Be lamb-like or sheep-like. Bow your head before the persecutor and "hump" your back to the shearer. Rejoice that it is given you to be fleeced for the glory of God. It is a good religion - for the man with the shears.

The Christ who is held up in the orthodox pulpit is rather a weak character. He is not the kind of man we would nominate for president. His followers have very little confidence in him as a practical teacher of business ethics. They have great faith in him as a revealer of spiritual things, but none at all as an organizer of the affairs of this world. If it were telegraphed over the country this afternoon that the president has resigned and that Jesus would take his place tomorrow, 95 percent of Christian business men would draw their money out of the banks for fear that Jesus would inaugurate a panic.

Jesus said of Himself, "If I be lifted up I will draw all men unto me." Well, He has not drawn all men, not even a majority of men, and I am inclined to think that He has never been lifted up. An unreal, imaginary character is being lifted up instead, and men are not being drawn by it.

Near a certain Indiana town there is a neighborhood peopled by an Amish sect. They all wear flat black hats and plain black clothes which they fasten with hooks and eyes, because buttons are not Christ like; they shave their upper lip, cut the beard square across the chin, and the hair square also. It is said that when one of the brethren needs a hair-cut his wife turns a bowl or basin bottom upward over his head and cuts away all the hair that comes below it. Attired in this fashion, and in a very strong odor of sanctity, two of these brethren were walking in the street one day, and were met by an old farmer, a typical Hoosier character. After looking them over critically, he accosted them thus: "Say, why don't you fellows get your hair cut an' shave?" "We attire ourselves thus," said one, "because we want to look like our Savior." "Did the Savior look like you?" asked the farmer. "We believe he did." "Well," said the old man, positively, "darned if I blame the Jews for killin' him, then."

The brethren were holding up a false Christ, and so the old man was not attracted; and I want to prove to you today that the church, everywhere, is holding up a false Christ; I want to show Him to you as He was and is, the Supreme Man - the Highest Type, the incarnation and revelation of that One Great Life which is above all and through all and in us all, lifting us all toward unity with one another and with Him.

It is my task to rescue Christ From Christianity.

In the first place, then, Jesus was not despised because He was a workingman. Custom required every Jewish Rabbi, or learned man to have a trade. We read in the Talmud of Rabbi Johanan, the blacksmith, and of Rabbi Isaac, the shoemaker, learned and highly honored men. Rabbi Jesus, the carpenter would be spoken of in the same way. St. Paul, a very learned man, was a tent-maker by trade. Jesus could not, in that time and place have been despised for His station or His birth. Indeed, He was popularly supposed to be an aristocrat by birth, a son of the royal house and was frequently saluted as the son of David.

Second. He was not despised for ignorance. He was a very learned man. Whenever He went into a synagogue He was selected to read the law and teach the congregation, as the one best qualified for that work. Luke says: "There went fame of him through all the region round about and he taught in their synagogues being glorified of all." In those times of fierce religious controversy no unlearned man could have held his own in such a fashion. He was thoroughly versed in the Jewish law; the way that He silenced his adversaries with apt quotations shows Him to have been letter-perfect. Even His enemies always addressed him as Master or Teacher, acknowledging His profound learning.

Third. He was not despised for His poverty. He had many wealthy and influential friends. Lazarus and his sisters were people of consequence. Luke says that Joanna, the wife of Chuza, the king's steward, and other women ministered unto him of their substance - that is, were supporters of His work. The king's steward was a high official, and his wife was a prominent lady. Joseph of Arimathea, who came after His body, was a well-to-do man. So probably, was Nicodemus. Jesus healed the sick in the families of rulers and of high officials, and they appear to have responded liberally in supplying His financial needs. True, He owned no real estate; but He dressed expensively, and never lacked for money.

When He was crucified His clothing was too fine to cut up, and so the soldiers cast lots for it; on the night of His betrayal, when Judas went out, it was supposed that he had gone to give something to the poor. It must have been their custom to give away money. In that country and climate their wants were few and simple, and were fully supplied. Jesus wore fine clothes and had plenty to eat and drink and had money to give away.

Read the four gospels, and you can come to no other conclusion. Jesus was not humble, in the accepted sense. He did not go about with downcast look, and a general attitude of asking permission to stay on earth. He was a man of the most impressive, commanding and powerful personal appearance. He "spoke as one having authority" and frequently we are told that great awe and fear came upon the people at His mighty words and works. In one place they were so frightened that they besought Him to leave; and John tells how certain officers sent to arrest Him in the market place lost their nerve in His commanding presence, and went back saying, "Surely never man spake like this man."

On the night of His arrest a bank of soldiers approached Him in the grove, and asked for Jesus of Nazareth; and when He answered, "I am he," such was His majesty and psychic power that they prostrated themselves; "they went backward" the account says, "and fell to the ground." Does this man I am describing seem to you like one of our Amish, or even like one of our Methodists? Yet this is the Christ of the four gospels. I would like to see one of His present-day followers knock down a platoon of policeman by saying "I am he."

Now, to be Christ-like in personality a man must be learned, well dressed, well supplied with money and be of noble and commanding appearance, speaking with authority, and possessing tremendous magnetic power.

What now, of the Christ-like attitude toward the world? One of the very best ways to understand that is by studying His reasons for taking the title He assumed - the Son of Man. He rarely spoke of Himself in any other way. This term, son of man, was common in the Jewish prophecies. It was simply an emphatic way of saying Man. If you wanted to emphasize your Methodism, you might say, "I am a son of Wesley," and if you wanted to emphasize your humanity, as Jesus did, "I am a son of man."

Why did He lay stress upon the fact that He was a man? You will note the position. The son of Wesley will stand for Methodism, and the son of Calvin will stand for Calvinism, but the Son of Man must stand for humanity.

The Roman empire was a great taxing machine. In the conquered provinces, the people were left, as far as possible, with their own local government and institutions of justice, the function of the Roman officials being to extort tribute, or collect taxes. Every form of extortion was practiced by governors, procurators and tax- collectors upon those who were able to pay. Open robbery, torture, kidnapping, false accusation, outrage of every kind might be practiced upon the man who had money to tempt the cupidity of the higher powers. And as the oppressed property holders had no way to meet the extractions of government but by oppressing the poor, the condition of the masses was pitiful indeed. You will readily see that the business and property-owning classes had to get the money to pay their taxes by exploiting the poor in some way.

It is an economic axiom which is indisputable that all taxation of whatever kind, upon whomsoever levied, is wrung at last from the hard hands of the toiling poor; that is the reason they are poor. To give you an idea as to how oppressive this taxation was, we may estimate from certain passages in Josephus that the private income of Herod the Great was three and one-half millions of dollars a year. That is not as much, of course, as the income of our president today, but he has a very much larger country, and more people to tax, and while he is not allowed to use some of Herod's most effective methods, he has others of his own which lay the crude ways of the monarchs of antiquity very far in the shade.

The enormous sums which were collected from that little province brought the unhappy toilers down to the last extremity of destruction; they could go no lower and live. In Judea, at this time there were several religious sects, which were also in a way political parties, scheming for place and power, and for influence with Rome. The Pharisees, Saducees, Essenes, Samaritans, etc., disagreed on various questions, as the interpretation of prophecy, the existence of angels, the resurrection of the dead, baptism, and so on. The strife between these parties was desperately acrimonious and bitter, often to the point of personal violence. Their arguments frequently ended in riots. You will notice, as you read, that they were always ready to "take up stones" to end a dispute; often only the commanding personality of Jesus saved him from being stoned by these religious mobs. These sects were intensely eager to make converts, or proselytes. Jesus says of them that they would compass sea and land to add one to their number.

Below all these middle-class disputants were the common people, sunk in the most abject poverty - taxed, beaten, outraged, robbed, slaughtered, and no voice lifted anywhere in their behalf. No one, Jew or Gentile, thought of demanding justice for the mongrel multitude. It is said of Jesus that He had "compassion on the multitude because they fainted and were amazed, and were like sheep without a shepherd." They had plenty of shepherds to baptize them, to interpret prophecy for them, to instruct them in "spiritual" things, and even to shear them; but none to demand a lightening of their burdens - none to cry out in their behalf for justice.

There are still shepherds who are far more concerned about correctness of doctrine than about justice. Into this maze of oppression, taxation, murder, outrage and theological discussion comes the grand figure of the Christ, saying: "The Spirit of the Lord is upon me, because he has anointed me to preach good news to the poor. I am no Pharisee; I am no Saducee; I am no Essene or Samaritan: I am a man! I come, not on behalf of Phariseeism or Samaritanism, but on behalf of humanity." A new note in religion; a new attitude. No wonder they were "amazed at his doctrine." No wonder His word was with power. No wonder they said "he speaketh as one having authority."

In John's gospel, Jesus says of Himself that the Father hath given Him authority to execute judgement because He is a man. I say that this is the only reason God ever had for giving authority to any man, and I say that if there is a man anywhere today upon whom the divine sanction rests it is not because he is a Pharisee or a Saducee, a Methodist, Presbyterian, Republican or Democrat, but because he is a man. And I also say that among all those who claim leadership today, by virtue of divine anointment, we may apply this test with certainty - that the man who stands for humanity, first, last and all the time, against all vested interests, religious and political, is the man who stands with God. He and he only, is in the true Christian attitude - the attitude that Jesus took.

And because He took this position; because He stood for humanity against the vested religious interests of His time, He was called an infidel; because He stood for humanity against the vested economic and political interests of His time He was called a traitor. Jesus was crucified on the charges of infidelity and treason; and He was guilty - legally - on both counts. I know no prouder titles, when justly acquired, than these: Infidel and Traitor! I pray that Great Intelligence, before whose eye all the affairs of men are spread, to write opposite my name in the book of His remembrance, Infidel - Traitor: Infidel to every church that apologizes for economic injustice; Traitor to every government that assists in the exploitation of the poor. The only sinful infidelity is infidelity to the truth; the only vile treason is treason to the weak. This was the attitude that Jesus took; He expressed all this when He assumed the title which made Him the champion of humanity - when He said, "I am the son of man." And He gave all this full expression in His teachings.

Let me quote from the sermon on the mount: "Ye have heard that it was said by them of old time, thou shalt not kill; and whosoever shall kill shall be in danger of the judgement; but I say unto you that whosoever is angry with his brother shall be in danger of the judgement, and whosoever shall say unto his brother 'Raca,' shall be in danger of the council, but whosoever shall say 'thou fool,' shall be in danger of hell fire." The expression "thou fool," does not clearly interpret the original; it would be better rendered by the phrase "you are no good," or "you are worthless.

Let me illustrate the meaning of this passage to you. I was sitting in a hotel lobby when the news came in of an Indiana coal mine horror, in which a number of poor fellows lost their lives. Two well-dressed men were discussing the affair, and one said: "Oh, well, it's only a couple of Hungarians less! A million more are ready to step into their shoes tomorrow. The world hasn't lost anything." Jesus says, whosoever shall speak of a man like that is in danger of hell fire. That is the exact meaning of this passage. The responsibility of all murder rests on those who degrade the public estimate of the value of human life. The killing of Filippinos on behalf of our commercial interests is paving the way for the killing of Americans in the streets of our own cities, on behalf of those same "interests." The talk of "inferior races" is but a prelude to the talk of "lower classes." Whoever talks so is in danger of hell fire.

The doctrine of hell itself, is born of the infamous idea that there are some classes of men who are specially valuable to God; and those who teach such blasphemies walk ever on the crumbling verge of that black pit, wherein gleam the fires of eternal wrath. If anybody goes to hell, it will be those who degrade humanity.

This is what Jesus said. Now, if you turn to the 12th chapter of Matthew, you will read that the disciples were crossing the fields on the Sabbath day, and that they plucked the ears of corn and ate as they went. This gave great offense to the Pharisees. They were not offended because they took the grain, for under law the right of a hungry man to life transcended the property rights of the owner of the field; none might say the famished wayfarer nay if he chose to pluck and eat. It was not, I say, because they ate, that the Pharisees were angry, but because the thing was done upon the Sabbath day. The Pharisees thought that the thing most valuable to God was their church, with its institutions and observances. They would not break the Sabbath to feed the hungry; they would not break it to heal the sick. God cared more for the institution than He did for the man.

And so they complained to Jesus; and He answered them: "Have ye not heard what David did when he was hungry, he and they that were with him?" and He went on to tell them how David and his companions - and David's companions at that time were a mighty tough gang - went into the temple itself, and took the shew-bread, which was sacred, and ate it - and God approved. "One standeth here," said Jesus, "greater than the temple." God cares more for a hungry man than he does for a holy house.

In Mark 2, where the same story is told, he adds: "The Sabbath was made for man, and not man for the Sabbath." Here is defined sharply the issue between Jesus and His opponents. They were exalting the worship, the temple, the Sabbath, the ceremonial. He exalted the man. And I for one, agree with Jesus. I feel no reverence for buildings, even though they may be magnificent structures, where a dim light falls through stained glass windows upon the structured forms of saints, and where robed priests chant in solemn ceremony; these things move me not at all. But when I stand in a school room and look into the bright faces of a hundred boys and girls - when I stand in the crowded market-place or in a factory, where my brothers and sisters toil to supply the needs of the world, and I realize that every life before me contains possibilities as boundless as the universe itself; when I stand in the presence of this toiling, suffering, loving, seeking, glorious, common humanity, I bare my head and bow in reverence, for here indeed I am in the very presence of Almighty God. One is here greater than the temple, greater than the church, greater than the Sabbath.

God has a higher call for men than the observation of certain days, or the keeping of certain places holy. This whole earth is a most holy place because it is consecrated by the love of God to fulfill His purpose in the high destiny of man.

Is not this the only rational interpretation of these sayings of Christ? Have you ever heard it so in church? Theirs is a metaphysical Christ, a false Christ. This Christ I hold up today is the real Saviour.

The trouble with the churches is that they are all too much like one in Washington. It was a Calvanistic church - a very solemn place. Washington is a solemn place anyway, for people who believe in hell - they are so near their finish. A good old Methodist woman strayed into this church one Sunday and sat down. The preacher was eloquent, and presently the old lady, greatly moved, shouted heartily, "Amen!" An usher touched her gently on the shoulder and whispered: "Madam, you will please keep still." She subsided, but under the influence of the eloquent sermon, she lost herself again directly, and shouted: "Glory to God!". Again came the usher with his whispered reproof. "But sir," she said, "I've got religion." "Oh, well, madam," he answered, "this is no place to have religion." You laugh. Perhaps you know of churches where anything is more welcome than religion.

"And Jesus took a little child, and set him in the midst and said:

'Whosoever shall humble himself as this little child shall be great in the kingdom of heaven.'" You have, no doubt, seen a great many pictures of Jesus as he blessed the little children, and you have always seen Him surrounded by prettily dressed ladies, who were bringing nice, clean babies - the kind of children it is easy to love; the kind you cannot help blessing.

The gentlemen who draw these pictures cater more to the artistic sense than to a desire to represent accurately the facts in the case.

That was undoubtedly a slave child; a child of the abyss; unwashed, uncombed, covered with vermin; human in His suffering, in His capacity for pain, but with the better portion of His humanity lying dormant in His soul visible to God but not to men. And He said, "Whoso receiveth one such little child, receiveth me."

There are a good many children in whom you find it hard to see the Christ, are there not? Let me do for you, my friends, what Jesus did for His hearers; let me bring a little child, and set Him here before you.

I went into a tenement building in the city of Chicago, one hot afternoon in the season when those buildings become great superheated ovens, with a doctor, to see some children who were sick. In one room we found a little boy - a very little boy indeed - who was dying with a fever. The room was squalid and intensely hot; there were three other children, dirty and uncared for. The mother was giving all her time to her sick baby, wetting his parched and bleeding lips, and trying by every poor device at her command to lessen his suffering. The doctor said to me that day: "I can go where grown people are dying, or dead, without being overmuch moved; I can go where children are dead, and thank God; but when I go in where these children are sick, and see what they have to bear, and how they bear it, it breaks me down and unmans me quite. I cannot bear to see it."

Poor little boy, with his bright eyes and flushed cheeks, he lay quite patiently, and only the restless movement of the wasted little hands upon the quilt betrayed his suffering. He spoke to his mother: "Mamma," he said, "it is time for papa to come in." The father was a stationary engineer, who worked nearby, and it seemed that it was his custom to leave his work, now and again to run in and see his child. "Yes, honey," the mother answered, "papa will be here pretty soon." "Mamma," the child said, "when papa comes he'll say 'how is my little man' and I'll say 'all right,' so he will be glad. Don't tell him I am dying, but I think I am."

He was thinking, you see, not of himself, even in the hour of his extremity, but of his father. Well, presently the father came into the room. He was a rough, wild looking man, with uncombed hair and beard, clad only in a shirt and overalls, his face and bare arms black with coal. I have no doubt he was an ignorant man, as books go. I have no doubt he was a bad man from the orthodox and conventional standpoint; I presume he sometimes swore, and played cards for the beer, and did other dreadful things.

As he came in, he glanced anxiously at his wife, and then at us, and read the worst of tidings in our faces. His own face quivered, and his bearded lips twisted strangely; then, for the child's sake, he forced a cheerful smile and came across the room toward the bed; and as he came, upon his coal-grimed features shone with transfiguring light a father-love as holy as the love of God Himself.

The father bent above the cot. "How is my little man?" he asked. And the feeble voice piped bravely, while the parched lips writhed in a pitiful attempt to smile: "I'm all right, papa; I'm all right." It broke the man down. He burst out sobbing, and springing to his feet rushed out upon the landing to struggle for self-control. The mother, also sobbing bitterly, bent over her child again; and down the poor child's cheek rolled just one tear - of pity - for his father. That was a "cheap" child; one of the "lower" classes. Not one of the "fittest" to survive - and so he died.

Jesus took a little child and set him in the midst of them, and said: "Whosoever shall offend one of these little ones it is better that a millstone were hanged around his neck, and he were cast into the sea." Yes, any man, or woman, or railroad system, or financial system or industrial order that stands between the child and life, is under the curse of God. I say, with Jesus, that it is more important that justice be done to one such little child than that all the corn crops of a thousand years be saved.

"Whoso shall humble himself as this little child, the same shall be great in the kingdom of heaven." How can you humble yourself as such a child? Does it mean to be childlike in spirit, teachable, credulous? No; there is only one way. Stand beside that child of the abyss and say, "Before God he is as good as I. He is entitled to everything I claim for myself and for my children, and I will never rest until all I claim for myself and mine is assured for him also." Then you will begin to be great in the Kingdom of God.

How can I love my neighbor as myself? How can I love that child as I do my own children?

One day Jesus was talking to the folks and He said: "Why are you worried about things to eat and wear? Seek a just and righteous order of things and you will have plenty." I am here to testify that Jesus told the truth. This world would produce food for ten times its population. It would clothe ten times its population more richly than Solomon was arrayed in all his glory. It would furnish building material to erect a palace larger than Rockefeller mansions for every family that lives on it. Our Father has provided the raw material for the things essential to life a thousandfold more than we can use. The race is rich, abundantly rich, as a whole. The satisfaction of human needs is a problem of machinery and organization. We have the machinery pretty well perfected. It is now a problem of organization.

Seek the Father's kingdom, says Jesus, and you solve the bread and butter problem. What is a father's kingdom like? A yonder comrade, let us say, is the father of a family, and he sees his children gather about a table where he has provided bountifully for them all, as our Father has for us. Well, the biggest boy gets to the table first, and he gathers all the good things around his plate, and gets his arms around them; his little sister reaches for a piece and he slaps her; he strikes back the outstretched hands of the others and says: "Get away! Our father put this here and I've got here first and it's mine! Get away," (strike, push, shove), and looking up to the father he says, "Our father (strike), thy kingdom come (biff), thy will be done" (bang). Would not that father say, "My will will not be done until your brothers and sisters have an equal chance." And if the big boy should say "Well then, father, I will hold it as your trustee, and I will give the others what they need, if I can spare it." Would not the father say, "My kingdom does not consist in benevolence or charity, or self-denial, or sacrifice, or worship, or Sabbath observance, but in justice for all."

Jesus pointed out that the birds are not worried about getting something to eat. They live in the kingdom of God. We live in the kingdom of Caesar. If the time ever comes when some of the smart birds get a corner on bugs or organize a worm trust, there will be worry among them also.

Now, so far as nature is concerned there is nothing to prevent me from loving my neighbor as myself. There is plenty for him and me, too. And just what does it mean this loving ones neighbor as himself? Suppose my wife and I sat down at the table and we had nothing to eat but a crust of bread and a piece of pie. And suppose I reach out and get the pie and say, "My dear wife, how I love you! I do wish you had some pie!" and I swallow it and leave her to gnaw the crust. Which do I love best, myself or her? If I love her as myself, will I consent to hog the pie? If I love her as myself what I try to get for myself I will try to get for her. If I love you as myself, what I try to get for myself I will try to get for you, and what I try to get for my children, I will try to get for yours and I will no more rest under an injustice done to your children than if it were done to my children.

Now can you imagine a state of society in which the good thing I do for myself shall be done for you also? I spoke one night in Chicago and at the close I got on a street car and stood beside a girl who had been one of the listeners, and she spoke to me. "Mister," she said, "I heard your speech and I liked it very much. I'm only a poor, ignorant girl but I've thought of these things, and the world as it is reminds me of one of these big jack screws they lift buildings with - you turn a handle round and round and the center part is lifted up. So, it seems as though we poor folks are at the handle. We go round forever and never get any higher. We are always in the same place. We go round to lift somebody else. And I thought it might be fixed like one of those winding stair-cases so that as we all went round we all might go up together, and the work we all do would help us all, and if a few people didn't get quite so high, some day we would all come to the top together and that would be better for us all." And I thought that if I had the power I would make all the college professors and preachers and the teachers go and sit at that poor girl's feet and learn a little political economy.

These things are hidden from the wise and prudent and revealed unto babes. The pure in heart shall see God. The average man is so wedded to the idea of the divine origin of the present order that he cannot conceive of the possibility of a change. He will not investigate, he will not consider; he simply says, "It can't be done." He is like the old Tennesseean who did not believe in railroads. They built a railroad through his vicinity and the neighbors got him to go down one day to look at the track. They had laid the track down to the river bank and had tunneled on the opposite side under a hill, but had not commenced to build the bridge. The old man took one look - that was enough. He didn't stop to ask questions. He threw up his hands and said: "Oh, by thunder, you needn't tell me that you can make an engine that will jump that river and hit that hole in the hill! It can't be did."

Have you ever thought, oh ye of little faith, that there is a way to bridge this chasm between individual effort and united effort? Consider for a moment our public school system. We are educating our children by uniting our effort. We hold the school property in common. You are a proprietor in the school property of Marion, Ind. I am a part owner of the school property in Cincinnati. So far as that work is concerned we are all one family, are we not? It is our father's kingdom, in part, established in the midst of Caesar's kingdom, isn't it?

Suppose, in my love for my children, I devise a new text book or a more convenient desk or a more comfortable seat, anything that makes their work easier or betters the school service - then I get it adopted, and I have helped my own children, I have helped your children, I have helped every child from Maine to California. I have brightened every life and added to the happiness of every home, I have loved all as well as my own. This is the spiral stairway plan. I like it better myself than the jack screw method.

Industry is on the other plan. If I invent a new laborsaving machine, I cause hundreds of my brothers to lose their chance to make a living, and make the problem more intense for all. Suppose the factory were like the school, an institution set apart for the supplying of a common need by united effort, would it be so? If I could, by some device, lighten my own task I would bring rest to all, and there, again, I would love my neighbor as myself.

The apostles understood it so. They started out to build a unified and harmonious world. Read the second and fourth chapters of the Acts of Apostles, and read the writings of the early Christian fathers, and you will see that the idea of Jesus and the apostles was not to build an institution for worship in a bad world, but to build the world itself into a united, harmonious, orderly and scientific society. To make society a spiral stairway, up which a redeemed humanity should march together into unity with God. They had all things common. There was no poverty among them that was not shared by all. The early churches were little commonwealths, and the purpose which they held with intense enthusiasm was the building of the world into one great commonwealth.

The Apostles were communist organizers. The purpose of Jesus, as understood by them, was the establishment of a scientific society, which he called by its true name - the Kingdom of God; a world of unified effort, centering in the development of the little child. It was this glorious vision which gave virility and power to the preaching of the early church, and the church of today has no power because it has no purpose and no hope.

Dr. Quayle, of Indianapolis, has written a little pamphlet in which he argues that the Apostles were mistaken in their sociology. He holds that they were all right in their theology - inspired and infallible - but they were poor business men. I would suppose that the same Holy Spirit who gave them their theology must have given them their social ideas also. The communistic regime was as much a part of the life of the church as the Lord's Supper, and was far more clearly drawn from the teachings of the Master. Dr. Quayle's attitude is equivalent to saying that the Holy Ghost is an excellent old personage, very correct on doctrinal matters, but a little off when we come to the practical affairs of life.

That is exactly the attitude of the church today toward Jesus. Every modern preacher, with few exceptions, denies his Master whenever he speaks of social problems. I am not going to rail at the church; but the church charges us with infidelity, with atheism and immorality, and I am going to reply with a statement of the case and with a counter charge.

Those of you who have read Elbert Hubbard's article on the cotton mills of South Carolina, will never forget that realistic description of the awful conditions. How the thousands of baby slaves are gathered in by fraud, misrepresentation and by tempting the cupidity of their fathers; how the long hours, the close application, and the flying lint combine to break down their feeble bodies so certainly and so speedily that the average life of a child condemned to one of these hells is only four years. It is organized murder on a wholesale scale; it is cruelty beyond words; outrage so infinite as to be inexpressible. And near many of these slaughter- houses you will find a church, built by the child-killing corporation, and there is a preacher whose salary is paid from the pitiful stipend of the dying children. In some cases it is even reported that a regular percentage is deducted from the weekly wages for the support of the gospel of that Christ who said, "Forasmuch as ye have done it unto the least of these, ye have done it unto me."

I suppose we all agree that that church is supported by the organized exploitation, even unto death, of little children? I suppose that we all agree that a business which works the lives of little children into dividends is wrong, and that a church which is supported by the fruits of such a crime is wrong, and that the spiritual life of any church cannot rise very far above the source from which it draws its financial nourishment? A church which lives by child murder cannot have much divine power in its ministrations, can it?

What is the difference, in principle, between a business in the South which takes all a child's life in four years, and a business in the North which takes a man's or woman's life in twenty years? What is the difference in principle between the business of Ohio and that of South Carolina? What is the difference in principle in competition anywhere? What is the difference in principle between the source of nourishment of the church here and the church there?

Let my brethren of the pulpit charge me with heresy and with infidelity if they will; I answer with this counter charge: I say that the same power which corrupts great corporations and bribes lawmakers, which suborns perjury and spots with foul stains the robe of justice, which plants the land with brothels and saloons, and makes city government a stench in the nostrils of God, is the power that feeds the church. Organized business! And I charge that down the no-thoroughfares of commercialism today, organized business and the church which bears the name of Jesus Christ, bound together like the Siamese twins, nourished by the same blood, fed from the same source, thinking the same thoughts, and loving the same loves, are walking side by side; and of the exploitation of men and the degradation of women, and the murder of children, equally guilty before God. If that be infidelity, let the church make the most of it. If it be false, let the church disprove it. If it be true, let her cleanse her robes of the innocent blood, attire herself in sack cloth and with the ashes of repentance on her head, cry for mercy to Almighty God.

In the time of Jesus they were very prone to compare themselves with one another, and thank God that they were not like other men. In the 13th chapter of Luke, you will read how Jesus said to them "Think ye that those on whom the tower fell the other day were sinners above all the other people in Jerusalem, because such a thing befell them? I tell ye nay, but except ye repent ye shall likewise perish!"

Do you think, my friends, that in the day when Capitalism stands up for judgement, and the blood of its slaughtered millions cries to God for justice, it will avail a man to say, "I was a Methodist: I was sound on justification," "I was a Baptist, I was put clear under water," "I was a Catholic, I said prayers with perfect regularity every day." I tell you no but except we repent we shall all likewise perish.

Ah, how I long to give my brethren of the pulpit this vision of the Christianity of Jesus and the Apostles; this concept of the real Christ. How I long for adequate words to convey His call to them and to you!

The call of Christ! What is it and where is it? Where do we hear it? Look and listen at the pageant of your civilization; see the gorgeous shows, the display of wealth, the wonders of color, the things of art: Hear the mighty uproar of the great world of commerce, the clamor of the market, the screaming of the whistles, the ringing of the bells, the puffing of engines, the crash and rattle of machinery, the clangor of music, the cheering of excited crowds - and now listen closer, bend down and keep still and through it all you hear another note, a minor strain growing louder and stronger day by day - the groans of despairing men, the sobs of outraged women, the feeble cries of dying children. The cry of the sorrowing for relief, the pleading of the disinherited for justice.

That, oh men and women, is the call of Christ to you. What does it mean to a minister of the gospel in the present day to answer that call? It means to stand, not for charity, but for justice; not for reform but for revolution. It means to close the doors of these splendid temples, rather than live another day by taking the gold of organized oppression. It means to go again upon the highways and the byways, saying, "The spirit of the Lord is upon us because he hath anointed us to preach good news to the poor." It means to work, not for institutions of worship, but for a commonwealth. It means to break at once and forever with the vested interests of Capitalism: to be infidel to its religion, traitor to its government: to cry with Isaiah:

"Thy princes are rebellious and companions of thieves; every one loveth gifts and followeth after rewards; they judge not the widow, neither doth the cause of the fatherless come unto them; the spoil of the poor is in their houses, their hands are full of blood! Bring no more incense, sing no more songs, pray no more vain prayers; observe no more ceremonies. I will have justice, before worship, saith the Lord of Hosts!"

Yes, the call of Christ to the minister is to break once and for all and absolutely with Capitalism. Render unto Caesar the things that are Caesar's and unto God the things that are God's means that all is God's: in a redeemed world there is no room for Caesar. And my brother, sister, the call is the same to you.

Matthew tells us that when Jesus hung upon the cross the Pharisees mocked Him saying, "If thou be the son of God come down from the cross." They wanted to be led by a Son of God but they wanted to be led in easy ways, to glory, place and power. They wanted a competitive Christ, who would lead them to competitive victory. They wanted a kingdom of God, but they wanted it to be on the general plan of this world's kingdoms. They wanted to give the poor charity not justice; to give the slave kindness not liberty. They would be good to the poor but they would not abolish poverty; they wanted to ride easily on the backs of others, not to bear others as a burden on their own shoulders. "If thou be the Son of God, come down!"

And current Christianity stands before the cross in the same attitude saying the same words, "Not that way, Master! Not to be crucified on behalf of humanity! Lead us the other way! Come down off the cross!"

My friends, the call of Christ is as it was 2000 years ago, and has ever been to bear the burdens of weak, wronged, outraged, robbed, oppressed and disinherited humanity. To join your lives to those of the poor. To feel their pains, to share their sufferings, to live for their deliverance - to bow beneath their sorrows in dark Gethsemane; to walk, thorn-crowned, with staggering feet up the steep way to Calvary; sustained because beyond the cross we see the river sepulcher, and through it shines the glory of a resurrected humanity. Lift up your heads! The day of your redemption draweth nigh; the kingdom of heaven is at hand.

Compare this call, my friends, with what you hear from the orthodox pulpit, the appeal to selfishness, the exhortation to save yourself; compare it with the appeal of orthodox politics to the appetite alone, and see if it does not move you more. Is not this Christ worthy of your following, this cause entitled to your highest service? Let us consecrate ourselves to it today. To the service of Christ in humanity, to the bringing in of the redeemed world, let us in emulation of our fathers pledge our lives, our fortunes, and our sacred honor.

BOOK SEVEN
MAKING THE MAN
WHO CAN

(OR HOW TO PROMOTE
YOURSELF)

FOREWORD

This book is a Live Wire. Make the right connection with it and success is yours.

How shall you do it? By reading it long and often; by going back to it every time you catch your confidence and purpose ebbing; and by acting up to its teachings in every way you can think of.

The Life of all success is The Spirit of Faith and Goodwill.

Whenever you feel your faith ebbing get back to this Live Wire again.

Live with it until its spirit is yours and you recognize yourself as THE MAN WHO CAN.

Elizabeth Towne, Editor and Publisher

The Nautilus Magazine of New Thought

Massachusetts, 1914

1. THE POWERFUL LIFE - WHENCE COMES THE POWER?

THAT there is a successful, powerful life; that it may be lived here; that it may be lived by anyone, we are obliged to concede; and having conceded this we cannot fail to wish to live this life, for rightly lived, it means health, wealth, power, happiness and all round success in life. Those who read this series of lessons are going to learn how to live it, and they need first to understand a little as to what the power is and whence it comes.

We are just passing from the physical, animal or material stage of development to the mental and spiritual stage. We are ceasing to be physical men and women and becoming mental and spiritual men and women. To make this change is sometimes a matter of considerable difficulty. The majority of people are not as yet making it at all. They are still entirely material in their beliefs and thought. They do not see the world of Spirit; they put their faith in houses and lands and money and so on, and because they believe in these things they are subject to them. The only powerful life of which they conceive is a life of physical power.

New Thought people, they whose spiritual eyes are becoming opened; who begin to see the inner and finer world penetrating the false appearances of the world of matter; who begin to see Spirit as the cause of matter and of what is called natural phenomena, these are they to whom Jesus referred in speaking to Nicodemus; they have been born of the Spirit and they begin to see the Kingdom of God. They get glimpses of a powerful life which may be lived in the flesh and here on earth; occasionally they enter upon it and live it for a time, but their great difficulty is lack of understanding as to what the power is and how the life must be lived. This we are going to find out.

The first step is to learn the great truth about the universe which is that all is one. All things are forms of one Substance; that Substance is conscious and intelligent; it is Spirit. In former articles and in my books I have referred to this Original Substance under various names, as the supreme, the Thinking Stuff, God, All-

Mind and so on; but here I shall use the one word, Spirit. Substance is Spirit; everything is Spirit; there isn't anything but Spirit.

Before you can fully believe this great truth you will have to learn to disbelieve much of what your senses tell you, and it is easy to do this when you understand how unreliable the senses are. The physical man depends upon the senses for everything. To him seeing is believing, and he accepts as real the appearances around him; but in reality he is grossly deceived; he lives in an unreal world, his whole universe is a deception, and not what it seems to him at all.

This man must believe that he lives on a flat world under a solid blue arch; the sun and moon travel over him and his earth is stationary and the stars are small points of life. These are the appearances of the physical world as given us by the senses, yet no civilized person now really believes in them; we know that the earth is round, that the sky is not solid, that the stars are very much larger than the earth, and that the earth goes round the sun. No well-informed person believes what he sees as to these things; he looks through appearances to the reality.

Take another illustration. Nothing appears more real than color and one can hardly doubt that the objects around us are really of the hue they appear; that the grass is green and the robin's breast is red and so on. But there is no color except in consciousness. When an object appears to us to be of a given color, as red, it is not really so. The "red" object reflects or refuses to absorb and receive the red in the ray of light which strikes it and throws it back to the eye; we see the color it rejects and not the color it is. Where there is no eye to receive the reflection, color has no existence. So it does not do to believe appearances to be true; we must look through them and see the only reality and the only reality of all things is Spirit.

The first step to be taken by those who would lead the Powerful Life is to cease to be misled by appearances, and to perceive truth; to cease to believe in what seems to be and to have faith in what is. They must get to the heart of things, and instead of trying to reason from appearances to realities they must believe realities and disregard appearances.

Spirit is Substance and all Substance is Spirit. There cannot be two Substances. The moment we admit that there are two Substances as Spirit and matter we are absolutely lost. If matter is distinct from Spirit then it has powers and potentialities of its own and may affect us for good or ill. So, if we believe this, we shall become more and more tied down to matter which we can see and have less and less faith in Spirit which we cannot see or can only feel; and the Powerful Life will become impossible to us. We must see that Spirit is Substance and that it is the only Substance. Nothing exists but Spirit.

Next we must come to understand that Spirit is life, and that it is all the life there is. Nothing lives but Spirit. Every thought of man, every volition of any animal, every unfoldment of leaf or blossom is Spirit, acting in the thing that moves. Spirit lives in the grass and flowers and trees; in flesh and insect; in animals and men. There is *no* life but the life of Spirit. "He giveth life to all." "In Him we live and move and have our being." Nothing has individual life or life of its own. It is all the life of Spirit.

Again, all power is Spirit. Every movement in nature or art from the flutter of a leaf to the rushing of the giant current through the dynamo formed by man is Spirit. And in it all and through it all Spirit is working intelligently to some great purpose or purposes of His own.

That there is intelligence through the power of nature is shown for one thing among many by continuity. Everything works under the same laws, yesterday, today and forever. But suppose one day the water pipes ran water and the next day gasoline; one day you weighed one hundred and ten pounds and the next day half a ton, the laws of gravity and chemistry working in contrary fashion; then you might suspect that there were two forces in nature or that the one force was an unintelligent one.

If you want to live the Powerful Life of Samson, Napoleon, or of the evangelist, - and you do, you are reaching out for more power. This is what we are all seeking. Whether we want merely to become rich or whether we wish to excel in society or to rear our children well or become benefactors of humanity, the only thing we require is power and ability to lead the Powerful life.

At the close of this first chapter I bring you to this fact, which if you can grasp it fully, will give you the foundation on which you must stand in leading the life, and if you go on with the succeeding lessons will certainly enable you to lead it.

We live and move and have our being in the limitless ocean of intelligent Spirit from whom we draw our life and power, physical, mental and spiritual. All power is in this Spirit. And we may learn to so unify ourselves with Spirit that more and more power shall be ours, in fact we may have all the power that He can trust us with, and it is only then, a matter of making ourselves trustworthy.

2. THE BUSINESS ATTITUDE

LIKE causes, under like conditions, produce like effects; business success is an effect, and cannot be an exception to the law of cause and effect. The cause of success is the person who succeeds; something in them has been applied to their work, and has produced a certain result. What is it in an individual which produces the result of success? It is not physical strength, although physical strength may be a great aid; all strong people do not succeed, however, and those who do have the ability to so apply their physical strength as to make it assist in producing the result of success. It is not intellectual ability, for all intellectually able people do not succeed; those who do have the power to so direct their intellectual ability as to make it assist in the achievement of success.

The potency which makes the successful person, therefore, is the power to so apply physical and mental ability as to produce results. This power must be an attitude of the individual themselves. It is not a special gift to a few, nor is it a rudimentary faculty which each may develop; it is a position to be assumed. If their abilities and energies are to be directed, it is the person themselves who must direct them; and if they direct them they are the potency which causes success.

Every human being has the inherent power to direct their own abilities and energies; and everyone is conscious of having this power. It is because a person has it that they are capable of growth and progress. To make a successful person, it is necessary to make one who knows what things result in success, and who will direct their energies to do those things; and the first essential to this is that they should assume the attitude of self-direction.

Every man or woman is either self-directing or directed by the suggestions which come from their environment. The individual who can is always a self-directing one; the one who is directed by suggestion is the one who cannot. The individual who is directed by suggestion has a "horoscope"; their destiny is decided by heredity and environment; the self-directing person does not allow their thoughts to be dictated by heredity, environment or the stars; they think what they want to think, and if their horoscope does not suit them they make a better one.

Business success depends upon business policy; business policy can only be formulated by thought; therefore, whether a person succeeds or fails depends upon the way they think.

The directed man or woman only thinks the thoughts which are suggested by their environment; and so they can only do what those around them think they can do.

The self-directing man or woman thinks what they want to think, and can therefore do what they want to do.

To become the man or woman who can, the first step is to take the attitude of self-direction.

Receive and consider every suggestion which comes from your environment, but do not act on the suggestion; act on your own conclusions about the suggestion.

Digest and assimilate suggestions as you digest and assimilate food; make them a part of your own thought before you use them, and learn to reject any that are indigestible.

3. WHAT YOU DESIRE

SUCCESS is becoming what you want to be, and is obtained by applying your energies to your work; and you will apply your energies in exact proportion to the intensity of your desire, and to your faith in your ability to become what you want to be.

The intensity of your desire will depend on the clearness with which you picture to yourself what you want to be.

Vague and indefinite longings will never call out your best effort. Form a mental picture of what you want to be, and of all that you want in person, property and environment; dwell upon it until it is clear and definite to you, and hold it until it arouses intense desire.

Think about this picture until you are always conscious of it, no matter what you may be doing, so that it is always in the background of your consciousness.

But even though you have strong desire you will not put forth your best effort without confidence; you will have to think you can before you can. And you cannot think you can unless you feel that you can; and so you need to have demonstrated to you the fact that you cannot feel that you can unless you have within you the power that can.

In other words, if you strongly desire to do a thing, it is certain proof that you have the power to do it.

Desire is the result of feeling, and the feeling which results in desire is a faculty seeking expression.

The desire to sing or play music is the musical faculty seeking expression, and if there were no faculty, or power, there could be no desire. We cannot desire things which do not harmonize with the forces within, for a thing which does not harmonize with the forces within is repulsive to us. Things only harmonize with those of the same essential nature; therefore, if you desire a thing it is because that thing is essentially and potentially within you.

What is within you essentially must be within you potentially. When we see a generous and sympathetic person we desire to be like them because the sight arouses generosity and sympathy within us; and the power to be, seeking expression, causes the desire to be.

When we hear a great oration or a beautiful song, we desire to execute a similar performance because the faculties of oratory or music respond to the stimulus and seek expression.

Desire is a power seeking expression. You cannot desire what is not potentially within you; and therefore, you can be what you want to be. The fact that you want to be is proof that you can be.

First, form a clear conception of what you want to be in person, property and environment; and then understand that in so far as your desires are not contrary to Eternal Justice it is absolutely certain that you can be what you want to be.

4. BECOMING WHAT YOU WANT TO BE

SUCCESS is a progressive evolution of the faculties of the successful individual. To understand this, remember that success is becoming what you want to be; becoming what you want to be consists in satisfying your desires, and desire is the effort of a faculty to come into action. Each gain in money or position that a man or woman may make enables them to bring into use a new faculty, or to make fuller use of an old one; this satisfies desire, and is success.

The man or woman who can use the most of their faculties is the man or woman who can; and because they are a person who can, they are a successful one.

Success, then, being an evolution of the successful human being, must follow the evolutionary principle of action; and the basic fact in evolution is that each lower plane contains all the potentialities required to perform the functions of the higher plane. On ascending to a higher plane, new faculties are brought into use; but we also see the continued use of the faculties which were active on the lower plane; and it is the complete development of these faculties, or their fullest possible use which makes ascension to a higher plane possible.

Evolution never reaches the higher plane from imperfectly developed specimens on the lower plane, but always from the most perfectly developed.

In other words, it is the evolutionary principle that those organisms which function most perfectly on the lower plane are nearest to the higher plane; and the way to approach the higher plane is by perfecting function on the lower plane.

More than this is necessary, however, for if no organism ever did more than to function perfectly on its own plane there would be no evolution.

Evolution begins when organisms begin to add to the necessary functions of the plane on which they are living; calling into use faculties which can be perfected only on a higher plane.

Your present work may not be the work you want to do; but unless you can do your present work perfectly you are not ready for the work you want to do. And even when you can do your present work perfectly, if that is all that you can do you are not ready for anything else.

It is only when you can do your present work perfectly, *and do some other work besides,* that you are ready to advance.

Evolution is brought about by developing the faculties which are to be used on a higher plane; and this is done by first doing perfectly the work of the lower plane and then adding to it, so as to bring other faculties into use, or to so develop those already in use that they become too large to find expression on the lower plane.

To rise, you must not only fill your present place, but you must more than fill it: it is that part of you which projects beyond the boundaries of your present place which gets hold on the higher place. The evolutionary principle of success is that you should more than fill your present place; and you can succeed in no other way.

5. PROMOTING YOURSELF

THE SUCCESSFUL life is the advancing life; and the advancing life is lived by obedience to the evolutionary principle. The evolutionary principle is that advancement which comes by more than filling your present place; and this is true whether you are an employee, or are in business for yourself.

However, a mere purposeless doing of more work than is required will not advance you; it will probably only tend to keep you where you are. If you are an employee and have no ambition to more than fill your present place, it will be to your employer's interest to keep you in your present place; and they will probably do so. You must know what you want to be, and you must more than fill your present place for the purpose of becoming what you want to be.

Do not do extra work with the idea that by so doing you may curry favor with your employer; that will put you in a servile attitude, and out of the attitude of self-direction. Do not do it in the hope that those above you will see your good service and promote you; they may find it more profitable to keep you where you are. Do what you do with the purpose of promoting yourself. You are more than filling your place in order to develop your faculties for filling a larger place; if your employer does not offer you one when you are ready for it, offer yourself to another employer. There are always places for the Advancing Man or Woman.

Keep your mind fixed on what you want to be, and more than fill your present place; your mental attitude will make you quick to see every opportunity for bettering your condition, and you will be competent to take advantage of opportunities when they come.

Do not wait for an opportunity to be all that you want to be; be all that you can today, and when an opportunity to be more is offered to you, take it. There is no such thing as lack of opportunities for the man or woman who is living the advancing life, and who has an advancing mind. Everything that touches your life is an opportunity, if you discover its proper use.

Every circumstance, every seeming misfortune, every person you meet, every dog that barks at you, or wags its tail as you pass - all have some element of usefulness to you if you will find it. Study them all, for they are your opportunities. Most men and women fail by waiting for some particular kind of opportunity, instead of being ready to seize every opportunity.

Steadily hold the picture of all that you want to attain in person, property and environment; live the advancing life within, by more than filling your present place; live the accumulative life without, by acquiring everything you meet which belongs in your picture, and you cannot fail.

The stars in their courses will fight for you; your success will be made by the evolutionary principle, the creative power of the universe.

6. THE ADVANCING THOUGHT

IF YOU are in business for yourself, the evolutionary principle of success is the same as if you were working for another. You must keep in mind what you want to become, and more than fill your present place each day. That does not mean that you are to try to do part of tomorrow's work today. You have nothing to do with tomorrow's work, except to be ready for it when it comes; but you must do all that is necessary for today's business, and something for increase. In every transaction you must keep the advancing mind; you must put the expanding thought into everything you do, and communicate it to every person with whom you have dealings.

If you sell a pound of sugar, do it with the thought that the purchaser's trade is valuable because they will soon be able to buy in barrel lots; if a child buy's a penny's worth of candy, put into the sale the thought that they will one day buy a five pound box; and in each case see that the customer gets the thought.

Put into every sale the thought of advance for the customer as well as for yourself; soon they will all feel that they are getting bargains in everything. And they will be right. If you thus put the advancing thought into every transaction, your customers will get it in regard to their own affairs; and they will begin to be more successful and will mentally connect their success with you.

This will strongly attract them to you; the best bargain you can give another person is to communicate to them the advancing thought in regard to their own affairs. No "premium" or "rebate" is equal to it.

When you send a person away feeling that they are advancing, and becoming a more valuable customer, you give them the strongest possible inducement to visit you again. If you communicate the advancing thought to your customers, they will begin to make successes because of it; and intuitively connecting their successes with you, will come to you for more power. You will build them up, and they, in turn, will build you up. *The person who can give the advancing thought to all who deal with them cannot fail;* they have exactly what they are seeking.

This principle holds good whether you are a merchant, an artist, a professional man, actor, singer - no matter what. You can more than fill your present place; so that your customers, patrons or audiences will know that they are getting a bargain.

It is not the quantity or quality of the goods that makes the bargain; it is the feeling of advancement, or increase.

The basic element of success in business is, therefore, to hold the thought and the mental attitude of advancement; and to more than fill your present place.

And you more than fill your place by so doing your work that those who deal with you are conscious of being advanced by you.

By study and application of the evolutionary principle, success is made a certainty, and failure rendered impossible.

7. THE LAW OF OPULENCE

"Except a man be born again he cannot see the kingdom of God."

IN LIVING the new life the first essential is to abandon the idea of competition and of a limited supply. Too many people who consider themselves practitioners of the new thought never entirely succeed in doing this.

Competition in business originates in the idea of a limited supply. It grows out of the supposition that because there is not enough to go round, people must compete with each other for what there is.

Many people who have a partial grasp of the new thought still suppose that it is necessary that some should be poor in order that others may have enough, and believe that wealth is possible only to those who have superior ability, or the power to attract to themselves a larger portion from the limited supply.

These people try to apply the new thought principles on the competitive plane, and they do so with a fair degree of success; they try to develop a superior attracting power; they inject new motives and new energy into competitive business methods; they assert, "I am success," all the while believing that they can succeed only because ninety-five per cent of all others fail.

The majority of these competitive new thought people do achieve a great measure of success because their faith gives them just the energy, push and optimism which are necessary in competitive business. The confidence born of their belief makes a majority of their actions successful actions; their partial application of new thought ideas makes them exceptionally able competitors, and they attribute their success to thought-power and to affirmation when it is almost purely competitive.

This so-called new thought is really only the highest and most fully perfected form of the old thought. It only sees Caesar's kingdom after all; it has no conception of the kingdom of God.

All the final results show that these new thought people are only a part of Caesar's kingdom. Their fortunes fluctuate. They meet with losses and their business suffers from panics. Their prosperity is checkered by periods of adversity. Their sense of safety is mere self- confidence; deep in the subconscious they always carry the germ of secret fear.

No one can ever be wholly free from fear who recognizes any limitation in the supply, for if there is not enough to go round, we know that our turn to go without may come at any time.

The lapses and failures of new thought people are traceable directly to the idea of a limited supply; to the idea that success and the attainment of wealth are possible only to a part of us.

Is there any truth in this idea that competition is necessary? Let us see. The things that are essential to life and advancement, mental and physical, may be roughly grouped under five headings, and these are: Food, clothing, shelter, education and amusement. For three of these, food, clothing and shelter, we look to the world of nature for supply. These three with their paraphernalia and extensions in the way of luxuries, decorations, art and beauty, constitute what we call wealth. Is there any limitation to the supply of these?

Take into consideration, first, the question of food supply. In this country we have not yet begun to sound the possibilities of intensive agriculture, making four blades of grass grow where one grew before.

It is a fact capable of mathematical demonstration that the single state of Texas, if all its resources were organized for the production of food, would produce enough to feed the whole present population of the globe, and feed them well.

Our food products range from wheat in the Dakotas to rice in Carolina; from northern fruits in Michigan to oranges in California and Florida. This country, intensely cultivated, would feed the inhabitants of ten worlds like this. There is no lack in the food supply.

When we pray to our Father, "Give us our daily bread," we should never forget to add a thanksgiving that He answered that prayer when He laid the foundation of the world.

Remember, too, that the work of men like Burbank has just begun; the food supply is capable of infinite development. There is, therefore, no need for men to compete with each other in order to get enough to eat.

As to the second essential, clothing, we find the same to be true. The United States can produce cotton for the world, but it is not necessary to dress the world in anything so cheap as cotton fabrics. We have sheep ranges to supply the woolen goods for all, and fields in which to raise the flax for fine linen; there are great wastes of land, now barren, where we might grow enough mulberry trees to feed the silk worms necessary to clothe the world in silks; we even have the deserts on which to raise ostriches for fine plumage. We have resources sufficient to clothe every man, woman and child in raiment finer than that of Solomon in all his glory. And there are undreamed of possibilities in the despised weeds by the wayside; some will presently develop into the raw material for fabrics more beautiful than the world has ever seen. The supply of clothing is inexhaustible. No need to compete with another here; no need for one to go in sackcloth that another may wear purple and fine linen; there is purple and fine linen for all.

Taking up the question of shelter we find the same conditions prevailing. There are great banks of clay waiting to be made into bricks and tile; there are vast ledges of building stone unquarried as yet; we have learned that brick may be made of sand and lime, and that cement is excellent building material. It is an indisputable fact that a mansion finer than Vanderbilt's might be erected for every family in America, and when all were finished we should hardly have made a scratch on the surface of our supply of building material. No need for some to live in hovels in order that others may be delicately housed!

And the supply for interior furnishings - for furniture, carpets, books, musical instruments, pictures, statuary, everything to delight the eye and mind of man is just as unlimited.

Truly, there is no scarcity of things; nor is there any lack of work that ought to be done. There is no necessity in nature for competition, either for things or for jobs. There is enough useful and beautiful work waiting to be done to keep us all busy all our lives.

And it may be well to point out here that there is no lack in the supply of finished products because labor is not productive enough to keep pace with the demand. Modern machinery has solved the problem of production. The producing power of labor has been multiplied by six hundred in a little more than a generation. In making nails, for instance, one man does the work which required a thousand men one hundred years ago; and the same is approximately true in all lines of industry; and the end of the increase in producing power is not yet. There is nothing in which further improvement is not possible. Six hours' work a day, by all of us, would produce all that we could use, including every known luxury.

With such abundance in the whole, we do not need to compete for a part; we do not need to take thought for tomorrow; we do not need to experience panics or reverses.

We need only to seek for the kingdom of God, and His righteous relations toward each other, and all these things shall be added unto us. And what is the kingdom of God?

"Whereunto shall I liken the kingdom of God? It is like leaven, which a woman took and hid in three measures of meal, until the whole was leavened."

THE KINGDOM of God is in nature like the leaven in the meal - in all and through all. It includes all nature, for God is the cause of nature; and when nature is perfectly natural, there is the kingdom of God in all its fullness.

If God be the Mind of nature, then there can be no more perfect expression of God than in the naturalness of nature.

The kingdom of God includes all life, for God is the Life itself; and when life is lived in a perfectly natural way, there is the kingdom of God in all its fullness; for there can be no more perfect expression of God than the living of life in a natural way.

And this brings us to the question, how may life be lived in the natural way?

The living of life consists in continually advancing into more life. Drop a seed in the center of a field; the life in the seed at once becomes active; it ceases to merely exist, and begins to live. Soon it produces a plant, and a seed head, in which there are thirty, sixty or a hundred seeds, each containing as much life as the first seed contained.

These fall into the ground, and in their turn begin to live; and in time there are a million seeds in the field, each containing as much life as the first seed contained.

The life of the first seed, by the mere act of living, has increased a million fold.

The living of life consists in continuously increasing life; there is no other way to live.

This necessity of life for increase is the cause of what we know as evolution.

There is no such thing as evolution in the mineral world. Minerals do not advance or progress. Lead does not evolve into tin, tin into iron, iron into silver, silver into gold, and so on.

Evolution is found only in the organic forms of life, and is caused by the natural necessity of life to find fuller and fuller expression.

Life on this earth began no doubt, in a single cell; but a single cell could not give sufficient expression to life, and so it formed a double celled organism; then organisms of many cells; then vertebrates; then mammals, and finally, man.

All this because of the inherent necessity of life to advance forever into more complete expression.

And evolution did not cease with the formation of man; physical evolution ceased, and mental and spiritual evolution began.

Man, from the beginning, has been developing more ability to live. Each generation is capable of living more than the preceding generation. The race is continually advancing into more life, and so we see that the living of life means to live more.

The action of consciousness continually expands consciousness. The primal necessity of mind is to know more, and feel more, and enjoy more; and this necessity of mind is the cause of social evolution, and of all progress.

If we take conscious life - as we must - to be the highest expression of God, or of the Mind of nature, then the purpose of all things must be to further the development of conscious life; and if man is the highest form of conscious life - and he is - then the purpose of all things must be to further the development of man.

And if the development of man consists in the increase of his capacity for life, then the purpose of all things in nature must be to further the continuous advancement of man into more and more of life.

Life finds expression by the use of things.

The measure of a person's life is not the things they possess, but the number of things they are able to use rightly; and to have fullness of life is to have all the things we are capable of using rightly. The purpose of the Mind of nature being the continuous advancement of man into more life, it must also be the intention of that Mind that every human being shall have the unrestricted use of all the things that they are capable of using and enjoying rightly; or that "their own shall come to them."

The purpose of God is that all should have life, and have it more abundantly.

God is the Mind of nature, and God is in all, and through all; therefore, the mind, or intelligence of God is in all and through all, like the leaven in the meal.

The desire for advancement is a fundamental fact in the action of mind; therefore, the desire for advancement is in all, and through all.

All things desire the advancement of every man.

If an individual desires any good thing in order to live their life more fully, that thing desires them also, for all life is one - the mind of nature is in and through all things.

The mind of things responds to the mind of man, when man desires advancement. All things work together for good to those who desire only advancement.

The greatest of all facts to us is the fact that there is a Mind in nature which desires us to have all the things we are capable of using, and willing to use, in the direction of fuller life, and that this Mind is in the things themselves, tending to bring them toward us; and that if we take the right course, recognizing this Mind and working with it, all things must come to us.

But this Mind is the Mind of the Whole, not of a part; and if we lose sight of the Whole and enter into competition with our fellows for a part we lose all.

For competition of a part is virtually a denial and rejection of the Whole. He who recognizes and accepts the whole cannot compete for a part. It is the idea of competition for a limited supply which prevents us from seeing and accepting the Abundance which is ours. We still keep up the foolish struggle of Caesar's kingdom, because we cannot see the kingdom of God, which is all around us and within us. "If my kingdom were of this world, then would my servants fight," said Jesus. We do not get fully out of the ideas of the kingdoms of this world; we still do more or less fighting.

But how are we to avoid competition, when the whole business world is proceeding on the method of competing for a limited supply? How can we get work without competing for jobs? Can we succeed in a competitive world without competing? Shall we withdraw from the world, and form communistic societies? Certainly not. To try that is to fail. A communistic society is a body of people who do not compete with each other, but who do compete with everybody else.

No community can be complete unto itself without greatly limiting its members in the means of life; and to do this is to defeat the end aimed at.

And if it is not complete in itself, satisfying all its wants, it must compete with the outside world for what is lacking, and this is what we seek to avoid. No separation of a part from the Whole in any way, will solve the problem. The community scheme is inconvenient, unnatural and impracticable.

Shall we establish socialism and the co-operative commonwealth? We cannot do it, because socialism and the co-operative commonwealth can never be established; it must establish itself, and it may take it a long time yet to do so. We cannot do away with competition by legislative enactment of any kind so long as the majority of men believe in the limited supply; so we must keep right on in business under the present system, and yet cease to compete. Can we do it? Yes. But how?

8. MAN AND MONEY

"I am come that they might have life; and that they might have it more abundantly."

GOD, the Mind of nature, produces the Abundance of nature with the purpose of providing for the development of man; not just of some men or women, but of mankind. The purpose of nature is the continuous advancement of life; and as man is the embodiment of God and the highest form of life, the purpose of nature must be the continuous advancement of every man and woman into more abundant life.

That which seeks the advancement of every man and woman cannot take anything from any one; therefore to be one with the Mind of nature is to seek the advancement of all at the expense of none; to seek to get for all what one desires to get for one's self.

This must lift one entirely out of the competitive thought. "What I want for myself, I want for all;" that is the declaration of independence aimed at the competitive system.

"Our" Father, give "us," - that is the prayer of the advancing life. This declaration and prayer are in unison with the Mind of nature; the man who so declares and so prays is mentally one with all that lives, God, nature and man; and this is the At-one-ment.

To be mentally one with the Mind of things makes you able to register your thoughts on that Mind, and your desires as well.

When you desire a thing, and your mind and the Mind of things are one, that thing will desire you, and will move toward you. If you desire dollars, and your mind is one with the Mind that pervades dollars and all things else, dollars will be permeated with the desire to come to you, and they will move toward you, impelled by the Eternal Power which makes for more abundant life.

To obtain what you want, you only need to establish your own at-one-ment with the Mind of things, and they will be drawn toward you.

But the primal purpose of the Mind of things is the continuous advancement of ALL into more abundant life; therefore, nothing will be taken away from anyone else and given to you unless you give to that person more in the way of life than you take away.

It will be plainly seen that the Divine Mind cannot be brought into action in the field of purely competitive business. God cannot be divided against Himself. He cannot be made to take from one and give to another. He will not decrease one man's opportunity to advance in life in order to increase another man's opportunity to advance in life. He is no respecter of persons, and has no favorites. He is equally in all, equally for all, and at the service of all alike.

To make the at-one-ment, you must see that your business gives to all who deal with you a full equivalent in life for the money value of what you take from them.

I say in life; that does not necessarily mean in money value. Here is what many critics of the profit system fail to understand: that a thing of small value to one man may be of inestimable value to another who can use it for the advancement of life. A box of matches would be worth more to an Eskimo than a combine harvester.

The value of a thing to an individual is determined by the plane of life on which they stand: what is of no value on one plane, or in one stage of their development, is indispensable on another plane, or in another stage. The life-giving power of any article may be out of all proportion to its monetary value. This book is not worth a dollar in so far as the cash value of the paper and ink are concerned, but one sentence in it may be worth thousands of dollars to any reader. You may sell an article for more than it cost you, making a profit; but the purchaser may put it to such use that it will be worth hundreds of times its cost to them, and in that case profit is no robbery. See that your business meets this fundamental requirement; that is the first step.

When you have done this you are one with that Intelligence in nature which is working for more life for all; you are "working together with Him," as St. Paul says; you and your Father are one. The aim of your work is that all may have life, and have it more abundantly. What you seek for yourself you are seeking for all, and the mental principle in everything that you need begins to gravitate toward you. If you need dollars, the Mind of things, in the dollars is conscious of the need; and you can affirm with truth "Dollars want me." Dollars will begin to move toward you, and they will come, invariably, from those who need what you can give in exchange. The Divine Mind will attend to the transference of that which is needed for the advancement of life to the place where need exists.

This will apply not only to all that you need to keep your business going, but to all that you are capable of using to enter into fuller life yourself. No good thing will be withheld from you.

Your unity with the Evolutionary Power, with the Purpose of nature, will be such that you will receive all that nature has to give. Because you will do always the will of God, all things are yours, and you need to compete with no one.

But you must bear in mind that your wants are impressed on the Divine Mind *only by your faith.* A doubt cuts the connection. Anxiety and fear cut the connection.

Exactly as you are in the matter of impressing your own subconscious mind, so you are in the matter of impressing the Mind of things.

Your affirmations fall flat unless they are made with the dynamic power of absolute faith.

The Mind of things will not act positively for doubt and hesitancy.

"What things so ever ye desire when ye pray, believe that ye receive them and ye shall have them."

We cannot walk and work with God and distrust Him at the same time. If you feel distrust, you impress the Mind of things with distrust of you, and things will move away from you rather than toward you.

The requirements for non-competitive success are very simple: First, desire for everybody what you desire for yourself, and be sure to take nothing from anybody without giving a full equivalent in life; and the more you give the better for you.

Then move out in the absolute faith that all you need for the fullest life you are capable of living will come to you. Pray with unfaltering faith to the Father that it shall come to you, and thank Him in every prayer, from a heart full of gratitude that it DOES come to you.

Everything that comes to you then will mean more life to someone else. Each gain you make will add to the wealth of someone else. What you get for yourself - life - you get for all. Your success adds to the life, health, wealth and happiness of all.

But someone says: Wherein does this differ from competition, after all? Are you not still competing with those in the same line of business? No! What you gain will not come from the limited supply for which others are struggling, but from the Whole.

Let me illustrate: It may be said that there is only a limited supply of money in the country; not enough to supply the needs of all. Suppose a large number of people enter this Way of Life, and dollars begin to move toward them all, there will not be enough to go around. That is true, but the thought of need impressed upon the Mind of things would react upon the minds of men; new currency laws would be passed; the bullion would begin to move toward the mints; and the printing presses to turn out bank notes if they were necessary to the advancement of life.

The Mind of things reaches beyond the coined cash, into the gold and silver lying in the hearts of the hills; and it will all begin to move forward when it is called for by the prayer of faith. The Mind of things can call in resources from the ends of the earth in order to meet demand.

And the same is true of everything else. Not only the mints, but the mills will start whenever a sufficient number of people have entered the way of the Advancing life.

If it be urged that the wage system prevents the workers from living full lives, the answer is that whenever the workers begin to live full lives, if the wage system stands in the way of their advancement it will be changed. Their demand for more life will be all that is required to change it.

Life cannot be advanced by changing systems, but systems may be changed by the advance of life.

There is plenty of work to be done in the erection of useful and beautiful things; all that is needed is a demand for those things by those whose sole purpose is to use them to give more life to all.

As the number of such people increases, the prosperity of all will increase, and a constantly increasing proportion of all classes will come into the Truth, abandoning competition and the way of the limited supply, until the kingdom will be established on earth as it is in Heaven. *"And God shall wipe away all tears from their eyes; and there shall be no more crying, neither shall there be any more pain: and there shall be no night there."*

9. TALK THAT BUILDS

DO NOT talk about poverty. It adds nothing to the wealth and happiness of the world to disseminate the information that you have always been poor, and have had a mighty hard struggle to get along. Poverty is no more a thing to boast of than ignorance is a thing to boast of. The old saying that it is no disgrace to be poor is only a half truth; in the true sense it is really a disgrace to be poor. Nobody is poor, or having a hard struggle but (a) the ignorant, (b) the lazy, and (c) the incompetent.

This sounds harsh, and you are ready to go "up in the air" about it; you want to tell me that the tenement dwellers and wage-slaves have no chance, and so on. But wait a little. The wage slaves really own the world; they have created it all, and they could take possession of it tomorrow if they would. They can begin, at any time, to use the factories to make things for themselves, instead of turning wealth out for their masters.

But they do not do it because they are (a) too ignorant to know that this is their world; (b) too intellectually lazy to THINK, and so discover that this is their world; and (c) incompetent, because they do not THINK.

Intellectual laziness is what keeps the masses down; those who work hard and willingly in other ways shrink from the effort of sustained and consecutive thinking; and because they let other people do their thinking for them, they are slaves.

The masses will be wage-slaves as long as the nickel and dime theaters are crowded and the public libraries deserted.

I tell you this because I want to make plain to you the futility of talking about poverty. Talking about poverty and adverse conditions will only lead people to run to the cheap shows, and to try in other ways to drown their miseries in temporary pleasures.

The more you talk, and think about your hard times, the more you will be inclined to seek some mental narcotic to dull the keen edge of your suffering; and the longer you will suffer.

No surer way to keep the masses poor can be devised than to continually write and talk about their poverty.

Talk about the good time coming.

The good time IS coming, and the rapidity of its coming is in exact proportion to the number of people who think about it and talk about it.

Instead of going about showing horrible pictures of the condition of those who live in the tenements, go about showing *beautiful* pictures of the conditions of those who will live in the *coming* city.

If you can inspire *one* person to go to work for the *coming* city, you have done more good than you can by sending *ten* people out with slaves and plasterers to relieve existing distress.

Instead of crusading against child labor and bad factory conditions, tell the working people what splendid conditions they will have when they wake up and begin to operate the industries for themselves.

The masses are not in bondage to anything but ignorance and intellectual laziness; they can have what they will if they will begin to THINK. And the way to make them think is to talk WEALTH.

That is the philosophy for the mass. *And the same applies to you as an individual.* If the mass is not ready or willing to rise, you do not have to stay down with it; you can rise above it.

But you can never rise above it if you keep talking about yourself as being down with it. If you keep talking of yourself as one of those who have hard times in getting along, you will continue to be one of those who have hard times in getting along.

Do not tell how poor your parents were, and what terrible times you had when you were a child. To talk of those things is to go back into those conditions, mentally; and to go back into those conditions mentally is to invite them physically.

Talk about the happy times you had in your youth, and forget all the unhappy times.

Do not tell how hard you used to work, and how little you got for it. If you worked hard for nothing, you were a chump; and you should not advertise yourself as a chump.

Tell of the good work you have done, and of the good wages you got for it; then you are advertising yourself as a competent person, who can earn good wages.

Do not, like Uriah Heep, tell how 'amble you are, and boast of living in a 'amble abode; declare yourself to be as good as the best, and describe the elegant home you are in the process of getting and furnishing. Don't apologize for your clothes, tell how few you have, or say you "have nothing fit to wear"; tell of the fine clothes you are making arrangements to get.

Don't talk poverty in any way; don't refer to it as existing. **TALK WEALTH.**

THE END

BOOK EIGHT
THE NEW SCIENCE OF LIVING AND HEALING

(HEALTH THROUGH NEW THOUGHT AND FASTING)

FOREWORD

STARVE and be a Samson!" That is the first line of an illustrated article in a recent number of the *New York World,* wherein are described the wonderful feats of Gilman Low who "lifted 1,000,000 pounds in thirty-five minutes." When he finds a car track obstructed by a disabled auto, Gilman Low lifts the 1,500 pound touring car out of the way as easily as you or 1 might move a baby wagon.

Gilman Low has broken all sorts of athletic records, but not on accepted principles of training. Once before, after using conventional methods, three meals a day with meat, etc., he attempted that 1,000,000 pound lift, which consisted in getting under a 1,000 pound weight and raising it on his back 1,000 times in half an hour. That time he raised it 500 times in twenty-five minutes and had to quit.

This time he trained for the feat by living first five weeks on one meal a day, consisting of three eggs, half a loaf of whole wheat bread and raw fruit, nuts or cereals, with one glass of milk taken afterward. During the day he drank plenty of cool, distilled water. Twice during the period he ate meat, but found it detrimental and ceased using it. The last three weeks he ate but four meals a week, of the foods before mentioned. At 10 a. m. of the day the lift was made, he ate six eggs and plenty of bread. During the eight weeks of training his exercise consisted principally of walking and deep breathing, combined with light gymnastics, and he kept out of doors as much as possible, being a *firm believer in the benefits of fresh air and sunshine.*

His 1,000,000 pound lifting was performed before a medical examiner and many witnesses. "When he had lifted the 1,000 pound weight 800 times his pulse registered only eighty-five, an increase of thirteen beats, showing a wonderful condition of heart and circulation. During the first one hundred lifts Low's arms were folded across his chest. After that his hands rested on a heavy bench and he lifted with arms, legs and back, increasing speed as he neared the close of his feat.

It cost Gilman Low exactly five and three-quarters pounds in the half-hour of lifting. And he prepared for it by living eight weeks on forty-seven meals, an average of one meal in over one and one-fifth days. And at only two of these meals he ate meat, finding afterwards that it interfered with his work.

When one thinks of Gilman Low eating air and lifting 1,000 pounds a thousand times in half an hour his imagination skips Samson as unimportant. Why not Atlas, standing on air, living on air and lifting the earth!

How much more can Gilman Low do by eliminating a few more meals? He has already performed wonders after seven to fifteen day fasts. During the physical culture show he fasted seven days and then with the back lift raised 2,000 pounds twenty-two times in nineteen seconds. What next!

All this goes to prove "The New Science of Living" as elucidated by Wattles in the first chapters of this book.

One of our correspondents asks, "If food is not necessary to maintenance of the physical being, why do all fowls and animals eat nearly continuously? Why does a babe cry for food at frequent intervals, though it sleeps much of the time!"

Nobody imagines that food is not "necessary to the maintenance of physical life." It is. *But food is not the source of physical power,* as the old physiology teaches. Food is to the body what raw material is to the builder. The power which receives food, dissolves and changes it, and builds it into muscle and tissue, nerves, *and brain,* is the Life Power which flows into us from the Infinite while we sleep. If we give this Life Power the right food materials, and the right amount of it, it builds beautifully, intelligently, ever improving and refining its work.

If we give too little food material this Life Power builder within us is hampered in its work, just as any carpenter would be if the mill failed to deliver the necessary lumber for the work planned. The body stores enough material for a forty, or fifty, or sixty-day famine, but not enough for eternal famine. Not yet, at least. If we give too much food material, or not the right kind, it is as if the lumber dealer kept delivering loads of all kinds of lumber until the premises were covered with it Imagine carpenters trying to build a house in the center of a lumber yard, with all kinds of timber piled about and more coming in with every revolution of the saw, and you will get a faint idea of the difficulties under which labors the builder which is you, when you pour in more food material than he needs.

And the danger of pouring in too much food if far greater than that of delivering too little. For the reason that too much food sets up a state of general inflammation throughout the body, which you interpret as a call for *more food,* when in reality it means there is already too much on hand. A baby suffering from indigestion acts ravenous. A grown-up stomach that is generating ferments calls for more, more. And another meal piled in gives *temporary* relief, just as kneading more flour into a batch of bread dough gives temporary relief from ferment.

What would happen to the dough if you kept on kneading it down with more flour, a dozen, a hundred, yes, thousands of times. The result would be unwieldiness and *poison.* The same thing happens in the continuously overloaded stomach, *and throughout the overloaded body.*

And no amount of mental or spiritual science will stop it, though it may retard the process, as cold retards the rising of your bread dough. In this way you may put off the day of reckoning with an overloaded stomach and body, but that is all you can do. The death-poison will get you sooner or later.

There is little danger of giving the builder within you too little material, *first,* because the body of every person carries enough building material in storage to last a complete famine of thirty to sixty days, or more; *second,* because the *normal* hunger of an un-stuffed and un-tempted body is an infallible guide to the *amount and kind* of food needed.

All our overeating comes from, *first,* the false belief that strength is gained from eating; *second,* the *habit* of eating so many times a day whether hungry or not; *third,* the continual tempting of the appetite through variety of dishes. Of course, the latter two causes are branches of the first.

The cure *and the proof* of the new physiology is to eat plain foods, cut out one meal a day, and take 36 hour fasts once a week for say four or five months. The improvement in feelings and endurance, and the change in appetite and tastes will prove the matter to all but the most hopelessly prejudiced minds.

Now, note that normal fowls hunt food "nearly continuously," but they come a long way from eating continuously. And the hunting and scratching enable them to make good use of all food they can find. Every poulterer knows that fowls penned up and overfed lay few eggs and suffer from numerous diseases. And no animals come anywhere near eating "nearly continuously" except cattle, and they exercise while eating, and if they get over the fence into a too rich field they soon die of over-eating. If you were to weigh the total amount a cow eats in a day, even in good pasturage, you would find she consumes less in proportion to her weight than the ordinary human being does. And she exercises nearly all the time and gives milk into the bargain.

Another correspondent takes exceptions to Mr. Wattles' statements about fear and digestion, and cites the case of an old lady who "has always eaten much, and anything she wanted, and does yet; who knows nothing about chemistry of foods, consequently has no fear of results of eating; and yet she has been a victim to sick headache, nerves and kindred troubles all her life." I should think so. Fear is not the only thing that causes such troubles. And fear of what one eats is not the only kind of fear that hinders digestion. The more fear of *any* kind one entertains the less food he can properly digest, for fear paralyzes digestive and other processes. *Any* fear. But over-eating and wrong eating are at the bottom of all sick headaches. If one adds fear to overeating he suffers more and oftener, that's all.

This same correspondent says she *must* have four meals a day, as she is "no good" with her stomach empty; and she can "work all around her daughter who eats half as much and sleeps twice as much." If she will cut her meals to two a day and fast thirty-six hours once a week, living thus, feelings or no feelings, for, say six weeks, *doing it with a will,* she will find herself doing still more work, with greater health and mental brightness than ever, and the gone feelings all gone for good. To merely assert that she *must* have four meals proves nothing. She will prove the opposite if she practices the new way.

And for one person to compare herself to another is futile. It proves nothing, for no two humans are alike. The daughter can cut *her* meals in two, and fast one day a week, and she will doubtless do more work than at present, and require less sleep.

For over-eating is one great cause of over-sleeping. Any sort of bodily exercise, including digestion, raises the demand for more sleep that the Life Power may accumulate energy to renew the broken down tissues. People of active living, like growing children, need much sleep. And people who eat much need much sleep, for it takes much Life Power to dispose of the food.

One person cannot be compared justly with another in such things; but one *can* try different methods of living, try them *faithfully,* and prove which is best, thus measuring himself by himself. So far this correspondent seems to have tried only one sort of living.

To eat all one really needs and *no more,* because the elimination of unneeded food requires Life Power or energy that would better be directed in other channels,—this is the intent of the new physiology. Sensible, is it not?

—ELIZABETH TOWNE.

1. THE SOURCE OF WORK-POWER

Life passes through us, we do not possess it. — AMIEL

IT IS PROBABLE that the late Edward Hooker Dewey, M. D., of Meadville, Pa., widely known as "the no-breakfast doctor," influenced more people in the direction of the simplification of life than any other writer, living or dead. His books, "The New Science of Health," and "The No-Breakfast Plan," have been read by many thousands of people and have indirectly influenced many thousands more; his theories are working a revolution, and yet scarcely one in ten of his followers comprehends the really revolutionary character of his thought, or the tremendous importance of his great physiological discovery.

In brief, as set forth in his last book, that discovery is this: That the strength—the work-power—of the human organism is not drawn from the food consumed, but is renewed in sleep. The storage battery of muscle energy and thought energy is not charged and recharged at the dining table, but in the bedroom. Food is to the human body what the soil is to a plant—merely raw material; tissue elements, to be built into the organism, but not in any sense a source of life.

The interesting points about this theory are:

First, that it is capable of mathematical demonstration, and is therefore true beyond controversy;

Second, that it absolutely overthrows current theories of the source of life and strength, driving the materialistic physiologist from the field by proving that life energy is not the product of functional action, and that most muscle workers would be healthier, stronger and longer lived on one-half, and most brain workers on one-tenth of the quantity of food they now consume. It gives good ground also for the argument that mind is not produced by the body, but that mind produces the body; that the brain does not produce thought, but that thought produces the brain; that there is no chemistry by which a piece of bread can become mind or thought; Third, it proves that most of the conclusions of the pseudo-science of medicine have been based on false premises, and are erroneous; and that most of the tick are greatly hindered in recovery by feeding, dosing and other interference.

It gives us, also, a solid foundation upon which we may base a really scientific investigation of the problems of the origin of life, and of the immortality of the soul; but that is beyond the scope of this article.

Let us now "make good" on our first proposition: That we do not get our strength from food. The brain is a storage battery of vital energy, which is charged in some unknown manner, and from some unknown source, during sleep. The stomach is a machine which is run by brain power, and the digestion of food is a tax on strength, and not a source of strength.

Now, as to the mathematics. A laborer will consume a beefsteak and a couple of potatoes, and will shovel twenty tons of earth to a height of five feet; was there sufficient potential energy in the food to perform the work? A Japanese soldier, carrying a heavy load, can march and fight all day and only consume a handful of rice; and he can do this for an indefinite period without loss of weight or strength. Can anyone seriously claim that the enormous amount of energy he displays was potentially in the few ounces of rice consumed per diem? No machine which science has been able to devise can extract one five-hundredth part as much energy from a pound of beef as the human body must draw from it if the old physiology is true; but it is not true. It is mathematically impossible. A man will eat a few slices of pork, and will "run down," catch and overpower two or three full-grown hogs, by the sheer excess of his physical power over theirs. Is the potential energy of a pound of dead pork greater than the kinetic energy of three *live* three hundred pound hogs?

Consider, next, the numerous cases of protracted fasts which have been recorded since Dr. Dewey's books were published. Leonard Thress, of Philadelphia, fifty-six days, and Miss Estella Kuenzel, forty-two days, *with a steady gain in strength from the first day,* are among the cases recorded by the doctor himself ; and some hundreds of others, perfectly authenticated, prove that a person can go from twenty to sixty days without food and can often do so without appreciable loss of strength. I believe it is the accepted *dictum* of the old physiology that a man will starve to death in ten days. This has been proved to be a mistake, and it is evident that most of the people who have perished of hunger in that limited time died because they thought they *had* to, and that, properly educated, they might have lived from twenty to sixty days longer. In death by starvation the brain and nervous system, which are the power plant, lose no weight; the other tissues disappear until the skeleton condition is reached, and death comes because the brain can get no more raw material with which to repair the heart, lungs, stomach, liver, etc. The organism grows weak and perishes from lack of raw material to replace the daily waste of its vital parts; it dies when the viscera are so attenuated as to be unable to perform their functions, but it dies not for lack of vital energy, but because the vital energy has no material to use in keeping up the organism. Set a plant in gravel, and it will die— not for lack of energy, but for lack of material.

Consider for a moment this claim that the body works with energy generated by its own digestive system. The digestion of food is certainly work, and it certainly takes power; those who remember the feeling of lethargy after a too hearty meal will not be disposed to deny that a very considerable amount of energy is required to operate the stomach. The old physiology claims that the heart, brain, liver, kidneys, etc., are machines which are operated by power which is ultimately traced to the action of the stomach; and that the stomach, in turn, is operated by power which is generated by the action of the heart, brain, liver, kidneys, etc. Here is a mechanical impossibility—the stomach generating power to operate the other machines and being in turn operated by power supplied by the other machines. That the body should perform its great amount of external work by means of energy generated by its own *internal* work is impossible; the claim that it does so is an absurdity. The functional actions of the viscera do not generate energy; they absorb energy. It uses up power to spade up the earth in the garden; and the heart and stomach cannot generate power to operate themselves, with a sufficient surplus to spade up the garden also. It is, I repeat, an absurd denial of all known chemical and mechanical principles to assert that the body works by means of energy generated by its own functional action. As well claim that a man can lift himself by his boot straps.

Power is stored in the brain during sleep, and is probably transmitted to the muscles and organs over the nerves in a manner similar to the transmission of electrical energy over a trolley wire; and there is no evidence that this power comes from our food at all. Food does not "strengthen" us; there is no such thing as a "strengthening" food. We need food to furnish the tissue elements, not to supply power; and every mouthful we eat in excess of the actual need weakens us and tends to shorten our lives. Most people expend more than half of their total life-force in the disposition of unnecessary food; if we only ate from one-tenth to one-half of what we now consume most of us would die of old age, and the average of life in the next generation would probably be beyond the century mark. This shocks you, doesn't it? Well, it is hard, scientific fact; I am just trying to write it in plain, common sense words.

But, you say, do not we *feel* more strength after eating?

Yes, but not after digesting our food. If strength comes from the assimilation of food it can only be after the food is completely digested; a partially digested mass in the stomach certainly cannot yield any work-power. Now it takes some hours, at least, to complete the process of assimilation; but the accession of strength is always felt *immediately* after swallowing the food. You are tired and weak; you swallow a cup of coffee and a piece of toast, and you rise and go to work refreshed; it has "strengthened " you, you say. But it has not; if you will pause to think you will see that your fresh strength cannot have come from the food, which has not had time to be changed at all; it is coffee and toast in your stomach, and will be, for some time; how can it strengthen you before it is digested? And three or four hours hence, when it *is* digested, you will be as weak as ever. If we get our energy from food, is it before or after we digest it?

You are stronger right after your noon-day meal, but at five p. m., when the food is digested, you are all tired out; and with all your eating you suffer a steady decline in power from the time you emerge from unconsciousness in the morning until you return to it at night. The accession of strength you felt after taking the coffee and toast did not come from the food; it was from the rally nature made, summoning her power to the task of disposing of the food. She drew on the brain for an extra supply of its stored-up energy to perform the work of digestion, and as this power was turned on you felt it throughout the body; but the power came from the brain, and not from the stomach.

We do not live by bread alone; we do not really live by bread at all. Beefsteak and potatoes are not the raw materials from which life and mind are made. The old physiology is controverted by the law of the conservation of energy.

So much for our first proposition; now for the second:

Most muscle workers would be stronger, healthier and longer lived on one-half, and most brain workers on one-tenth of the food they now consume.

Since Dr. Dewey's books were published some hundreds of thousands of people have adopted the no-breakfast plan, going entirely without food until noon; and nearly all of them have found, to their astonishment, that they were stronger, brighter, and had more work-power without the breakfast than with it. And the exceptions are nearly always those who cannot grasp the idea that the possession of strength does not depend on keeping the stomach full. This is the philosophy of the no-breakfast plan: You awake with the brain fully charged with work-power, and your blood contains the tissue elements of the previous days' food; you are, therefore, in the best possible condition for work. Why should you eat? It takes power to run the stomach; why not save the power for your other work? You are not realty hungry; there is no such thing as a normal hunger on arising in the morning, in a person who has been sufficiently fed on the previous day. Your morning appetite is a matter of habit; of mental attitude. You eat because you are afraid you will get faint later in the day; or you tickle your palate with sweet foods until you arouse a taste for more; but you never eat breakfast because you are genuinely hungry.

If you do not believe all this, put it to the best possible test; try it on yourself. Get up and go to work without eating; and if you are in anything approaching a normal condition you will find that you are in better condition for mental or physical labor with an empty stomach than with a full one. Mind, though, much depends upon your mental attitude; remember that many people who believe in the old physiology have starved to death in ten days, while others, better taught, have fasted forty days without much discomfort. If you *expect* that because your stomach is empty you will have a fainting fit about ten o'clock, the fainting fit will probably come; you will get just about what you look for. On the other hand, if you put the thought of food resolutely aside, and go to your work without fear of any disagreeable consequences yon will have a forenoon of such mental cheer, and of such physical vigor as you have seldom experienced; but you will not feel so well after your noon meal.

Why? Because you will overeat; you will mistakenly suppose that because you have done without breakfast you must eat enough, and more than enough at noon to make up the deficiency; and during the afternoon so much of your brain's energy will be required at the stomach that you will have very little left for mental or physical work. This ought to convince you that your stomach is a machine which absorbs energy, instead of being a generator for producing it. The object in dispensing with the breakfast is not to increase the quantity consumed at noon but to prevent the waste of energy in the disposition of unnecessary food. If you want to be strong, and full of snap and vigor, drop your breakfast entirely, leave off half your noon meal and two-thirds of your evening one. Eat just enough to maintain your weight; not a mouthful more. If you can hold your weight on one cracker a day, and you eat two crackers, the disposal of the superfluous one will be a waste of your life force; it will weaken you by just the amount of power required to dispose of it, and if you overeat as a matter of habit the surplus will be a source of danger, disease and premature death.

You don't believe it, do you? Well, it won't cost you a cent to prove it. If you want to have strength for your work, whether mental or physical, get eight hours of sleep every night in a well-ventilated room; eat plain, hearty food, and the smallest quantity which will maintain your weight. If it takes power to run the stomach it is foolish to keep it in operation more than is actually necessary. "For this cause many are weak and sickly among you, and many sleep." said St. Paul, writing to the Corinthians about overeating at the Lord's supper. Wise St. Paul!

Most of the dietary conclusions of the pseudoscience of medicine are based on false premises, and are therefore erroneous; and the recovery of most of the sick is greatly hindered by feeding, dosing, and other interference.

Most physicians accept the theory that we can add to the strength of a sick man by inducing him to swallow food; when the fact is that every mouthful is a tax on his strength, and decreases his power of resistance. It takes power to run the stomach. In every case of severe sickness Nature takes away the appetite, because there is no power to spare for the digestive process; she wishes to conserve her energy for combat with the disease. In severe sickness Nature's way is to suspend digestion and let the brain live on the tissues of the body, which can be spared. That is why a sick man loses in weight. If you feed him, and he still loses, it is proof positive that the food is not assimilated; if it *were* assimilated there could be no loss in weight. And if you continue to feed under such conditions you may be absolutely certain that you are loading up his system with waste matter which must be eliminated at a fearful cost in vital power. You may lay it down as a general law which is amply proven in practice, that in the absence of appetite the patient who is fed will lose weight and strength more rapidly than the one who is not fed. When the desire for food is absent, and the tongue is heavily coated, it should be interpreted to mean: "Busy; nothing wanted within." It is homicidal folly to feed under such conditions; the food decays in the alimentary canal, and generates poisons which are dangerous to life. No matter what the books say, it is foolish to feed the sick man whose breath tells in unmistakable language that his digestive tract is already filled with rotting filth. The sick horse will not eat; and it is to be hoped that sick men, women and children will someday be allowed by their physicians and friends to exercise horse sense. Nature would have the severely sick man sleep much, and not eat at all; *we* try to induce him to eat all he can, and we wake him every few minutes to force into his protesting stomach some nauseous or poisonous compound of drugs. Nine-tenths of our interference with the sick has no scientific justification, and is injurious to them. Put the sick man into a well-ventilated room; make him as comfortable as possible; shut out the neighbors, the family, the preacher— everybody but the nurse, and possibly the doctor; in most cases leave the doctor out, too. It would be a great deal better if two-thirds of the doctors had to resort to some other means of making a living; the other third could easily take care of all the cases where they are really needed. Give nature a chance with your sick one; and if he dies you may at least feel sure that you did not help to kill him.

The stomach is a machine which uses up power, and it is operated by power supplied from the brain, which is charged during sleep. Remember this physiological fact, and regulate your life accordingly; get sleep enough, and get it under favorable conditions, and eat less.

> *Sleep, that knits up the raveled sleeve of care,*
> *The death of each day's life;*
> *Balm of hurt minds, great nature's second course,*
> *Chief nourisher in life's feast.*
> —SHAKESPEARE, *"Macbeth"*

2. SLEEP.

He giveth His beloved sleep.—Ps. 127:2.

IN THE PRECEDING CHAPTER we considered some of the arguments for the new physiology, which holds that vital energy is renewed in sleep, and is not generated by the digestion of food. Man is not, as we have been taught to suppose, an engine whose power comes from the combustion of fuel, or food. If he were, he would never need rest or sleep; supplied with food he could keep on eating and working indefinitely, as an engine can work indefinitely if it is supplied with coal; whereas no matter how much or how often he eats, we know that he must have frequent lapses into the silence and unconsciousness of sleep in order to recharge his brain with that mysterious energy by which he lives and works.

We find by observation that the fact that vital power is received in sleep is universal with all forms of life. Men, animals, reptiles, fish and insects sleep; and plants sleep also. You will notice that I speak of vital power as being received, not generated; if the law of the conservation of energy holds good as applied to the energy displayed by the human body, then the energy of man is received from some source outside himself; for it is a mechanical impossibility for the organism to generate within itself the power to maintain itself, renew itself, and perform external work also. The human body cannot be regarded as being anything but a machine; and since it is found to be impossible for a machine to operate itself, and to do additional work with power generated by its own operation, 1 am compelled to accept the hypothesis that there is an inflow of life, which is received by all living organisms during sleep. Let me write this again, and call your attention to it for it is the greatest and most important scientific fact that has been given to the world in a century.

There is an inflow of vital power, which is received by all living organisms during sleep.

I do not know where this inflow of life comes from; I do not know whether it results from some combination of other forces or is a force which is eternally self-existent; I am simply stating the facts as I observe them, and giving the inevitable deductions from them. If the facts disprove the theories you have been holding, you will have to readjust your theories to fit the facts. It is a fact that the human body cannot possibly manufacture its own vital power and at the same time be manufactured by its own vital power; and it is a fact that it receives its vital power in sleep; and necessarily, from some source outside itself.

Life comes to us from somewhere; we do not make it; we receive it. I do not say that it is received only in sleep; I do not know but that there are conditions under which we may receive it when awake. Neither do I say that we always receive it directly from the unknown source; there may be individuals who can become so charged with it as to be able to communicate it to others; I do say, however, that no individual has power to create it in himself; he can only give what he has received, so that ultimately we all receive from the unknown source.

Now, as to the importance of all this. Hold up your finger, and examine it carefully. What made it? It is made of different chemical elements taken from the food you have eaten; but what combined those elements and built them into a finger? Life! You slept, and your brain was charged with power; that power was applied to the stomach and bowels and digested your food; it took the separate elements and emptied them into the blood; your heart, which beats by brain power, forced them along through the arteries until they came to the finger; and vital energy from the brain built them into bone, muscle, nerve and connective tissue. Life built the finger; and nothing but life can make another like it. All the science in the world cannot duplicate it; we may make something which looks very much the same, but it will not be like your finger at all. Be careful, therefore, about the gentleman who tells you that he has a "remedy" which will renew your finger or fix it up all right if there is anything the matter with it. Nothing can repair or renew the finger but the force which created it—vital power. Nothing can make a finger, nothing can mend a broken or injured finger, and nothing can cure a sick finger but life. There is no remedy, and no known force that can unite a broken bone save life only; and there is no remedy and no force that can make a heartbeat save life only. Nothing ever made a heartbeat but life; all the other powers in the world cannot send a single pulse-throb through the arteries of a dead body. No medicine ever made your heart beat, and none ever will; nothing ever made a heartbeat but vital power. The force which operates your heart is stored in your brain during sleep. The only manner in which a medicine could make your heart beat would be by causing the vital power to flow from your brain to your heart. I do not say that medicine can or cannot do this; I will touch upon this point again.

What is true of the heart is necessarily true of every other organ of the body; they are all operated by brainpower, and cannot be operated by any other power. We hear certain medicines spoken of as having power to move the bowels; but a little study must convince us that the only power on earth which can move the bowels is that which is stored in the brain. If a medicine causes the bowels to move it must do so by causing the brain to move them; you understand that I do not say that it is impossible for medicine to do this; I simply say that it is impossible that it should be done in any other way. The vital power which is stored in the brain during sleep is the only power capable of producing functional action in any part of the body. Your heart, stomach, liver, kidneys and bowels are not separate and independent machines, operated by different and extraneous powers; they are all parts of one machine, which is run by brain-power; and the brain is charged in sleep.

Now, if there is defective action, or congestion, or inflammation, or pain in any part of the body, the only possible way to effect a cure is by directing the brainpower to the affected part. If a medicine can do this it is of value, provided its benefit be not neutralized by reactionary or other effects. Local applications produce their curative effect in this manner; a mustard plaster cannot increase functional action in the organs over which it is applied, but it is possible that by it a chemical effect upon the tissues may cause the brain to turn its power in that direction, and so increase functional action. This is the only theory of medical action which is in accord with the facts; and we must apply it also in explaining the effects of exercise and massage. Neither exercise nor massage can build up a weak part; but either may cause the brain to build it up, by directing its power to it. Mental healing is accomplished in exactly the same way; it is done by consciously and intelligently directing the brain-power by concentration of mind; and it is by far the most scientific and effective method of healing, when not complicated by speculative absurdities which befuddle the mind and prevent direct and positive action.

Now, again, perhaps you do not see the importance of all this. Go back over this chapter, and the preceding one; examine the facts and study the logic of the deductions. You will hardly fail to become convinced that your body is a machine which is operated by power which is stored in your brain during sleep; and that no other agency can heal it, build it up, or keep it well but this brain-power. If you are sick or weak you know now where your cure is to be found; and you are ready to begin to act intelligently.

First, if the power which is to heal you is to be stored in your brain during sleep, you had better study sleep, and learn how to surround yourself with favorable conditions for the charging of your storage battery with power; sleep intelligently, and with a purpose, so as to get the best results. There are laws which govern the process of charging the brain with vital force; some of them are known; enough to enable you to set to work with a reasonable certainty of getting good results.

Second, having learned how to charge your brain with vital power you must learn how to conserve the power; how to keep yourself from throwing it away, and expending it uselessly; and this is more important, perhaps, than you imagine. Most people waste at least half their vital power.

Third, you will need to learn how to turn this force to the part where it is most needed; and this involves the consideration of all medicines, treatments, exercises, and mental processes.

What we need above all else is to be scientific in our methods of arriving at conclusions. We must avoid speculation, and fanciful theories based on the supposed need for retaining old medical or religious dogmas, and stick to the facts and to the deductions which are the inevitable corollary of the facts. If the facts do not accord with the teaching of the doctor and the physiological authorities, we will have to disbelieve the doctor and the authorities, and accept the facts; and if the facts disagree with the dogmas of the preacher we will have to ask the preacher to revise his dogmas; we must keep to the facts. And here, again, are some of the facts, and some of the things which the facts prove:

In death by starvation the brain loses no weight, but is nourished at the expense of the other tissues of the body. Death does not come so long as there are other tissues available for the brain to feed upon. This proves that the brain, not the stomach is the alpha—the center of vital power.

The structure of the body goes to prove that the brain is the power-plant; the afferent nerves carrying sensation in, and the efferent ones carrying power out. It is an absurdity to suppose that muscular power is generated by the muscles themselves; it is far more reasonable to assume that power is transmitted to them over the nerves in a manner similar to the transmission of power over an electric wire.

The strength of the body is not drawn from food; because (a) It would be impossible to extract the amount of energy displayed by the body from the quantity of food consumed; (b) Work-power does not increase in proportion to the quantity of food digested; (c) If work-power came from food we would not be obliged to sleep for the purpose of renewing our strength; and (d) The digestion of food is work in itself, and requires the expenditure of power; it cannot, therefore, be done with power drawn in the ultimate from its own processes. Work cannot do itself with power furnished by itself. It is a manifest impossibility that the body should work with energy manufactured by its own internal processes, which are themselves a part of its work, and consume its power.

Lastly, we see that every living thing goes regularly to sleep, and wakes with renewed energy.

From all this we deduce:

That the external work of the human organism is done, and its internal processes carried on by means of a vital energy which is accumulated in the brain during sleep.

That this vital energy is the only power by which the body may be healed, repaired, renewed or maintained.

Were I to adopt a pet idea as so many people do, and fondle it in my embraces to the exclusion of all others, it would be, that the great want which mankind labors under at this present period is sleep. The world should recline its vast head on the first convenient pillow and take an age-long nap. It has gone distracted through a morbid activity, and while preternaturally wide awake, is nevertheless tormented by visions that seem real to it now, but would assume their true aspect and character were all things once set right by an interval of soul repose. — HAWTHORNE, "Mosses from an Old Manse"

The mind grows wiser by watching, but her sister, the body, of coarser materials, needs the support of repose. — SCOTT, "Talisman"

3. TO USE SLEEP.

HAVING SETTLED that the brain is charged with vital power during sleep, the next important thing is to study the process, and see if we may arrive at any conclusion as to the laws which govern it. In observing the phenomena of sleep, the most noticeable thing is the change in the manner of breathing. The sleeping person breathes deeply, strongly and with a more rhythmic movement than the waking one; a much larger quantity of air is taken into the system in a given time during sleep than when awake. Very few persons breathe audibly when awake, while frequently the deep, strong breathing of a sleeping person can be heard throughout a house of ordinary size. Since deep and rhythmic breathing is universal during sleep, I conclude that it is an essential part of the process of charging the brain with vital power, and that a large quantity of air is necessary to the operation. I notice an apparent connection between air and vital power, as shown by other phenomena. When I am about to undertake a heavy lift, or to perform some feat of strength, I instinctively fill my lungs with air, as if by so doing I could add to my muscular power; and if I exercise violently nature compels me to breathe with great force and rapidity, evidently needing an increased quantity of air because of the strenuous exertion. There appears, I say, to be a direct connection between air and energy. But I find that deep breathing is not all; I cannot renew the energy of the brain by deep breathing without sleep; I must go into the silence and become unconscious. And I do not know *what* it is in the air that is essential to life. It is not oxygen alone, for if you put me in an atmosphere of undiluted oxygen I will die. I must have air.

It is essential, too, that the air be pure. When I sleep in a room with no ventilation I rise in the morning unrefreshed; the battery has been very imperfectly charged. It is therefore necessary to have air which is in motion; since motion is essential to the purity of air. It will not answer the purpose to set a spool of thread under the window and put the bed's head back in the corner, out of the "draft." The draft is just what I want to get into. The object of ventilation is to produce motion in the air, so that we can breathe air which moves. It is not enough to raise the sash well up, if that is the only opening, for the air in the center of the room, or in the corner where the bed's head stands may be absolutely motionless and stagnant and remain so throughout the night.

There is not the slightest reason for the universal fear of drafts; a draft is air in motion, and motion does not impart any evil quality to air; on the contrary, moving air is far more likely to be pure than that which is stagnant The chemical processes by which air purifies itself depends on motion. There is no reason to suppose that cold air is dangerous; that is, if it is not so cold as to actually freeze one. The night air is not less salubrious than day air. Night air is air with the light out of it, and taking the light out of air does not make it noxious. There is no evidence to support the idea that damp air is harmful ; damp air is air with a little water in it, and water is not a poison.

If you lack vitality of power and wish to proceed scientifically in charging your brain with it, you must first disabuse your mind of the notion that pure air, in any place or under any condition or in any quantity is harmful; and you must come to understand the fact that the first great necessity of life is a plentiful supply of absolutely pure air during sleep.

So, attend first to the ventilation of your sleeping room. If there is only one room in the house that can be ventilated sleep in that room no matter how inconvenient it may be otherwise. Begin by providing for a current of air across the room. Open a door or window on each side; wide open. Do not be afraid of burglars; better be carried off by a burglar than by the undertaker. When you have arranged for a current of air through the room, pull your bed out so that your head will be right in the middle of the stream. If you are not quite free from the old fear of moving air, you had better do this gradually, bringing the bed out a foot or two at a time; otherwise you may scare yourself to death with your fears of the dreadful "draft!"

Now understand that no matter what your disease may be, there is only one power which can cure you. You may have consumption, typhoid fever, appendicitis, cancer, liver complaint, a broken leg or a sore toe; but the only power which can make you whole is your own vital energy. The life that is in you is all the life there is; and you must accumulate enough of it to overcome the diseased or morbid condition. And you get it in sleep, and fresh, pure, *moving* air is absolutely necessary to the process. Do not close the window because it is damp; breathe

the pure air, water and all. Do not close the window because it is cold; pile on bed clothes or make a fire. Do not "air" your bedroom during the day and close it at night; better reverse the process. Sleep the year round with your head in a running stream of pure air, fresh from out-of-doors.

There are certain other things which are pretty well established. In a vast majority of cases eight hours is about the right length of time to pass in sleep every day. More than eight hours is too much It is generally better to sleep six hours than ten. Don't ask me why, because I do not know.

And a condition of absolute physical and mental relaxation and passivity is demanded for the best results. It is a mistake to eat before going to bed. The digestion of food is work, and if you wish to gain strength you should not work while you are sleeping. I know, if you are mentally excited or disturbed you can often become unconscious more speedily after eating; that is because the stomach is robbing the brain of power, but unconsciousness while the brain works is not genuine sleep, and the charging process is very imperfect under such conditions; and you will lack power the next day. And you cannot make up the loss by eating more; the more you eat the weaker you will be. What you lose in sleep cannot be recovered at the table. There are better ways of curing insomnia than by overworking the stomach. Never mind what anybody tells you about the necessity for stuffing; go to bed with your stomach empty. The digestion of food is work, and you cannot have a natural, effective sleep while you are at work.

So far, you will please notice, I have written on physical energy or work power; not of will power. Will power, or spiritual control is also acquired in the silence, but with this difference— we do not become unconscious. We will talk about that in a subsequent chapter, but I want to call attention here to the fact that certain thought conditions are essential to perfect sleep. A brain whose power is being drawn upon for thought cannot sleep. You cannot sleep and dream at the same time; the more you dream the less perfect is the renewal of your vital power. I do not wish you "pleasant dreams" or any other kind; I hope you may sleep.

Absolute quietude of mind; the cessation of all physical and mental activity, the relaxation which comes only with perfect trust in God, is a necessary condition for "restful" sleep; but while this is true, there is an element of positive thought which may enter in, possibly with advantage. It is a demonstrable fact, as I will show you later, that the brain power may be directed to or withheld from any part of the body by thought; and there is pretty good evidence that the character of the last thought on going to sleep may influence the course of the brain current during the night. Those who indulge in lascivious waking dreams are apt to have lascivious sleeping dreams; and to become unduly stimulated in the sexual system by an abnormal turning of power in that direction. I am quite sure that it is possible to turn the vital energy toward any weak or defective organ, ongoing to sleep; but I am not so confident as to the wisdom of this, for it seems to me that sleep is for the gathering of force, and not for its expenditure in healing, or any other activities. I would be careful about setting the mind at work to heal myself or others during sleep; the best time to think your healing thoughts is when you are awake. Suppose, when you lie down tonight you try a formula like the following:

"I have opened my windows, and the pure air, filled with vital power, comes streaming in; the One Great Life is seeking to find me, and to fill me with Itself. I relax, and open my soul as I have opened my windows; I shall be filled with Life while I sleep; and it will give me power to overcome every ill, and all weakness. Flow in, oh, Life, and give me strength; and I will use it, by the guidance of Thy love, to do Thy will. Amen."

The first wealth is health. —EMERSON

Oh, thou that pinest in the imprisonment of the Actual, and criest bitterly to the God* for a kingdom wherein to rule and create, know this of a truth, the thing thou seekest is already with thee, here or nowhere, couldst thou only see! —THOMAS CARLYLE

4. SCIENTIFIC LIVING AND HEALING

NOT MANY THINGS are harder to over come than the persistent auto-suggestion that life is of material origin, and that vital power comes from food. It takes a great deal of argument to make the average man (especially if he is a woman) understand that his strength is renewed in sleep, and that he grows weaker, not stronger by eating. Possibly not many of our readers are firmly grounded in this faith as yet; I shall have to argue it a little further for you, even at the risk of repeating myself.

Let me call your attention, first, to the fact that loss of appetite nearly always accompanies severe sickness. Now, if strength comes from food, why does nature "go back on us" just when we need strength most? Why does she not make the sick man ravenous with hunger, as she does the woodchopper? The latter needs food in large quantities to replace the tissues destroyed by his strenuous toil; he has digestive power, and hunger is given to him. Why should not hunger be given to the sick man, so that he can generate vital power from the food, build up his strength and get well?

The appetite is taken away in severe sickness because nature needs all her power for the work of restoring normal conditions, and there is none to spare for the labor of digestion. The digestion of food is work, and hard work; the sick man's brain has not the power for it. So nature says, "Keep out; we are busy inside; when we are ready for food we will let you know." Sick horses never eat; but sick people--or at least their friends and physicians— seldom have horse sense. When the appetite is taken away it is considered a sign that nature requires "light" foods; or that the earth should be ransacked for tempting dainties to create an appetite; whereas, nature simply wants to be let alone. Food given when the tongue is coated and the appetite gone is seldom digested; it decomposes, and the condition within the stomach of the unfortunate one becomes something horrible to think about; a putrid, poisonous mass, the dreadful odor of which can often be distinguished throughout a large apartment

The person who fasts loses weight, but the loss all falls upon those tissues which can best be spared; and even in death by starvation, the brain and nervous system lose no weight at all. That is, the brain *eats up* the other tissues; and death does not come until the skeleton condition is reached, and there is nothing more for the brain to absorb. The brain must be sustained; when there is no other food it draws its nourishment from the body itself. The sick man loses in weight by just this process; and it is the intention of nature that he should do so. I am not speaking of the sick man who *has* hunger, you understand, but of the severely sick one who has none. Nature desires his brain to live on its stored-up resources for a few days; she wants to economize power. And if you feed him he generally keeps right on losing weight; and the more you feed the faster he loses which is proof positive that he does not assimilate food. If he did, how could he lose weight? He lies still, and is not destroying any tissue; if he assimilated food he could not fail to gain in weight. And, I repeat, the patient who is fed generally loses weight and strength faster than the one who eats nothing at all; proving that the disposition of the food is a tax on his energy. It would be as logical, and as scientific, to set the sick man chopping wood as to feed him; working his stomach is as bad for him as working his arms would be.

Even when the sickness is chronic, and there if some appetite, the greatest care should be used not to overeat. Where little or no exercise is taken, the amount of food required is very small indeed, and there is nothing to gain and everything to lose by eating more than is readily assimilated. Very, very many invalids are kept weak and low because their brain power is wasted by overeating; sick or well, if you are eating more than is required to maintain your body you are robbing yourself of vital power, and charging your system with deadly poison besides.

In case of severe sickness, do not offer the patient food nor mention it in his presence; put him in a cool, airy room and make him as comfortable as possible; give him a chance to sleep; do not let him be talked to, or fussed over; keep out the neighbors, the doctor and the preacher; and if the disease is curable, he will get well. The scientific use (or non-use, as the case may be) of air, water, food, exercise, sleep and thought will cure any disease that is curable at all.

Be sure you do not mention food until the sick one asks for it with well-developed hunger. Do not fear that he will suddenly starve to death, and drop off all in a minute when your back is turned. He will starve faster if you feed him than if you do not. Trust nature; when she is ready for food she will let you know.

If the sickness is not severe, and there is little appetite, bear in mind that the way to conserve brain power is to eat no more than is actually demanded, and that a sick person, who exercises little needs very little indeed. One egg makes a pretty fair day's ration for the average sick person—even for one who is "up and around"; and if most of the sick who are trying to eat all they can, and racking their brains and those of their friends to think of "something they can eat," would cut their day's food down to one egg, or its equivalent in weight and value, they would surprise themselves and their doctors by an immediate gain in weight and strength. Save your brain power, and get strong and well.

Let us now give a little thought to the phenomena we see in the class of diseases called catarrhal—coughs, colds, hay fevers, etc. In many cases an enormous quantity of matter is expectorated or discharged; and the question I wish to press upon you is, Where does it all come from? Clearly, nothing can come out of the body through the mouth, which has not been put into it -, and as things are generally put into the body through the mouth, is it not apparent that what is blown out of the head must have gotten into the body by way of the stomach? Is it not an unavoidable conclusion that catarrhal discharges are taken from the food consumed; that they are simply food matter gone wrong? If there is a discharge from the body we know that one of two things must be true; either the tissues are breaking up and coming away, or the discharge comes from the dining tables.

This is the process of "taking cold." A pound of food is needed in the system, and we eat, say, two pounds. Digestion being good, the whole quantity is taken into the blood. Nature has use for only one pound, and she uses that, repairing bone, muscle and nerve. The other pound she has no use for, but it has been forced upon her, and she must dispose of it. She may deposit a little of it on the body in the form of fat, and eliminate more through the kidneys, lungs and skin; but there will still be some ounces left to decay in the blood—for food matter will decay in the blood. So there is a little rotten matter—sewage— left in the blood as the result of that meal. At the next meal the process is repeated; and at the next, and the next The quantity of decaying waste in the blood gets greater, until at last the arterial flow is like a stream into which the sewage of a city is emptied, foul and thick with decaying refuse, which all comes from the dining table.

At last the stream gets so thick that nature must call a halt; she cannot carry on the processes of bodily renewal with that foul blood; it must be purified. So there is a chill; a congestion in some part of the mucous membrane, and the impurities begin to be strained off. When you take cold you cough up and blow out the surplus food you have been eating; it would kill you if you did not get rid of it. The cold is an effort of nature to save your body from dissolution. It is not caused by drafts or exposure; it is caused by overeating. If you do not overeat you may sit in drafts, or sleep in them, or expose yourself as you please, and you will not take cold. You "catch" cold at the table; you cannot get one anywhere else. That is where we get catarrh, which is a chronic cold. A year of scientific living will cure the worst case of catarrh that ever happened, climate or no climate. And this is the way the new physiology accounts for catarrh, and catarrhal diseases. You may easily avoid these ills if you only realize that you do not have to stuff yourself with large quantities of food in order to generate vital power. Your life is more than meat. It is not drawn from material things, and food does not contribute to life or strength in any way. You need food only to supply the spirit with material from which to construct a body, and the quantity required is very, very much less than most of you have believed.

Let us talk a little now about "germ" diseases. The people of the city of Chicago have dug great tunnels out under the lake a mile or so, to get pure water. They want to get far away from the water of the river, which is thick with rotting sewage, like the blood of a glutton. There are plenty of disease germs in the river, but none out in the lake; disease germs cannot live and propagate in water which does not contain sewage; and it is also a fact that they cannot propagate in blood which does not contain sewage. If your blood is like the pure water of Lake Michigan no disease germ can live in it; but if it is like the Chicago river it will be a breeding ground for any organism that may be introduced into it This is bedrock, scientific fact. If your blood is pure yon are immune to germ diseases; you cannot have typhoid, la grippe, smallpox or diphtheria, nor can you catch cold. Disease germs can only propagate in impure blood, and blood is made impure by overeating, and by not breathing enough.

How much more sensible and scientific to purify the stream than to try to neutralize the germs by loathsome counter-poisons!

Let me close this chapter outlining a sane regime of living. We do not need food on arising in the morning. We have slept, and the brain is fully charged with power; there is no demand for food, for there has been no destruction of tissues. No one is really hungry in the morning; the appetite for breakfast is a forced and unnatural one. Most people do not eat breakfast because they are hungry, but for fear of collapse later in the day; they think to store up energy in the stomach against a future need. Drop off the breakfast altogether, and as soon as you get your mind adjusted to the plan you will find that no matter whether your work is mental or physical you can do more of it "on an empty stomach" and do it better. At noon, eat a moderate meal of any plain hearty food that your taste may call for; and eat a very light supper between six and seven o'clock. If you are a brain worker, make your dinner very light also; by "light" I mean small in quantity, not of chaffy materials.

Bo not bother your head about carbohydrates and nitrogens; eat what you like best. The invalid and the brain worker need exactly the same foods that the woodchopper needs, but not nearly so much. Tour taste is the safest guide as to what you shall eat; let it be beans, potatoes, sauerkraut, hog and hominy—anything that will stay on a Christian stomach, if you desire it, but not too much! And above all things, *never* eat when you are not hungry.

Life is an energy which is stored in the brain during sleep. If we understand that material food plays no part in the generation of this energy, and govern our appetites accordingly, we shall have perfect health. If we live according to the simple law of life no material thing can harm us. We are spiritual beings; we get our life in the Great Silence, out of which we came. We shall live after we cease to eat, for we do not live by eating now; our physical bodies are kept up by a mysterious power which comes to us while we are unconscious. God is Spirit; and He giveth life to all.

It is notorious that a single successful effort of moral volition, such as saying "No" to some habitual temptation, or performing some courageous act, will launch a man on a higher level of energy for days and weeks, will give him a new range of power. The emotions and excitements due to usual situations are the usual inciters of the will. But these act discontinuously; and in the intervals the shallower levels of life tend to close in and shut us off. Accordingly the best knowers of (he human soul have invented the thing known as methodical, ascetic discipline to keep the deeper levels constantly in reach. Beginning with easy tasks, passing to harder ones, and exercising day by day, it is, I believe, admitted that disciples of asceticism can reach very high levels of freedom and power of will. Ignatius Loyola's spiritual exercises must have produced this result in innumerable devotees. But the most venerable ascetic system, and the one whose results have the most voluminous, experimental corroboration is undoubtedly the Yoga system in Hindustan. — WILLIAM JAMES, "Energies of Men"

5. MIND CURES

IN THE SECOND CHAPTER I asserted that nothing can repair, restore, heal or renew the body or any part of it but vital powers—the energy which is stored in the brain during sleep. Nothing but brain power, conducted to it over the "motor" nerves, can make a heartbeat; and nothing but brain power can "strengthen" a weak heart. Nothing but brain power can cause a liver to secrete bile; and a "torpid" liver is one to which the brain power is imperfectly conducted or applied. Nothing but brain power can cause a movement of the bowels; the only power which can cure constipation is that which is stored in the brain during sleep. This is pretty hard for you to believe, if you have been taking medicines to "strengthen" your heart, "act" on your liver, and "move" your bowels; but it is a demonstrable scientific fact nevertheless. How much medicine will it take to make a dead man's heart beat, his liver act or his bowels move? Can medicine move heart, liver or bowels when the brain is not charged with life? The most that can be said of medicine it that it (or the belief in it,) causes the brain power to be applied to certain parts of organs. You must understand that your liver like every other organ of your body is built and planned to be operated by brain power; it cannot be operated by medicine, or by anything else, any more than an electric motor can be made to run by turning a steam jet against it. The electric motor is only built to be run by one kind of power; and the same is true of the liver. There is not the slightest evidence that there is any "remedy" which can "act" on the liver, or cause the liver to act; and this is true of all the viscera.

How, then, do we get effects from medicine? Let me show you. Suppose I begin to write here a detailed description of things good to eat—fried chicken, lemon pie, strawberries and cream—yum, yum! You read a little way, and you notice an increased flow of saliva into your mouth; it "makes your mouth water." How can the thought of strawberries and cream cause the saliva to flow? Only by causing the brain power to be turned on; nothing but brain power can cause the salivary glands to act. Tickle the inside of the mouth with a straw and the saliva will flow; why? Because the afferent nerves carry the irritation to the brain and cause the power to be turned on. The power is turned on to the whole digestive system by the thought of eating; and it is withheld by anxiety, or the fear of indigestion; but that is another story, which I will tell you a little farther on.

Suppose, instead of strawberries and cream, I tell you of something horrible and disgusting,—say a dead cat. Pretty soon you begin to be nauseated; and you may even vomit How can the thought of a dead cat cause vomiting? Only by causing the brain power to be turned on to the stomach with that intention; and that is the only way an emetic can produce its effect Nothing but the brain can cause vomiting; an emetic introduced into a dead man's stomach lies inert and powerless. Some emetics act through belief only; others, perhaps, irritate the sensory nerves of the stomach in such a way as to cause the power to be turned on; but it is always the brain which really empties the stomach.

Of course there are medicines which act directly on the parts with which they come in contact—corrosive chemicals which affect the lining membranes of the alimentary canal. These ought never to be taken, and the ignorance which prescribes them is homicidal. Irritation of the sensory nerves, in any part of the body, causes the power to be turned on in that direction. That, as I have mentioned in a previous chapter, explains the action of all "strengthening," "soothing," "healing" and other applications. A mustard plaster has no power to increase action in the parts beneath it; but its irritation causes the brain to act. Liniments, etc., cannot overcome morbid conditions; but by reflex action or by the patient's faith, they may cause the direction of an increased amount of brain power to the affected part And there is not the slightest evidence that medicines do or can "act" except as described above.

What I say of medicine applies also to massage and exercise. Massage may shake and work loose the obstructions to the circulation in a congested tissue; and it may cause the brain power to be turned on. It cannot increase "local action" because, strictly speaking, there is no local action; all action is from the brain. Shaking and pounding a torpid liver, loosens the morbid matter in the ducts and channels and draws power from the brain to move the matter on; but it does not cause the liver to act, for the liver never acts; the brain acts through it. This ought to be understood in applying massage: That there are two things to accomplish, the thorough loosening of the tissues and opening of the channels, and the turning on of power of the brain. Massage cannot "build up" a weak or defective part; only brain power can do that.

This is also true of exercise. Exercise does not strengthen weak parts; the brain does that Exercise does not make big muscles; the brain does *that* also! Don't fly off the handle, you physical culture enthusiast; let me explain. How do you build up a weak part by exercise? Flex and relax the biceps muscles vigorously for a few moments; the quantity of blood flowing to it is greatly increased, and the blood carries the food; the muscle is fed more just in proportion as it is used more, and it grows larger and thicker. The benefit of exercise is that it turns the brain power to the part you wish to build up; and with brain power goes an increased blood supply, which carries the nourishment. So it is the brain which makes the big muscles, you see. Exercise really tears a part down, and the brain restores it. And let me give you a gentle hint right here. If the above is true— and it surely is—*all* exercise is not beneficial to a sick man, but only those movements which direct the power to the afflicted part. If your back is weak and you take arm and leg exercises, you are drawing power away from the part you wish to help; that is the reason why "physical culture courses" under the guidance of pugilists and ex-champion wrestlers are as apt to do the sick harm as to do them good. For a weak back, take ten minutes night and morning of exercise which uses the muscles in the weak place; and do not neutralize the effect by going through other movements which draw the power to other parts of the body. Remember that ten minutes twice a day is worth more than two hours at irregular intervals; what you want to do is to regularly, systematically and continuously demand of the brain that a little more power and nourishment be sent to the weak part. *That* is the way to exercise scientifically for curative effect. Ask, and keep on asking, and ye shall receive.

That is you will receive if you put your mind into the demand. And now we are at the *crux of* this whole healing business. Neither medicine, massage nor exercise can produce effect if opposed by the mind of the patient. I hope you will read and consider carefully what follows. It is the most important of all, so far.

Let a person be laid on his back on a bed, accurately balanced so that the head and foot may swing up and down; now let him be asked to perform severe mental labor, and the bed's head will tip down, because of an increased flow of blood to his head. Let him go through a series of leg exercises and the foot of the bed will tip down, because of the increased flow of blood to the legs, and mark! Let him *think* out the leg exercises, without moving a muscle, and the foot will go down, showing that it is the *intention* to move which sends the blood to the legs; and if the intention is formed in the mind, the power goes whether the movement is really executed or not. It is the *thought* of exercise, and not really the exercise which sends the blood to the muscle; and if the thought be withheld the exercise accomplishes next to nothing as a building process. That is why exercise which is taken under compulsion, which is a drag and a task, does no good. That is why mere muscular toil and drudgery rarely make strong men and women, but generally make weaker ones. Work or exercise to be beneficial must be done freely, joyously and confidently; if it be mechanical and automatic it is useless expenditure of power, and tears down instead of building up.

And if the positive thought of action can send power and nourishment to the muscles of the legs, it necessarily follows that the same must be true of all parts and organs of the body. The firm, steady concentration of thought upon the "torpid" liver with the positive will and purpose to make it "go" will certainly cause action where action is possible at all. This is true of all cases of arrested action, unless there is some mechanical obstruction which requires massage, manipulation or surgery. If there is a part of the machine which isn't working, turn on the power by steady, concentrated, purposeful *thought;* understand that you possess at all times the power to control and direct your own vital power. And if there is a thought that turns on the power, so there must be thoughts that shut it off; and this we find by experiment to be true also. Fear or anxiety instantly arrests action. If you think of your liver with fear you shut off the power from it; if you think of your stomach with anxiety you deprive it of energy; if you think with fear or anxiety of the bowels yon paralyze them. In most cases of constipation the cause is entirely in a habit of mind or thought which withholds power from the bowels. All cases of indigestion are greatly aggravated by anxious thought about the digestibility of foods. When you begin to worry about what you shall eat you begin to have dyspepsia. Don't think about the values of digestibility of different foods; eat what tastes good to you, but only eat from one-fifth to one-sixteenth of what your friends would like to have you eat. That is all that is necessary to cure stomach trouble. We hear it said of melancholy people that they have the blues because their livers are bad; that is generally the reverse of the truth; their livers are bad because they have the blues.

Remember that the calm, confident, purposeful thought of faith sends the life power flowing out; and the fear thought locks it in. And can we cultivate power to think the thoughts of faith and cheer, and avoid those of anxiety, fear and discouragement? Yes, and that will be the subject for a subsequent chapter of this series.

Every man has experienced how feelings which end in themselves and do not express themselves in action, leave the heart debilitated. We get feeble and sickly in character when we feel keenly, and cannot do the thing we feel. —ROBERTSON

The flighty purpose never is o'ertook,

Unless the deed go with it; from this moment

The very firstlings of my heart shall be

The firstlings of my hands.

No boasting like a fool;

This deed I'll do before the purpose cool.

—SHAKESPEARE, "Macbeth"

6. NATURE AND DEVELOPMENT OF WILL POWER.

"Burnt offerings for sin thou wouldst not.
Lo, I come to do thy will, Oh, God!" —Heb. x: 8-9.

IN HUMAN LIFE I seem to see three different forms of manifestations of energy, which for convenience's sake I am going in this article to call physical, mental, and spiritual. Physical energy is what we have been treating of in this series of articles; proving that it is not drawn from food, but is received in sleep. It is the life force of the organism, the work power of the body. Mental energy is thought power. I do not know what the difference between physical work power and thought power may be; I do not know whether there is a difference or not; but I know that there are individuals who have a great deal of physical power and apparently very little thought power; and there are others who have a great deal of thought power and very little vital energy; and so I will consider them as separate forms of force. We will, therefore, adopt this hypothesis; that you display three forms of energy; first, the physical power, which carries on the work of the material body, and second, the power which runs your think-machine. I do not know what your think-machine is, or where it is; I do not know whether you think with your brain or not; I am inclined to think that you do not; but anyway, I know that you have a thinker, because you think; and I know that it takes power to operate your thinker, because thought is a force itself, and cannot be produced without the expenditure of force. So I know that you have a thinker and that it takes power to run it; and I am assuming that this power is different from physical energy, although I do not know that it is; but it makes my point a little clearer to speak of physical energy and thought power as if they were different things.

Now, this thinker of yours is absolutely indifferent to moral considerations. It knows nothing, and cares nothing about good and evil. There is no connection between thought power and goodness. Bad people often have much thought power, and many excellent souls have very little. A devil may be a very keen and acute thinker, and a saint may be almost destitute of reasoning power. Your thinking machine works in the direction in which you set it running. If you start it planning to execute a noble deed of charity, it will go on and arrange all the details, and if you put it at work on a plan to rob a bank, it will work on the details of that plan just as readily. I think you will agree with me, however, that you have, at least in a rudimentary way, the power to control and direct your think-machine. You tell it to think about this, and it does; or to cease thinking about this, and to consider that, and it obeys you. So you see here are the three forms of power I have mentioned— first, physical power; second, thought power, and third, the power to control and direct the thought

Now, it is this power to control and direct the think machine that we wish to develop. The trouble is that there are too many other forces operating it Someone, or something, starts it running on the fear thought or the thought of despondency and discouragement, and it runs away from us; we want to master it completely, so that it will only work on the thoughts of hope and faith and love and health; how to do it is the question; how to develop this power of control. For it is not a thing to be acquired, but one to be developed; we have it within.

Did your thinking-machine ever run away with you along the line of self-pity? First, it says, you are not appreciated; you are not understood; those around you do not realize how fine your nature is, and how delicate your sensibilities are! They are all blind, callous, selfish; they do not love you as they ought, they do not see, or seem to care how they make you suffer! Ah well, they will be sorry, when it is too late! And then your imagination runs on and you see yourself sick, dying, dead—and your weeping friends stricken with awful remorse, standing around your coffin and wishing they had treated you better—did your thinker ever get started on that line? And when it reached a certain point did not something else seem to rise up within you and say: "Nonsense! You know better than all this! Stop it, and think sense!" It was as if the engine ran away while the engineer slept, and he suddenly awakened and assumed control. This engineer is always within you. You have always faith and hope and love at the center of your being. You do not have to acquire them from without, but to arouse them within. The engineer is there, but he is like one in a tomb, asleep; he must hear the voice and come forth. That is salvation. "You who were dead in trespasses and sins hath he quickened," said St. Paul, who was very scientific. To be dead in trespasses and sins is simply to have lost control of your thinker. The engineer is in a dead sleep, and the sin thought and the fear thought and the disease thought are running the engine. The force works undirected. How shall we waken the engineer, and get him "quickened" so he will stay awake? How shall we vitalize this third principle, and get the power of control over our own internal forces? This is the supreme question. We know how to charge the battery of vital power in sleep; how shall we energize the soul?

Let me point you to the connection between silence and physical power. When you want vital energy you have to quit reaching, snatching, and grabbing for it, and just lie and shut your eyes and let it come. To charge the brain with power you must get still; stop the busy hand, close the eye, suspend the action of the senses; and life comes in. Cease all activities, and couple on to the one Eternal Life as to a dynamo, and get charged. That is the process. Why not try it in charging the will? Suspend all other work and make connection with the Eternal Will, and receive spiritual power as we receive physical energy; why not?

I wonder if any of our readers were ever in an old-fashioned Quaker meeting, where the congregation sat in silence for an hour? If you were, you know something of how it feels to be in an atmosphere surcharged with spiritual power. For a hundred devout men and women to sit together in perfect silence for an hour, with their thoughts withdrawn from earthly things and their souls open toward God—it is no wonder that the early Quakers were spiritual giants and giantesses. It is a great pity that the friends of the present day have fallen in line with the practices of their competitors and fill every moment of their meetings with gibble, gabble, gobble,—words, words, words! The marked spiritual power which once distinguished the Quakers came to them in their silent meetings, and they have lost it with the discontinuance of the practice. The silent meeting was scientific; it was in line with the law of transmission of life, and to that law you must individually conform if you are to have energy of soul.

So, this is the method. Go into your closet and shut the door. Get by yourself in the quietest place you can find, and where you may be free from interruption for a little while. And sit down; relax the body; rest. And now, stop thinking. You have not gone apart to meditate, or to think about God, or about anything else. Stop thinking; silence; be still. And when you are still begin to pray. Now this is a wordless prayer, and a prayer without thought. You are not to pray with the thinking-machine but with the will. You are not to think thoughts and tell them to God; nor are you to ask Him to think thoughts and tell them to you. You are not seeking God's thoughts but His energy. You do not wish to hitch your thinker to His thinker, but to unite your will to His will. You will readily see that if there is a purpose in the universe, there must also be a will behind the purpose, and this will must be the source of all will power. Get rid of the notion that there is any connection or similarity between stubbornness and will power. Will power is power to control and direct your own thought. It is spiritual energy and comes by connection with the universal will, in like manner as physical energy comes by connection with One Life.

What manner of prayer, then, will connect your will with the will of God? Only this, and no other:

"I will do Thy will., Oh, God!"

That is all the prayer you need. "Not every man that sayeth onto me Lord, Lord, but he that willeth to do the will of my Father shall enter the Kingdom." To will to do the will of God is the sum of all religion. It is the highest possible assertion of self-hood. It comprehends all possible good effort, and shuts off all evil. It suspends all activity but God's and holds the soul in silence before Him. It is the greatest assertion of will power of which man is capable. Angels can do no more. And that within you which wills to do the will of God is the power which can direct and control your thought Exercise it; call it into activity. Sit in the silence and hold your soul on the will to do the will of God. When you cannot or do not wish to concentrate longer, arise and go out Do this every day or twice a day; and whenever your thinker gets beyond your control for an instant, will to do the will of God. You will find yourself in the way of power and life; you will draw spiritual power from God in the silence by day as you draw vital energy from Him in the silence of night.

"For I do not my own will, but the will of Him that sent me." "Not my will, but thine." "I do always His will."

That, beloved, is the way to get will power; and will power is the spiritual ability to control and direct yourself in thought and deed, internal and external.

And now, here are the conclusions: Never eat unless you are hungry. If you are a hard worker or a young person, eat two moderate meals a day. If a brain worker, an invalid or an old person, eat only one meal and not much at that.

Sleep in pure air. Think good thoughts. And acquire power to do all these things by willing to do the will of God.

7. THE LIVING ONE.

AT THE RISK of being guilty of wearisome repetition, I must here re-state some of the things which have gone before. I want you to have them fresh in your mind, so that you will fully grasp the arguments which follow, for the point is one which is rather difficult to state. Life is a force, a form of energy, as truly as heat and electricity are forms of energy. That which performs work is force, or energy. There is no distinction to be made between the life of the body and its work-power. Life *is* work-power. The work-power of the body is not drawn from the food consumed; this we have proved by the following facts:

1. The anatomical structure of the body, which proves that the brain, not the stomach, is the power plant of the organism.

2. The phenomena of sleep prove that the brain is charged with work-power during the period of sleep.

3. It is a mechanical impossibility that the enormous amount of work-power displayed by the body should be in the food consumed. A handful of rice cannot possibly furnish power to carry two hundred pounds over twenty miles of rocky ground.

4. People can fast, if properly instructed, from twenty to sixty days without material loss of strength. This would be impossible if the work-power were drawn from the daily food.

5. In death by starvation the brain loses no weight. Nature preserves the power-plant intact until the last.

6. The accession of strength felt after eating must come from the brain. It cannot come from the food, which is still an undigested mass in the stomach.

7. In severe sickness Nature always takes away the appetite; proving that the digestion of food is work; a tax on strength, and not a source of strength.

8. All the other phenomena of life point us irresistibly to the conclusion that food is merely raw material, to be used in building up the body; and that it is used by an energy which is stored up in the brain during sleep.

Now, as a form of energy, life presents one peculiar characteristic; it seems to be an exception to the law of the correlation of forces. Heat, light, and electricity are convertible, each into the others; but none of them, so far as we know, is convertible into life. Every living thing came from a germ, which contained part of a preceding life, and contained it as life, and not as something else to be converted into life. Life only comes from life; we cannot originate, generate or create it as we do electricity, by changing or combining other forces. It does not appear, so far as our observation goes, that there was ever any new life, or that life has ever come into existence where there was none before. We, with all our wisdom, skill and science, can only watch life reproduce itself; we cannot originate it.

It is the work-power of the life in the seed germ which produces the organism. It is the function of life to produce organisms. The life in the seed produces the plant; the plant does not produce the life. Life is not a result of organization, but is the cause of it. Living organisms are not machines which generate life; they are machines which are built and operated by life. Life is not the result of functional action, because it is the cause of functional action; it cannot be at once the effect and the cause. The external work of the body, as I have shown in a preceding chapter, cannot possibly be performed by power which is generated by its internal work; for the power which does both the internal and the external work is one and the same. There is no difference between the power which does muscular work and that which operates the heart, liver and stomach. It is all one, and comes from one source. It is, therefore, an absurdity to say that the work-power of the body is the result of the performance of its internal digestive or other functions.

Life is the cause of all function, including the digestion of food, and cannot be the result of that which it causes. We are therefore driven to the conclusion that the body receives its power from some external source. It certainly expends energy, we have seen that it does not and cannot generate this energy; it must, occasionally, be charged anew. And when we witness the phenomena of sleep we conclude that we are witnessing the vitalizing process; the sleeping organism is being charged with power.

But where does the power come from? Oxygen, as we have seen, is necessary to the charging process, but oxygen is not life. It is a chemical element indispensable to functional action, and to the operations of vital power, but it is not life. Nor does it appear that there is any possible combination or recombination of the elements of the atmosphere with those of the body which can produce life. For if life be drawn by chemical processes from atmospheric air, it can only be done by internal functional processes, and we have seen that it is a mechanical impossibility that life should be the result of functional action. It is as impossible that the body should manufacture life out of air as that it should manufacture it out of food. All the arguments which I have used in the one case will apply in the other. If vital power cannot be received by the body in the form of potential energy in food, and converted into life by functional action, then it cannot be received in the form of electrical or other energy from the atmosphere, and converted into work-power by functional action. It must, therefore, be received directly as vital power, for the body is not a generator or transformer of energy. When the body receives life it must receive life; it cannot receive something else which is to be converted into life, for this would make life to be its own creator, the effect becoming its own cause.

Therefore, life is not drawn from the atmosphere, for the atmosphere is a compound of dead gases. It is not drawn from the earth, for the earth is dead mineral, vegetable and animal matter. There are forms of potential and kinetic energy in both earth and air—heat and electricity, for instance—but as I have shown you, these are not life, and it is not mechanically possible for the body to convert them into life. If there is life in the air it must be there as life, and not as something else; and it must *be in* the air, *not of* the air. If there is vital power in the earth, it must be there as life, and not as some other form of force; it must be a force; separate and distinct from all other forces, and not an inherent property of matter. For, if life were inherent in all matter, death and disintegration would be impossible. The body without the spirit would not be dead, but just as much alive as ever. We cannot escape the conclusion that vital power, or life, is seen by us only in the bodies of living organisms; whatever forces we see in dead matter are not alive, nor capable of being alive; for we receive life, not something else. If vital power is present in our material environment it is there as a living force—a living presence, a life,— not as a dead material force, which we must convert into life in order to live.

There is one other supposition which we must consider briefly here, which is that life comes from the sun. This idea probably originated from observing the phenomena of the seasons; the forth putting of life in the spring, when the sun's rays penetrate air and soil, creating the right chemical conditions for the building of organisms by life. There is no evidence, however, that the life of the springtime comes from the sun. A certain amount of heat is necessary to the constructive processes of vital power, but heat in excess is destructive to all the work of life. Life does not come from fire, or work in fire, or with fire; and the sun, so far as we know, is pure fire. It is unthinkable that there should be life on, or in the sun. And, so far as the facts go, life only comes from life. If there are no germs of life in the son, then reasoning from the facts of life as I see them, I cannot accept the theory that life comes from a body where there is no life.

Whence, then, does life come? I do not know. I can only say with Swedenborg that there appears to be an inflow of life into the world, which is received by all living things according to their forms; or I can say with St. Paul that there is a Living One, in whom we live and move, and whose offspring we are. But this I know by all the laws of force, that we must get our life from a living force which surrounds us. There is no escaping this conclusion. It is mechanically impossible that we should generate life, or that we should convert some other force into it; we receive it as life, and we receive it *from* life.

Do you remember what happens on the window pane on a cold morning when a fire is kindled? The pane acts as a condenser, changing the form of the moisture in the air; it becomes tangible. Wherever heat and cold, positive and negative, come into contact there is a precipitation.

The surface of the brain is this point of contact between positive and negative, Uncreate and Create, Spirit and Matter.

The positive ever acts upon the negative; the higher and finer forces upon the lower or coarser.

The natural attitude of man is one of aspiration toward the Uncreate and command toward the Create; negative to the Highest, positive to all beneath. — ELIZABETH TOWNE, in "Constitution of Man" (1896)

8. NEW LIGHT ON IMMORTALITY

FINALLY, in the light of all the foregoing, what about the immortality of the individual? Well, the new physiology gives us, for the first time, a really scientific basis for the hope of a continued existence. You must remember that if the old physiology is true, immortality is simply impossible. If you get your vital power from food, then your soul comes from the beef trust; and when you cease to eat, that will be the end of you for time and eternity. The theory that the soul draws its vital power from God, while the body gets energy from corned beef and cabbage, is improvable; all the evidence goes to show that there are not two kinds of life, one of the body and one of the soul, but that there is only one life. The life of the soul and the life of the body are one, and come from the same source; therefore, if the old physiology is true, the death of the body is the end of all.

To prove individual immortality we must demonstrate two things to be true:

First, that there is a spiritual organism which the ego, or individual intelligence can inhabit after the dissolution of the physical body; and

Second, that the ego can and will keep the spiritual organism so in harmony with the constructive principle of nature that it, in turn, shall not be dissolved.

It is unthinkable that life should continue individualized without an organism. There must be a separate organism for every individual life; and when the life can no longer preserve its organism against the attacks of nature's destructive principle, then it must cease to be an individual life, and be merged into that Universal from whence it came. What evidence have we that there are spiritual bodies?

1. We have the testimony of clairvoyants and other psychics who claim to see them. Take this evidence for what it is worth to you. Personally, I believe some of it.

2. We are able to demonstrate mathematically that personality is not the result of functioning of the physical body. Mind is not produced by the physical body, for mind controls the physical body. Mind is not the result of functional action, for mind can and does control functional action. There is no organ of the body whose action is not controllable by mind, properly applied. To have mind control the machinery which produces it would be to make the effect become its own cause. If mind were the result of functional action, it could not cause or control functional action. There is no more evidence that the brain thinks than there is that the heart thinks, or that the liver thinks; the most we can say is that the brain appears to be the organ through which the ego applies thought to the physical body. It does not appear to be at all impossible that there is a spiritual organism, formed of finer material, in and through the physical body, permeating it as ether permeates the atmospheric air; and that this spiritual body may continue to exist after the dissolution of the physical body.

But its continued existence must depend upon its power and willingness to co-operate with the constructive principle in nature. Look where we will, we see two principles in operation; all about us are the phenomena of construction and destruction, integration and disintegration, combination and dissolution, growth and decay, life and death. In our own bodies construction and destruction are continuous; and the length of physical life depends upon our living, so that the process of construction shall equal or exceed that of destruction. In the very nature of things, it is not possible that there should be any such thing as essential, inherent and intrinsic immortality for any living organism. Every living thing, whether spiritual or physical, must be subject to the same fundamental laws; and each must receive its vital energy from the same source. You know that you are not necessarily and inherently immortal, in so far as your physical body is concerned. You may have a long and merry life, or a short and miserable one, just as you choose. If you eat and drink and sleep and think in a constructive way, you will live a good while—I cannot undertake to say how long. You may achieve physical immortality, for all I can prove to the contrary, although I do not believe you can; and I do not know why you should want to unless you are afraid to pass out, and try the other plane. On the other hand, if you eat and drink so as to turn your constructive force into the destructive channel; if you do not give the constructive principle an opportunity by sleeping under proper conditions, or if you think destructively, you can commit physical suicide in a very little while, or you can prolong the process over a number of years, but it will be suicide all the same.

Permit me now to point out that the same must be true of your spiritual body. I believe that you have a spiritual body, for the reasons given above, and because I see phenomena in your life which I cannot possibly account for on any other hypothesis than that there is a personality which uses your brain but which is not produced by your brain. All that, however, is another story, and I shall not go into it now. But you will note now that it can be no more a necessity that your spiritual body shall live forever than it is that your physical body shall live forever. You are endowed with the power to commit physical suicide, and it necessarily follows that you must also have the power to commit spiritual suicide. The spiritual bodies of those who persist in thinking the destructive thought and living in the destructive way must eventually be dissolved into their original elements, and the life principle be merged into that Universal life from whence it came. They who persist in violation of the law must eventually vanish from the universe; the "soul that sinneth, it shall die." Immortality is a privilege, but not a necessity. Conscious individual existence on either the physical or spiritual planes can be long continued only by working in harmony with the constructive principle; by intelligent and continuous co-operation with God. And this is the great, stern fact that underlies the New Physiology: That the individual cannot create or renew his own life, or vital power of soul or body; he must, therefore, so harmonize himself with the source of life as to receive from it, or he will inevitably perish.

> *How wonderful is Death!*
> *Death and his brother, Sleep.*
> — PERCY BYSSHE SHELLEY

Everything in nature contains all the powers of nature. Everything is made of one hidden stuff. — EMERSON.

9. SUFFERING IN SICKNESS.

MY ATTENTION has lately been called to the case of an old lady—seventy-six years old— who is suffering from a severe attack of asthma, complicated with la grippe. Her sufferings are distressing to witness. She coughs almost continuously, especially during the night, and expectorates vast quantities of mucous; there is much retching and straining in the desperate efforts nature is making to eliminate this filth from the overburdened system.

Now this old lady belongs to that vast army of excellent women whose greatest pleasure is to feed their families, their visitors and themselves. It is not an exaggeration to say that most of her life has been spent in cooking, in eating and in thinking of eating, and in planning and preparing for meals.

When she was younger, an active and hardworking housewife, she ate heartily, and with some reason, because of her physical activities; but for some years now she has done very little work, and she has gone on eating, just the same. I do not know that she has eaten leas than during her years of active life. She thinks and talks continuously of eating, and of things good to eat; she frequently munches apples, etc., between meals; she "lunches" at all hours, and often at bed time. And for some years she has suffered intensely with rheumatism, asthma, and frequently recurring attacks of the grippe.

It is impossible to make her believe that all her sufferings are caused by the terrible struggle her physical organism is compelled to make to rid itself of the filth with which she is continually gorging it; but such is actually the case. And the same is true of nearly all old people who suffer from the so-called infirmities of age. It has been said that when a man "retires" nature usually retires him permanently in a very short time; but the fact is that he usually destroys himself by continuing to eat as if he were still at work. Professor Metchnikoff discovered that old age is caused by a germ which originates in putrefying matter in the intestinal tract; and he hit on the marvelously scientific scheme of drinking sour milk to kill the bad germs, as the sour milk germ is an enemy to the old-age germ. And by the way, what has become of the professor's great "discovery" that drinking plenty of sour milk would make us all immortal in body? Like most of the medical discoveries it seems to have fallen flat. It is about time for some other great "scientist" to come out with an elixir of life. Instead of trying to find a counter-poison for the old age bug why did not Metchnikoff simply advise people to eat less, so as to have no putrefying filth in the intestines? This was the plan followed by Lewis Cornaro, the feeble Italian, who lived to pass the century mark, often subsisting a whole day on half an egg, or a single bunch of grapes. And Cornaro, a broken down wreck in middle life, recovered his health and lived and died without suffering. There is no reason in nature why there should be aches and pains and physical miseries attendant upon old age -, it ought to be a period of physical rest and wholesomeness, and mental cheer and joy; and the reason why it is not is generally to be told in one word—overeating! The old lady mentioned above is very cross and crabbed; hating everybody, and disliked by most of those around her, she leads a loveless and wretched life; her vital power is so fully expended in eliminating the filth she continually shovels into her stomach that she has no strength to expend in loving people. And even in her misery, her whole thought is of something to eat It is the first thing on awakening in the morning, and it is referred to hourly during the day. "Isn't there something I can eat? Get me a Little of this, or that" and so on. The poor thing eats enough to supply the needs of a hardworking man, and lingers on in excruciating torments while her enfeebled system tries to rid itself of the poisonous accumulating filth.

Another neighbor of mine, also an aged woman, passed out the other day. This was a similar case. She, also, was "a great sufferer." For weeks before she died her continuous groans and screams were heard by the neighbors; she ate three or four meals during the day, and was also fed at four o'clock in the morning. She was a heavy woman; she could have lived through the entire period of her sickness without food and had she done so she would have lost less in weight, for her system would have been spared the dreadful labor of eliminating unused food; and not only would she have lost less flesh but she would have had a painless illness, and an easy death. Most of the agonies of all kinds of sickness are due to feeding.

Five years ago I was asked to advise a young man who was in the last stage of tuberculosis, with the end very near at hand. Surrounded by loving friends, who, unable to think of any other way to show their sympathy, were continually forcing food upon him, he was coughing his life away, and suffering severely in the struggle of his feeble body to eliminate the filth. I said to him: "My boy, if you want to spend your remaining days in peace and comfort, do not eat except when you are decidedly and unmistakably hungry," and I gave his family a lecture on the difference between selfish and unselfish love. That young man never ate another mouthful of food. In a few days his coughing and expectorating ceased; he slept well, and was free from pain; he became bright and cheerful, and *four weeks* later, he fell asleep, like a little child. In my last illness, may I be delivered from the love that feeds!

And that is about all, dearly beloved. Most of the suffering in sickness is caused by feeding the sick. Oh, I know! You don't believe any such stuff! But you try it, and see. When you are sick, stop eating. Do not think about eating; do not talk about eating; ask your friends to kindly refrain from talking about eating; and wait until you are sure you are hungry; and then wait a few hours to make sure you are sure; and then eat enough to satisfy your hunger, and *then* wait again. And if you are getting along in years, and especially if you have quit work, remember that it takes only a very little raw material to maintain the body of an old person who does not work. Find out the least quantity of food upon which you can live and keep up your weight, and live on that. If you can live on one bunch of grapes, or half an egg a day, and be well and free from aches and pains, and also be bright and happy, is not that better than to eat forty bunches of grapes or a couple of dozen eggs, and be a wretched, suffering invalid, a burden to yourself and a trial to your friends?

And, by the way, this applies as well to you who are *not* growing old; find out the smallest quantity of food upon which you can live and work without losing weight; and live on it!

THE END

BOOK NINE
HELLFIRE HARRISON

(A NOVEL)

1

THEY were tremendous times. Governments were going to pieces, and kings and queens were losing their crowns, and sometimes their heads also; the many-headed beast was giving his keepers an immense amount of trouble. The air quivered with revolution, and politics was a warfare of the gods; the greatest figures in the world's history were on the stage, and acting mighty parts. England was on the verge of anarchy, and highwaymen plied their trade as actively on the streets of London as on lonely country roads; the hardest-working man in the United Kingdom was the hangman, and his labors were in vain so far as increasing the safety of life or property was the object.

The tide of religious sentiment had reached its lowest ebb, and it was said that zeal for godliness would look as oddly upon a man as the clothing of his greatgrandfather. Sincere men, recoiling from the emptiness of ecclesiastical officialism, became skeptics and stoics; they organized hell-fire clubs and made it their fashion to repress every sign of human interest or feeling, pretending to believe in nothing but themselves, and to consider themselves as not worth believing in. Duels were of daily occurrence; every man carried his life in his hand. Yes, they were certainly tremendous times; and it was during the maddest stage of this terrific period that Harrison came from Virginia to England to see his son, who had wintered in the mother country; and so it came about that for the first time in thirty years he visited Wycherly Castle, his birthplace and the ancestral home of his family.

He left his coach to wait at the gate and walked in through the grounds alone. He had given his elder brother, Lord Wycherly, no intimation of his coming, which was a proceeding quite in keeping with his usual ways.

Mr. Gerald Harrison, tobacco planter and member of the Congress of a certain very small but very pugnacious and self-respecting republic, was an uncommonly handsome man of fifty-two; straight as an arrow, of powerful build, and with the suppleness and activity of a youth. He was faultlessly dressed in the fashion of the time, from the silver buckles on his shoes to the crown of his three-cornered hat. Every garment that he wore was a triumph of the tailor's art; his hair was freshly powdered, his cheek was smooth and rosy, and his eye was very bright; his smile, although a trifle cynical and scornful, was good to see withal. He scanned the castle curiously as he drew near to its weather-beaten front, and laughed aloud.

" A little dirtier and more ruinous without," said he, " and I doubt not, a little draughtier and chillier within. Gad, what a place to pass away one's life in; I would rather live in jail! Thank the kind fates for making me the younger son!"

He drew a handsome box from his pocket and took snuff, using great care lest any should fall upon his spotless waistcoat, or on the ruffled bosom of his shirt; and then he walked up the steps and plied the great iron knocker lustily.

" Tell Lord Wycherly," said he to the liveried footman who opened the door, " that his brother waits."

The man gasped with astonishment, then showed him into a room and went away; presently he came back and bade him follow. In a great upper chamber he found Lord Wycherly, who arose and came across the room to greet him; and though they were the only children of their father, and had not looked into each other's faces for thirty years, they shook hands as calmly as if they had parted but the day before. After the fashion of the cynical cult to which they both belonged, it was their pride to show neither feeling or affection; neither of the pair would, under any consideration, have betrayed emotion in greeting the other, especially in the presence of the footman, who was just leaving the room. Lord Wycherly was two years the elder, but, though very like his younger brother, he showed his age far more; his face was wrinkled and careworn.

" Time has used you well, Gerald," he said, admiringly, after they had talked awhile. " Egad, you look but little older than your son. A fine boy that; you should be proud of him."

" I should be proud to remember his mother, rather," said Harrison, " for his bringing-up was more her work than mine. And I believe he is a passable young fellow."

" He is like you, and yet not like you," said Lord Wycherly. " He has little of the dare-devil disposition you showed at his age; and which, if half we hear is to be credited, you have not entirely outgrown. Some strange stories have come to London of the doings of a Virginia planter whom they call Hell-fire Harrison." He shot a single keen glance at his brother's smiling face.

" The name comes from a time some years back," said Harrison calmly, " when a few of us heard that Hell-fire clubs were the fashion over here, and we must needs organize one. I was active in it, and the more strait-laced of our godly neighbors gave the name to me; and it has clung."

" I can readily believe that it has," said Wycherly grimly, " and that it has not, in all ways, been amiss. Yours has been the easiest lot, after all, Gerald; you have had the best of me. New soil, new people, new methods, and liberty to take your own way; while I have had to uphold the family name on these exhausted acres, so hampered by silly traditions that I dare not leave the old rut, or change the antiquated system in any part. Richard tells me that your plantation brings you more than all my rent-rolls bring to me, and you can do what I have never done; live as you please! Well, we could not both have the luck to be younger sons, but if 'twas to be done over, I should try to wait and let you make your advent first. I see you still wear the old sword. Let me look at it again? "

Harrison drew his sword, and gave it to his brother, without speaking; and the other inspected it with a curious smile, making the flexible blade whistle through the air with a dextrous movement of his wrist. The weapon was a rapier, of unusual, and evidently of Oriental design, somewhat heavier than the dress swords generally worn by gentlemen in those days, double-edged for a little distance back from the point, and sharp as a razor; a tool made for service, not for show.

" Our father loved it," said Wycherly quietly, " because of the family traditions attached to it. I hardly know whether he was most pleased or sorry when you asked for it on going away. But it was yours by right; your equal in handling it never lived. Has your hand lost any of its juggler's cunning with the sword? "

Harrison took the weapon without answering, and stepped toward the great window, formed of many small panes of glass. On one of these, at about the level of his face, a blue-bottle fly was slowly crawling; he indicated it to his brother by a gesture. Then he held the sword at half arm's length before him, with the blade pointing straight upward, and with a slight but powerful movement of the wrist, caused it to bend forward with a hissing sweep. The keen point flicked the fly from the pane without a sound to show that the glass had been touched. Harrison sheathed his sword and sat down, and the brothers took snuff, smiling at each other; for an instant the bars of their cynical pretence were down, and they looked into each other's hearts; but only for an instant.

" I remember well," said the elder, " the night you cut the French Count's nose in half with that same stroke."

They talked on for some time, exchanging reminiscences of their younger days, and then Harrison said:

" I saw your coach made ready as I came up the drive; were you about to go away? "

" I was for London; the house sits to-night. But now that you are here — "

" You will go right on, Richard. My own coach waits at the gate. I am going on to Farnham to see Alicia."

"Hah," said Lord Wycherly. " Yes. Alicia will be glad to see you, Gerald. She lives alone with her servants at Farnham Court; and you will find that she shows her years even more than I show mine. After her husband died she fixed her whole heart on her son; and he grew up a fine fellow, very like your boy. But he was killed, unfortunately, in his first duel. Yes, go and see her; she always liked you. I remember that we thought at one time you were going to make a match of it."

She never thought so," said Harrison smiling, " nor did I. We were only the best of friends. Yes, I think she would be pleased to see me, and I need not keep you from your seat among the lords; I know there are great matters pending. I will go on to Farnham, and we will meet later."

And presently the brothers parted at the door, with a farewell pinch of snuff, a few courteous phrases, and an air of calm indifference.

2

I WAS never so pleased," said Lady Alicia, " to see any person in all my life, as I am this day to see you."

She sat in the pleasant drawing-room at Farnham Court, and Harrison, bright-eyed and smiling, sat across from her.

" I take that to mean," said he, " that I am better worth seeing — "

"Don't flatter yourself! It is because I have need of you; you come in the very nick of time. But of that we will speak later. And yes, my friend, I am glad to see you for your own sake; to see how fresh and young you look, although you make me sense my wrinkles and sunken cheeks more keenly. Do not interrupt me; you know 'tis so. Women grow old faster than men in these times, for we must sit at home with our sorrows and let them eat out our hearts, while you forget yours in battle and diplomacy. Well, never mind. I was delighted with your son, Gerald, when I met him during the one week I spent in London last winter; a right noble youth."

" As of course he must be, with my example — "

" Chut, chut! If he does well, it is in spite of your example, and not because of it. And he is a splendid young fellow; even in these days of loose living, he has no bad habits."

" One," said Harrison. " He will go to church."

" Why, so I heard," said she, " and I rejoiced that you had not been able to make him into a case-hardened, sneering cynic, like Wycherly and the rest of you. His mother must have been a rare woman, Gerald."

" She was, Alicia," he answered. The change in his tone was very, very slight, but she noticed it and understood; and she changed the subject instantly.

" Now, as to the matter I mentioned awhile ago," said she. " Gerald, do you remember Andrew Hogg? "

" Ay; very well indeed."

" And do you, by any chance, remember his son? "

" A dark-faced little boy, when I left England?"

"Yes! Dark-faced and sullen, like his father, and with a worse temper, even then."

"I remember; I cuffed him, once, for torturing a helpless kitten. And has he grown up to fulfill the brilliant promise of his childhood?"

" He is a very devil! Drunken, brutal, licentious, fearing neither God nor man. He lives at Hackthorn Hall with three ruffians he brought with him from the wars, who are well dubbed the bloody three; renegade fighting men. He keeps no other servants than these three; they are all good swordsmen, and more than one life has been lost hereabout by incurring their ill-will. Andrew is nearing forty now; and as he grows older he grows worse in every way. The country people call him ' The Black Hogg.' He and his men are often away for long periods; 'tis thought that they go far from home and play the highwayman. When they are here, they spend their days in sleeping, and their nights in roistering at the hall, or at the Blue Goose Inn, in Farnham village. The whole county is afraid of Andrew Hogg."

" And what, Alicia," said Harrison, as she paused, " have I to do with this merry gentleman? "

" Do you remember Janet Ainslie? " " " Oh, right well! Gad, but she had spirit! She married Billy Chester, so they wrote me."

" Sir William Chester; and he died when their child, little Mary, was ten years old. Then, after three more years, Janet, being homeless and dependent, and very proud, married a squire of this neighborhood, Sladden by name; and shortly afterward she also died, leaving him to rear the child. Sladden was a somewhat dull and stubborn man, and he has grown duller and more stubborn with the passing of the years, but under his care Mary has grown to be the fairest girl in all England, and ' The Black Hogg' has set his mind on marrying her."

"Well?"

"Well? It is not well. Sladden favors Andrew Hogg with all his stupid strength, and they have sworn, together, that the marriage shall take place before the end of June, and 'tis near the middle of May."

" But, Alicia, surely there is little harm in a maid's being married against her will? Why, she is not supposed to have a will afterward, in any case! "

" Not the least harm in the world," said Lady Alicia, calmly.

" Even if she does not love him," Harrison went on, " she will undoubtedly come to do so, if he flogs her frequently enough? "

" And he will certainly do that," agreed the lady.

Harrison took snuff, regarding her with his bright eyes, and his most cynical smile.

" Oh, hang it, Alicia," said he, " what do you wish me to do? "

" Why, sir," said she, knowing her man perfectly, " but you are conceited! I have not asked that you shall do anything. What can you, a single man, do against Hogg and his bloody three? I have merely given you a bit of neighborhood gossip, so that you might understand the situation and guard your tongue; for I am, going to call on Mary this afternoon, and you shall ride along to protect me on the highway. It was for that I said I needed you. The roads are not safe for a woman with no protection but a couple of footmen. While you are here, I may go a-visiting."

" Humph," said Harrison.

So they set forth presently, Harrison riding a horse beside Lady Alicia's sedan-chair, and they passed the gates of Hackthorn Hall before they came to Sladden's farm, which was a little further on. When the Virginian was introduced to Mary Chester he drew one quick breath of astonishment, and owned to himself that Lady Alicia had told the truth when she called her the fairest girl in all England. He talked with her for an hour, and found that she had a pleasant wit, and that she lacked not for a double portion of her mother's spirit.

" I have come to England," he told her as he was leaving, " seeking a wife. Are you ready to receive proposals?"

" Oh, surely, sir," said she. " What maid is not? "

" I do not seek for myself," he went on, " but for my son; and I have taken a mighty fancy that I should like you for a daughter-in-law."

" Thank you, sir! But is your son to have no voice in the matter? "

" He is a very bashful youth. But he is coming down from London in a day or so, and he shall fall in love with you."

"Ah! And can you make him do that, sir? "

" If he is so stupid as not to do it, I will flog him till he does."

" Oh, poor young man! What a dreadful alternative!"

" And if you do not fall in love with him," Harrison went on, " I will pull your ears."

"My precious ears! I'll not let them come to harm, sir. I think I love your son a little already. And does he take his bashfulness from his father, sir? "

" I think so."

" I think so too; for if you ever had any, someone has taken it."

So they bade each other a laughing farewell, and Harrison rode away beside the sedan-chair. Once out on the highway, they saw coming toward them a strange looking fellow, whose spine seemed afflicted about the hips. He wavered from side to side as he walked, and flourished his arms as if he found it hard to keep his balance. Lady Alicia stopped her bearers and Harrison at sight of him.

" See, Gerald," said she, " yonder comes Dicky Dirk. When he was born his mother was a servant at Hackthorn Hall; it was during the old Hogg's time. Young Andrew had a petty spite against this woman, and one day he snatched the babe from her breast and dashed it on the floor. Still he held his grudge against her, and a few months later, in a drunken rage, he killed her husband, and she died of a broken heart. The boy grew up to walk as you see him; strangely crippled about the hips, and yet he is said to be as strong as a very giant in the arms and shoulders. He carries a great knife, and so got the name of Dick o' the dirk, now shortened to Dicky Dirk. He lives, the Lord knows how, mostly by doing odd jobs for the country people, and he rarely speaks, even when spoken to. Dicky, this is Mr. Harrison, of Virginia."

" Give 'ee good day, zur," said Dicky, wavering past them, and looking neither to right nor left.

" Good day, Dicky," said Harrison, riding on; and he performed the difficult feat of taking snuff on horseback, with more than his usual carefulness. Lady Alicia watched him closely, but in silence.

" Alicia," said he, after a while, " this Hogg of yours seems to be a rare soul."

" Why, so he is; and I have told you only a few of his pleasant eccentricities."

" I think I will stay in the neighborhood for a while; I was always fond of Farnham. And to prevent scandal, I will take quarters at the Blue Goose Inn."

He beamed upon her with his most pleasant smile, but she shuddered and grew cold, even as she felt that her point was gained, for the thought came to her that she had caused sentence of death to be passed on Andrew Hogg. Harrison went on quietly:

" I will write Richard, and have him down to stay with me. Get up a party of some sort for next week, Alicia, and invite Mary Chester. I will bring the boy, and we will trust in the Lord, who does all things well — with proper management on our part."

" Don't scoff," said Lady Alicia, " I will give the party on Wednesday."

3

SO young Richard Harrison first met Mary Chester at Lady Alicia's party, and, because their curiosity had been artfully aroused beforehand, the two young people took a mighty interest in one another.

" I've heard much of you, sir," said she, as they sat together.

" We famous men are always being talked about," said he. " And I have heard much of you, sweet Mistress Chester."

" We famous ladies are always being talked about," said she.

" Famous indeed," he answered. " Lady Alicia told me that you were the fairest girl in England; I was a little doubtful at the time, but I will swear now that she might have included Scotland, Wales and the Continent."

" Why not America also?" she asked. " But no doubt you have left someone there who is fairer than I."

" In America," he replied, " most of the good looks are given to the men, as you may have noticed."

" Why, so I had," said she, " and yet the men are not conceited, which is very strange. But I must believe all you say, for your father told me that you were a most proper youth."

" I respect my father too highly to question anything he says," said the young man.

" He told me," she went on, daringly, " that if you did not fall in love with me you should be flogged."

" I never willfully gave him cause to flog me," said he, " and I shall not do so now."

" And he said," Mary continued, " that if I did not fall in love with you he would pull my ears."

" Such beautiful ears shall never be pulled; I shall see to it that you fall in love with me."

Most of that evening they were together, and in a day or so he called at Sladden's farm; and from that time on it was evident that they were in truth falling very deeply into love with each other. Young Richard rode to Sladden's every day, for he was no slack wooer; and Lady Alicia looked on, trembling for what might come to pass, but with a thankful heart; Harrison looked on, bright eyed and smiling, and was always near at hand when the boy passed Hackthorn Hall; Dicky Dirk, hiding in the bushes or lurching along the road, looked on, muttering to himself; and Andrew Hogg looked on, cursing. Presently he summoned Sladden to a conference, and the latter, a square-built, square-jawed, square-headed man of sixty, took his stepdaughter to task.

" What do you mean, you hussy," he demanded, " by letting this young cockerel come upon the place? Dost want to see me pitch him out upon the highway? "

Now, though Mistress Mary had received but little kindness from her stepfather, she had never treated him with disrespect, or disobeyed him until he began trying to make her accept the love of Andrew Hogg, but upon that issue she was in open war with him.

" Yes, sir," said she with a curtsey. " I think I should much enjoy looking on while you undertook to pitch Master Harrison into the highway."

" His father's a dirty rebel," said Sladden.

" But for your life, you dare not say so to his face," said she.

" If you were my own daughter," he growled, " full-grown as you are, I would whip you till you took up with Squire Hogg."

" If I were your daughter," she said with her head held very high, " no doubt but I would be willing to marry Squire Hogg; but my father was a gentleman."

" I shall forbid that whelp to come on the farm," shouted Sladden in a passion.

" And he'll come, none the less," said Mary.

Sladden did not forbid Richard the place, but when, on the next day, Mary told the young man what had happened, he urged her to marry him at once, and she refused.

" We have known each other scarcely three weeks," she said, " and if we wed now, people will say 'twas but the fear of Andrew Hogg drove me to you. Sir, I wish to be courted with all due pomp and circumstance. I sometimes think I like you very well, but again I am not sure of it, nor am I certain that you love me. Make me sure of both, and I will marry you, but I will not be driven to do so by Slad-den and the black Hogg."

" By Heaven, they shall not hurry you! " said Richard, looking very like his father. " Take your time, sweet mistress, for all of them. But I will not say that I shall not hurry you myself; for I am asking you to marry me because I love you. I am as sure of that as if I had known you all my life. And love me you shall, and marry me you shall, and I am coming to see you every day, Hogg or no Hogg, Sladden or no Sladden, until you say yes tome.

And so he did, riding into the farmyard every day, tossing his bridle rein and a coin to the stable boy, and receiving Sladden's sour look with a high head and a careless smile. But Hell-fire Harrison, having been told all, redoubled his watchfulness, for he knew that the crisis was at hand.

And it was; for sitting over their liquor at Hackthorn Hall, Hogg and the bloody three were taking counsel as to the safest way of killing Richard.

" Meet the cub on the road, and run him through," said Trainor, the most reckless of the four, and the best swordsman.

"Ay; but his father is always with him, or close at hand," said Hogg.

" And they say he is the best swordsman in England. Some of us will lose blood if we try that, and why run needless risk? Here is a better plan: When the young whelp is safe at Sladden's tomorrow, Harrison will ride back to the Blue Goose Inn to wait until nearly sunset; then he will come out to meet the boy and convoy him home. Now, an hour before sundown, let Trainor go to the Inn and get into conversation with this rebel. Drink with him, if he will, and fall to arguing if he will not; quarrel, but do not come to blows. Carry it off in such a way that if he leaves 'twill appear to the bystanders that he is afraid, but do not cross swords, or he will do for you." Trainor sniffed doubtfully, but Hogg went on, " Keep him there until after sunset, and then get away; apologize and eat humble pie if you must; you shall give it back to him later. Meanwhile we three will settle the young popinjay, and if the old one attacks us here, later, we will meet him at the door with our pistols, and give him no chance to come to close quarters. Will that do? "

The others accepted the plan, and so on the following afternoon, as the sun was getting low, Trainor set off for the Blue Goose Inn, and shortly after, the other three rode out upon the highway, and took their stand beneath a clump of trees to wait for Richard.

4

TRAINOR found the elder Harrison sitting by a table, in the tap-room of the inn, with a bottle of wine at his elbow. Sitting down, the ruffian pushed the table so roughly that the bottle was upset. Harrison, who instantly comprehended the whole plan, rose to his feet and drew his sword.

"Draw!" said he to Trainor.

" You seek to provoke a quarrel, but I bandy no words with a scoundrel of your kidney. Draw, or by Heaven, I will run you through, where you sit!"

"Would you murder me? "blustered the fellow, as half willing, half afraid, he slowly rose and drew his weapon.

"No; but I will find out whether you are the swordsman you are said to be. On guard!"

They crossed blades, and after a few passes had been exchanged, Harrison's smile grew more contemptuous.

" I see that you cannot fence," said he, " and so we may as well make a finish of it. Look out, now; I am going to slice your nose across the middle, and cut the sign of the cross on your left cheek." And, with three lightning strokes of his razor-edged sword, he carried out his threat.

"You are the devil!" cried the bully, staggering backward as he wiped the blood from his face. " I will not fight you more! "

" You are easily satisfied, my friend," said Harrison, wiping his sword carefully and sheathing it, and then he took snuff, smiling, while the innkeeper hurried the wounded ruffian away to the village leech.

So, half an hour later, when Hogg and his two remaining scoundrels saw Richard coming in the distance, it happened that they also heard the hoof beats of a horse coming from the opposite direction, and turning, saw Harrison, who rode past them with a courteous salute. Joining his son a little way down the road, he turned about, and the two came on together.

Hogg and his friends perceived that Trainor had failed in his mission, but they did not guess how grievously, and they were puzzled as to what to do. They discussed the situation hurriedly for a few minutes, and then Andrew burst out with a great oath, declaring that the whole matter should be settled then and there. They took their stand in the centre of the highway, facing the Harrisons, who were coming in a walk, chatting carelessly together.

Andrew Hogg was a powerful man, more than six feet tall and very muscular; his swarthy face was bloated and swollen by hard drinking, and he wore his long hair unpowdered and badly combed, while his dress was slovenly. But he did not lack for brute courage, nor did either of his two companions, who were like him in a general way. They were all good swordsmen, and fighters of experience, and they awaited with confidence the coming of the Virginian and his son, who now rode up and drew rein, seeing that the way was blocked.

" Good evening, gentlemen," said Harrison. " What would you have of us?"

" A pinch of snuff! " growled Hogg, expecting a refusal.

Harrison drew his handsomely engraved snuff-box from his pocket, and riding close to Hogg, presented it, open, with a courtly gesture, and the other, who did not use snuff was so confused and taken aback that he took up a pinch with clumsy and not over-clean fingers. Harrison instantly tossed the box, with its remaining contents, into the ditch beside the road.

" What do you mean by that?" roared Hogg, his dark face turning fiery red.

" I can feed swine," said the American with his most pleasant smile, " but I will not root in the trough with them."

"By Heaven!" shouted Andrew, " be careful, or you will feel the swine's tusk! " and he laid his hand on his sword.

" Be careful yourself! " replied Harrison, unmoved. " I am too much of a Jew to eat pork, but just enough of a Christian to kill hogs, especially those possessed of devils."

Young Richard burst out laughing, while the three ruffians sat hesitating; the calm assurance of Harrison, and his evident anxiety for a fight daunted them. He faced them in silence for several seconds, still sitting within arm's length of Andrew; and then as they made no move, he spoke again.

" If you dare not fight, draw aside and let us pass," said he; and under the compelling power of his steady eye, the three involuntarily reined their horses toward the roadside. The father and son rode on slowly, conversing as if nothing had happened; and though they knew that their discomfited enemies had pistols in their holsters, neither of the pair so much as turned his head.

"We have them cowed," said Harrison. " I think we shall hear no more from them." But in that he was mistaken, good judge of men as he was; he underestimated Andrew Hogg.

That night Hogg and two of his men rode away toward London, leaving the wounded rascal, Trainor, alone at Hackthorn Hall, and no one about Farnham saw either of them for a week. During this time young Richard's wooing progressed smoothly, and his father relaxed his vigilance a little, for he came to believe that Hogg, seeing only formidable and dangerous opposition ahead, had given the whole matter up. At the end of the week came a surprise; for a Captain Keatley, with an escort of half a dozen troopers, appeared in Farnham village with a letter from the King, requesting the presence of Gerald Harrison at Saltire Castle, thirty miles away, where his majesty was making a short visit.

The letter merely set forth that the King, learning that Master Harrison, brother to his well-beloved Lord Wycherly, had but lately come from the United States of America, requested the presence of Master Harrison, so and so; and as the audience was set for the day following the one on which Harrison received the letter, it was imperative that he should set off at once with the escort. The Virginian was caught napping; he did not think of connecting Andrew Hogg with the King's invitation, which he supposed to be due to Wycherly's influence; he knew that his brother and other liberal statesmen were working to eradicate the ill feeling toward the new republic which existed at court, and he never once thought of refusing to comply with the request, which was, indeed, tantamount to a command. Richard was at Sladden's farm when the message came; so, after hastily writing him a note bidding him exercise all possible care and watchfulness, Harrison rode over to Farnham Court to bid Lady Alicia farewell for a day or so. Her suspicions were instantly aroused, and she became very anxious. " I do not like this message, coming at this time," said she. " If you go away, I am afraid for Richard — and for Mary. There is more in this than we see, Gerald. It is only the fear of you that has held Hogg in check so long, and when he gets you away he will do some devilish thing. I would you did not have to go, but the King's commands must be obeyed."

"Tut, tut!" said Harrison. "You are frightened at shadows. I do not think our Hogg has influence enough at court to have brought all this about; it is not his doing. He and his crew are away on some cut-purse expedition; we have scared them out. I have left a word of caution for Richard, and hang it, Alicia, the boy is no baby; he can take care of himself. If I did not know that, I would stay for all of fifty kings." Lady Alicia shook her head reprovingly; in those days the conservatives clung to an exaggerated respect for the pretensions of royalty, for which the radicals manifested an equally exaggerated contempt.

" Blaspheme not the Lord's anointed! " said the lady. " But there is only one man in England who is a match for black Hogg and his bloody three, and that is you, Gerald. Go, since you must, and come back quickly. I shall have no peace until I see you again."

So, smiling at her fears, he kissed her hand and went. It was well on in the afternoon when he rode out of Farnham with his escort. They had planned to ride until after midnight, for the moon was full, and then to lie at Shoresby until morning, reaching Saltire Castle early in the following day.

Now, the King's invitation had been brought about in this way: Hogg, going up to London to devise some means of getting rid of Harrison, had fallen in with an American tory named Cunningham, who hated the Virginian and all things connected with the republic overseas, and who had some influence at court. This man had impressed Andrew with the danger of meeting Harrison in fight, because of the latter's almost supernatural skill with the sword; and, by putting their wits together, the two had formed a cunning plan for getting him out of the way. Cunningham had procured the invitation to an audience with the King, and had seen that the letter was intrusted to Captain Keatley, an honest but somewhat thick-headed soldier, who was violently prejudiced against republican ideas. The tory had intimated to the Captain that in case Harrison should insult Royalty by declining the invitation he was to be brought to Saltire Castle by force, and the soldier, understanding that his mission was to make an arrest under pretence of an invitation to court, was quite prepared to use strenuous measures. As soon as the Virginian's back was turned on Farnham, Hogg and his three villains were to waylay Richard and kill him; and then, when Harrison returned, they were to take refuge in Hackthorn Hall and stand guard with loaded pistols, trusting to shoot him down before he could come to close quarters. They had arrived at the hall during the night previous to the coming of the King's messenger, and they watched the Virginian from a distance, as he rode away with his escort.

5

JUST at sundown on that same evening, Richard left Sladden's house and started toward Farnham village and the Blue Goose Inn. He was on foot, and he walked briskly along the highway, whistling a merry tune. He had just passed the gates of Hackthorn Hall when up from the grass where they had been sitting, rose Andrew Hogg and the bloody three, and sauntered out in front of him in such a way as to bar his progress; and they stood looking at him in evil fashion. Young Richard saw murder in their eyes, and he sent one swift glance up and down the road, thinking of his father whereat black Andrew laughed aloud.

" Useless to look for father to protect you, little man," he mocked. " He's many a long mile on his way to Saltire Castle. So you must fight your own battle for once."

" I have no doubt that he is gone, Hogg," said Richard coolly, " else you four would not dare show your heads abroad. Say what you want, you cutthroat scoundrel, or get out of my way."

" Oh! " said Hogg. " Now hear him try to roar, this puppy who is pretending to be a lion's cub! Why, this is what I want, my dear young friend.

I want you to go back to London, and never come near Farnham, or see Mistress Mary Chester again."

" And what if I refuse your very reasonable request? "

" We'll run you through the body, and leave you lying here for the carrion crows to peck at."

" Do you want Mistress Mary yourself, Hogg?"

" Ay, and mean to have her."

" If you were not such an infernal coward," said Richard, as if considering, " how easily you and I might settle this whole matter."

" What do you mean, whelp? "

" Let your three thieves sit down again while you and I fight it out without interference, and let the best man have her. If you can best me fairly, I will go back to London as you say."

"Good!" roared Andrew, drawing his sword. "Sit down, men, and watch me clip this young cock's spurs. On guard, boy, and you shall howl for quarter, or I'll run you through." The other three sat down upon the grass, and the two men in the road crossed swords.

We have said that Andrew Hogg was a good swordsman; but he was not long in learning that young Richard was a better one. The youth had been carefully trained by his father, and had a fair share of the latter's marvelous skill. It was but a few moments until Hogg was bleeding from a wound in the shoulder, and was looking greatly worried and amazed.

Richard pressed the fighting, for he hoped to disable his adversary and take to his heels before the other three could come upon him., knowing that he had no chance against all of them; but this opportunity was not to be given him, for Andrew, hard pressed, called for help and the other three rushed to his assistance. Richard defended himself gallantly, but without hope. Attacked on all sides, he was soon wounded in the sword arm and disarmed, and two of his enemies grasped him by the wrists while a third, kneeling behind him, clasped him about the knees. Andrew stood in front, furious with his defeat and the pain of his wounded shoulder.

"I'll finish you now!" he shouted, presenting his sword's point for a thrust. Young Richard saw his deadly purpose in his eye, and his own glance wavered for a single instant; he was young, and he loved, and it was hard to die. Then his look grew steady again, and he stood very straight with his eye on Hogg's, and smiled while the cowardly villain ran him through the body. His knees gave way and he sank in the dust of the highway, but as he went down he swayed forward and spit in Andrew's face.

"For her!" he whispered, as his eyes closed. Hogg, frothing with fury, raised his sword for another thrust; but just at that instant there came a strange moaning howl from a thicket beside the road, and he held his hand and stood glaring into the shadows, for it was growing dusk.

The four drew close together around the body of their victim, and stood trembling; they were all superstitious, and moreover, the dread of Hell-fire Harrison was coming heavily upon them.

" Let be!" said Trainor, tremulously, grasping Hogg's arm as he raised it again. " He's dead enough. Come on," and the four started off toward the Hall. As soon as they were out of sight, Dicky Dirk came from the thicket, lurching from side to side in desperate haste. He bent over the prostrate body for a moment, and then, by exercising all the strength of his powerful arms, hoisted it upon his shoulders and staggered off toward Farnham Court.

It was quite dark when he kicked open the great door and shambled into the entrance-hall with his bloody burden. Lady Alicia chanced to be at hand, giving her servants some directions for the night. When she saw what Dicky carried she screamed aloud, for Richard's arms hung limp on either side of his bearer's neck, and his blood was dripping from his own and Dicky's clothing; so she was justified in thinking him quite dead. She. turned upon one of her two footmen, like a fury.

" Take the best horse in the stable," said she, " and ride toward Saltire Castle. Kill your horse, if need be, but overtake Gerald Harrison and tell him Andrew Hogg has killed his son!" And the man ran out instantly.

They carried Richard into Lady Alicia's own room, and sent the other footman for a physician; and meanwhile the lady and Dicky Dirk, who had spoken not a word since coming into the house, worked together to stanch the flow of blood. Presently the Farnham apothecary came, and relieved them of their task. He was well-skilled in dealing with wounds, as were most of the surgeons of that day, and he worked long and patiently before Richard's condition was to his liking. It was ten o'clock when he turned to Lady Alicia and said:

" No vital part was touched, my Lady; it was almost a miracle. With the best of nursing, the lad will live."

"Thank God!" the lady gasped, but Dicky, turning in silence, left the house and went swaying off across the fields toward Sladden's farm. Notwithstanding his disability he got over the ground rapidly, and it was less than an hour later when, under his hand, the heavy iron knocker woke the sleeping echoes of the farmhouse. He knocked continuously until he heard footsteps within, and then stood waiting.

6

SLADDEN himself opened the door a very little; but a heavy fist was dashed against it, sending it flying wide, and Dicky Dirk came lurching in. The cripple's hands and face were stained with blood, and his clothing was soaked with it; his manner showed excitement, and his look was wild and fierce. The farmer, knowing well the strength of those long and hairy arms, kept out of his way, staring in blank amazement.

" Where's Mistress Mary?" demanded Dicky.

" What's that to you?" growled Sladden. " Get out, you villain; I want to lock my door again."

"Will zee Mistress Mary," said Dicky.

" You can't see her, you bloody ruffian! What pot-house brawl have you been into? Get out. Mistress Mary has been in her bed these two hours."

" Call her."

" Now, curse your impudence! Get out, or I'll call help to throw you out. What do you want with her? "

"I'll call her zelf," said Dicky, starting toward the stairway. He knew the house well, having been often employed there. Sladden sprang before him with an oath, but the cripple put his hand on his knife and came on, and the Squire stepped aside. Dicky went up the stairs, and knocked at Mary's door, and it was quickly opened by the girl herself. She had been sitting at the window, looking at the moon and dreaming of her lover, and was fully dressed. She cried out, when she saw her bloody visitor.

" Dicky," she said sharply, " is it Richard?"

"Ay," said Dicky. " T hog met un on t' high rowd, an' t' four fought un, an run swourd through un." She leaned against the wall, with her face as white as snow.

" Is he dead? " she whispered, trembling.

" I carried un on back to Farnham Court," Dicky replied, " an' t' leech says a'll live, if un has good nursin'." The color came back to her face with a rush.

"Why, that he shall have, Dicky!" said she. " Wait you for me," and she began throwing some of her apparel into a portmanteau. When it was filled she turned again to the cripple, who stood waiting at the door.

" Take me to Farnham Court," said she, and they went down the stair together. Sladden, with two of the farm-hands whom he had called, was waiting in the hall below.

"What does this mean?" he asked, astonished. " Where are you going? "

" I am going to Richard Harrison," she said, " who was attacked upon the road to-night by that cowardly murderer Andrew Hogg and his crew, no doubt with your full knowledge and connivance."

"You shameless hussy! Will you go to him unwed? " Her cheek grew hot, and her eye flashed hotter still.

" Dicky," said she, " if yonder man lifts hand to stop me, kill him!"

" I wull! " growled Dicky, drawing his great knife and lurching forward; and Sladden and his bumpkins backed against the wall and let them pass. It was midnight when they reached Farnham Court, where Lady Alicia greeted Mary with joyful astonishment, and yet with an anxious face.

" How is Richard? " were the girl's first words.

"He is conscious, Mary; full of hope and courage, but very weak from the great loss of blood."

"But will he live?"

" With proper nursing; so the surgeon says."

" I have come to nurse him." Lady Alicia looked perplexed.

" But Mary — " she said, and hesitated. She was thinking of Andrew Hogg, and the fear possessed her that when he heard of Mary's presence at Richard's bedside he would come in a rage to finish his work and carry the girl away. And Mary, seeing her hesitation and remembering Sladden's insult, misunderstood her. She raised her head high, and turned instantly to Dicky Dirk.

" Dicky," said she, " will you do me a kindness? "

" Ay," said Dicky, promptly.

" Then go to Farnham parsonage for Vicar Slade, and bring him here; bring him, Dicky, whether he will or no. Tell him he is to marry me to Richard Harrison, and then we shall see who will keep a wife from her husband."

Dicky wavered out into the night, and Mary turned again to Lady Alicia, with a heaving breast and a triumphant look.

" Will anyone have a better right than I? " she demanded.

The lady's eyes shone as she clasped the girl in her arms and kissed her.

" It was not of that I was thinking, Mary," said she. "But of — well, never mind; you have chosen the right way." She turned suddenly to the sleepy footman, who was sitting in the hall.

" Thomas," she said, " what weapons have we in the house? "

" Only a couple of muskets, my Lady."

" Load them, and bring them here, and keep the front door barred. Let no one enter until you are certain that he is a friend."

" You fear Hogg? " said Mary. " I had not thought of him."

" God send Gerald Harrison back before Black Andrew hears of this!" said Lady Alicia. They put their arms around each other, and went up to the door of Richard's room, and the woman who was watching whispering to them that he had fallen asleep, they sat down outside to wait. After a little time, Dicky Dirk came, leading the shivering clergyman by the arm.

Vicar Slade was a typical parson of those times; a fox-hunting, gambling, hard-drinking man of the world, very much more rogue than saint; the type of ecclesiastic who brought religion into disrepute, and drove men like Gerald Harrison to the profession of open atheism. In common with all of Farnham, the Vicar was much afraid of Andrew Hogg, and it was evident that he was badly frightened; his clothing was disheveled, and Dicky grasped him tightly above the elbow.

" A was feard o' t' hog," said Dicky, " an' wouldn't come; zo I browt un."

" This is a most outrageous proceeding, Lady Alicia," said the clergyman in a quivering voice.

" It is not Lady Alicia's doing, Mr.Slade," said Mary, gently. " It was I who sent for you, to exercise your holy office in marrying me to Richard Harrison. Let him loose, Dicky."

" No," said Dicky, " a'll run off." And he kept his grip upon the parson's arm.

" I know enough of all this," quavered the vicar, " to be aware that I must answer to Andrew Hogg if I marry you."

" Must answer to me if ee doan't," said Dicky, putting his hand on his knife.

" You are surely between two fires, Mr. Slade," said Lady Alicia, smiling in spite of herself, at the man's terror, " for without doubt Dicky will do you a mischief if you refuse to perform this ceremony."

"That I wull!" growled Dicky.

" I call upon you to witness then," said Slade, " that I do it under compulsion, and in fear for my life. If you have a prayer-book in the house, Lady Alicia, have it fetched; and then I am ready, since I must."

They sat waiting until Richard awoke, and then went together into his room, Dicky keeping near the parson, with a watchful eye upon him. When Mistress Mary saw the white face upon the pillow she came very near losing the self-possession she had retained so bravely. She stopped short, and stood for an instant with both her clenched hands pressed against her throat. Then she went quickly to the bedside, and bent above him, smiling. And seeing who it was, he looked with wonder for a moment, and then smiled back at her.

" Angel!" he whispered softly. She stooped, and laid her cheek against his.

" Richard, my dear love," said she, " do not try to move or speak. You are sorely hurt, and I have come to be with you night and day. And I have brought the parson to marry us, if you will have me, Richard."

"Will I?" he whispered, smiling. " Ay, and be run through fifty times to get the chance." She put her finger on his lips.

" You are only to say yes and no, sir," said she, " and not to excite yourself at all. Do you understand? "

" Yes and no, sir," said he. She drew a ring from her finger, and placed it under the poor nerveless hand, which lay upon the cover.

" It was my mother's wedding ring, and shall be mine," she said. " When the time comes, I can slip my ringer into it; do not try to raise your hand. Dicky, you have been our friend this night, and you shall give me away. Go on, Mr. Slade; we are ready."

So they were married, with Lady Alicia and the serving-woman for witnesses ; and Dicky Dirk gave the bride away. Then Mary put them all out of the room, and sitting down beside her husband, held his hand and sang to him softly until he went to sleep again. Day was breaking when all this was over, and Lady Alicia sat down in the hall, with her one footman and her two loaded muskets, to watch for Andrew Hogg, while Dicky Dirk hurried off across the fields, weaving from side to side and clutching at the air in his haste, and reaching the gates of Hackthorn Hall, sat down to wait for Gerald Harrison.

7

HARRISON and his escort rode in a leisurely fashion along the road to Saltire Castle, beguiling the time with pleasant conversation. The night air was cool and fresh, and the moon was shining brilliantly. The two gentlemen rode abreast in front, with the troopers following a little way behind. It was past midnight, and they had come in sight of the lights of Shoresby, where they were to rest until morning, when they heard a horse galloping hard behind them, and drew rein to see what the occasion of such haste might be. And the rider proved to be Lady Alicia's footman, bareheaded and splashed with mud, who rode up and spoke to Harrison.

" My Lady sent me, sir," said he, " to tell you that Andrew Hogg has killed your son." And he added: " I saw his body brought in."

Captain Keatley cried out in horrified astonishment, and turned sharply to Harrison. An instant comprehension of the whole plot came to the Virginian. He realized that Lady Alicia had been right, and that the King's invitation had been procured to get him out of the way while his son was murdered. But whatever passed in his mind, his countenance did not change in the least, and his voice was calm and natural as he answered:

" Ah! In that case, much as I regret to lose your pleasant company, Captain, I suppose I must turn back." He waited an instant for a reply, and then slowly turned his horse about.

Captain Keatley hesitated in some perplexity. He had been very favorably impressed by Harrison, and he felt a keen sympathy for the man who met such dreadful news with so gallant and unwavering a front; and also, there began to dawn upon his mind a suspicion that he, himself, had been made an instrument in carrying out some vile plot. On the other hand, he had his instructions from Cunningham, and his almost superstitious reverence for the King's command, and, for a moment, he could not decide between his sympathy and what he conceived to be his duty. As the American started his horse on the backward way, Keatley found voice, and said:

" But, sir, his Majesty ordered me to bring you to him, and if I return without you, what shall I tell him?"

Harrison slowly turned his horse about again, coming face to face with the soldier; he rode up until his horse's head overlapped the captain's thigh, and their faces were scarcely twelve inches apart. The moonlight fell full on the Virginian's countenance; he was smiling pleasantly, but Keatley's blood ran cold as he caught his look, for his eyes were like coals of fire, yet when he spoke his voice was soft and low.

" Tell him," said Harrison, " to go to Hell!" Captain Keatley leaned backward as if he had received a blow, and uttered an exclamation of horror.

" And tell him," the other went on, " that if I had believed you to be a co-conspirator with Andrew Hogg in this, I would have run my sword through you the instant I had the news. Good morning, Captain." He wheeled his horse about for the third time, and rode back past the troopers in a walk, and no one lifted a hand to hinder him. Captain Keatley rode on to Saltire Castle, and reported simply that Harrison had turned back on hearing of the death of his son, and that he had thought it right to let him go. So great was his admiration for the American's courage that he never mentioned the affront which had been offered to Royalty.

Once out of earshot of his escort, Harrison gave his horse the spur, leaving Lady Alicia's man to follow at a slower pace, and rode with all speed toward Farnham. At the first tavern he secured a fresh mount, leaving his own steed for the serving-man to bring along. What passed with him during that lonely ride, whether he laughed or cried or kept his stoical composure through it all, no one will ever know. He dearly loved his son, and he believed him dead, and his heart must have burned with a fierce lust for vengeance upon the murderers, but when, in the early morning, he sprang from his saddle at the Blue Goose Inn, his face was as serene as ever. He went straight to his apartment, exchanging no word with any one, and there he removed all traces of his rapid ride by a bath and a change of garments. The sun was just rising when, immaculately dressed, and with every frill and ruffle in its place, with his hair freshly powdered and his rosy cheek smooth shaved, he set off afoot and at a careless pace toward Hackthorn Hall. No one was astir at the inn save the lout of a stable-boy who had taken his horse. No one yet knew of the happenings overnight, and so he went on, still believing that his son was dead. As he entered the gate of Hackthorn Hall, Dicky Dirk rose up beside him.

" Been waitin' for ee," said Dicky.

" How came you so bloody? " asked Harrison.

" Picked up thy boy."

" Hah! Yes. Well, Dicky, what do you want with me? "

" To zee ee kill Hogg."

"No, Dicky," said Harrison, "I will do this work quite alone. I want neither help nor spectators." He was about to start on, but Dicky stopped him by throwing up one of his huge hands.

" Look ee! " he said, and his hoarse voice trembled in a sudden outburst of rage, " Hogg broak ma back; killed ma fayther with swourd, an' broak ma moader's heart. I've carried dirk for vifteen year to kill un, an' by Goad, I'll zee un die." Harrison stood quite still for a moment, gazing into cripple's passion-distorted face.

" Ay, ay? " said he. " Well, Dicky, your claim seems to take precedence over mine; though I am sorry for it. Come on, then, you shall not only see him die, but you may finish him yourself." He started on, and Dicky followed at his heels.

They walked slowly up the graveled drive which led to the house, a strangely paired couple indeed; the smiling, splendid gentleman, looking about him with an air of half indifferent interest as he sauntered along, and behind him the blood-stained cripple, beating the air with his huge hands, and making fearful grimaces in the sudden giving way to his long hidden hatred of black Andrew Hogg.

Hogg and his men had held high carnival all night, celebrating the murder of Richard, and as day was breaking they had decided that Trainor should stand guard in the grounds with his pistol, against the possible coming of Harrison, while the others went to sleep. They had been in their beds but an hour or so when the Virginian arrived, and Trainor, sitting at the foot of a great tree beside the driveway, was drowsing also, with an empty bottle beside him. So Harrison walked up to him, and stood for a moment looking down at the nodding head and bandaged face.

"Kick him awake," he said to Dicky, and the cripple brought one of his heavy hands down on the sleeper's head with a resounding slap.

Trainor leaped to his feet on the instant, and seeing at the first glance who his visitors were, he proved his readiness by firing his pistol, which had been ready in his hand, point blank at Harrison. The Virginian sprang aside, and Dicky struck up the fellow's arm, so the bullet went wide of the mark, and Harrison, whipping out his sword, ran the man through. He fell upon the driveway, and Dicky, bending over him and seeing that the sword-thrust had gone rather low, drove his dirk with great precision through the ruffian's heart. Harrison drew a handkerchief from his pocket and wiped his sword carefully before sheathing it; and Dicky wiped his knife upon his bloody sleeve.

"You seem to have a good workman's taste in these matters, Dicky," said the American as they started on. "You do not like to leave an imperfectly finished job behind you."

When they came to the front of the house, Harrison paused and inspected the silent building reflectively; he expected to be fired at from the windows, but nothing of the kind happened, and there was no sign of life.

"They must be still asleep," he said to Dicky. "I wish we had a way to break down the door."

"Wait," said the cripple, shambling of! around the house, and presently he came back carrying a great axe. He went up the steps, and swinging the tool with all the strength of his powerful arms, began to batter at the lock of the heavy oaken door. The sound of the crashing blows reverberated through the house like thunder, and Harrison kept close watch upon the windows, but still he saw no sign of life. Presently, the thick wood about the lock having been beaten to fragments, the door swung open, and the Virginian stepped in with Dicky close behind him.

8

FROM across the entrance hall came three pistol shots in quick succession, but the bullets whistled harmlessly above Harrison's head, for the nerves of Hogg and his two remaining scoundrels were not in condition for effective target practice. After carousing until nearly daylight, they had been aroused out of their first drunken sleep by Dicky's crashing blows upon the door, and tumbling out of bed half-dressed, as they had retired, they had run down the stairs carrying swords and pistols. When Harrison stepped inside the door they fired hastily, and now, their firearms which had been their chief reliance against the terrible Virginian, being empty and useless they dashed them to the floor and drew their swords. They were truly a loathsome sight as they stood huddled together by the farther wall; their uncombed hair hung in tangled masses about their bloated and desperate faces, and the fear in their burning eyes was like that of rats caught in a trap. Stepping at once between them and the stairway, Harrison came on, smiling and calm. At a little distance from them he halted and drew his sword, and then clapping it under his arm, took a pinch of snuff. Returning the box to his pocket, and carefully brushing off a speck which had fallen on the front of his ruffled shirt, he saluted courteously.

" Good morning, gentlemen," said he. " I am sorry to disturb you so early, but my business is urgent; I have come to rob the hangman of a job."

At that, Andrew Hogg knowing that he must fight for his life as he had never fought before, burst out in cursing and sprang forward, calling out to his men, and the three fell upon Harrison. And now Dicky Dirk, looking on, saw such an exhibition of skill in fence as few have witnessed in this world. Harrison's sword became a glittering wall of steel; it seemed to encase him from head to foot like a suit of armor. He did not leap and spring about to dodge their thrusts, but stood still, beating aside their blades with his own flying weapon. His quickness of eye and hand, his strength of arm and wrist, were marvelous; it was the skill of a wizard, a prestidigitator, rather than that of a merely expert swordsman. They could not reach him with their thrusts or blows, they could not even make him give back an inch, or step aside; and they were compelled to keep in front of him by Dicky, who, whenever one of them stepped out to take the fencer on the side, came quickly in behind the fellow and made him jump toward the front again for fear of getting the huge dirk between his shoulders. And so the fight went on for several minutes.

Then Harrison laughed out suddenly, a ringing laugh, which echoed through the house above the sound of clashing steel, and panting breaths, and muttered curses.

" It is time," he said. " Let us finish." He made a quick forward stroke with his sword, so deadly swift that the blade sung with a shrill whistling note; and one of the two henchmen of Andrew Hogg went down with his throat cut, his head being nearly severed from his body.

"Richard!" said Harrison softly, and though he smiled, his eyes were terrible to see. Another lightning stroke pierced the other ruffian through the heart, and Andrew, now mad with fear, faced Harrison alone. The Virginian dropped the point of his sword and stepped back.

" Hogg," said he, " I came to kill you; but I found Dicky on the same errand, and his rights to be your executioner seem to precede mine. You made him fatherless and motherless, and the crawling, staggering thing he is, while you have only made me child-less. Dicky shall kill you, Hogg, but I will put out your eyes first. On guard!" And they crossed swords again.

It was soon over. Two dextrous strokes of the razor-edged blade, and the point was slashed through each of Andrew's eyes; he dropped his sword and clapped his hands to his bloody face, howling with pain and fright; and Dicky, laughing as fiends may laugh in hell, lurched forward, and driving his great knife through the black villain's heart, left it sticking there.

They left the house without a word, and walked out to the highway. There Harrison paused, and said quietly:

" Is my son's body at Lady Alicia's, Dicky? "

" A' bain't no boady," said Dicky. " A's livin'."

" What? " cried Harrison sharply, startled for once out of his composure.

" I zaw Hogg run un through, right yonder," said Dicky, " while t'others held un fast; a' stood straight, an' spit in t' hog's face when swourd went home. I picked un oop, an' carried un vor dead to Farnham Court; but t' leech says un'll live, if has good nursin'."

" Now, by all the gods!" cried Harrison. " But this is the greatest news man ever told to man! Good nursing, sayest thou? Why, that he shall have, Dicky."

"Zo Mistress Mary zaid," said Dicky.

What? "

" I went to t' farm at midnight," said the cripple, " an' to her bedroom door, an' told her. 'Why then' says she, 'good nursin' he shall have an' packed her portmantle. Sladden would stop her, an' says she, 'Dicky, kill him.' Zo I pulled dirk, an' Sladden run."

" Go on, thou bravest-hearted knight that ever stood by lady in distress," said Harrison. " What happened next? "

" When we coom to t' Court," said Dicky, " t' Lady was for not lettin' maid stay; an' Mistress Mary zaid to me, ' Dicky, go bring Parson Slade to marry me to Richard; we'll zee who keeps wife from her husband.' Zo I browt parson, and a' married un."

" Now, by all the gods! " said Harrison again, but very softly now, and somewhat as if he choked, " but here's a lady! A right noble lady, on my soul! And what more, prince of storytellers?"

" No more," said Dicky. " I came here to wait for 'ee. An' now t' hog is dead I've nowt to stay here for; will 'ee tak me to Ferginny? "

" Will I take you? Ay, that I will. Whither I go, thou shalt go, and my people shall be thy people; unfortunately for the rest of the quotation, I have no God, but if ever I find one, he shall be thy God also, Dicky."

" Doan't woant no Goad," said Dicky Dirk.

Lady Alicia, still watching with her loaded musket, greeted Harrison with joyful relief when, serene and smiling, he came a half hour later to Farnham Court.

" All's well," said she, " now that you are here to protect your own. I have been in dreadful fear lest Hogg should come with his bloody three to finish his work and carry your daughter away."

" Hogg and his bloody three will trouble no one more, Alicia," said he, " for Dicky Dirk and I have been to Hackthorn Hall."

She was silent in awe for a moment, well knowing what his words implied.

" What word did you send the King, when you turned back? " she asked. He laughed at this, truly a woman's question at such a time.

" I sent him word," said he, " that he might go to Hell!" Lady Alicia, trained to the greatest reverence for Royalty, cried out in horror.

" Do not be alarmed, my dear Alicia," said Harrison, taking snuff. " Now that things have turned out so much better than I thought, I shall not insist upon his going; I will write Wycherly this morning to tell him so. And now, how is Richard?"

" Doing well, and happy in the love of his dear young wife; thank God! "

" Why then," said Hell-fire Harrison, " it will be the first time in forty years, but I think, Alicia, that I shall have to say Amen! "

THE END.

Made in the USA
Middletown, DE
12 June 2018